Scotts

Sprinklers
& Watering Systems

Meredith® Books
Des Moines, Iowa

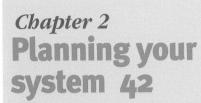

Chapter 2
Planning your system 42

Discover how easy it is to measure your lot and plan a versatile system that is right for you.

Chapter 1
Understanding irrigation 4

You can't control the rain—or the lack of it—but having an automated watering system is the next best thing. Here's essential information about water's relationship to plants and soil, and ways you can tailor a watering system to meet the varying demands in your yard.

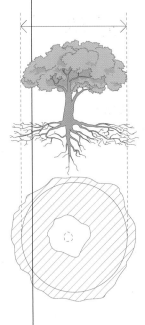

Chapter 4
Using your system 148

Here's help for planning your system's schedule and tips on how to keep things running smoothly.

Chapter 3
Installing your system 100

Learn how to install your system, from hooking up to your water supply to snapping in the last microemitter.

Troubleshooting and repair 172

Here are a few of the most common problems you might encounter with your system and steps you can take to correct them.

Understanding irrigation

No matter where you live in North America, if you are an avid gardener, there have been days when you have cursed the weather. It is either too hot and dry or too cloudy and wet. Whichever it is, you want to be able to control the amount of water that reaches your plants. With a modern, automated irrigation system, to a great degree you can.

With new irrigation technology, it is easier than ever for homeowners to plan and install an efficient watering system suited to their unique needs. By adding an irrigation system to your landscape, you will help all of your plants reach their fullest potential, you will increase the value of your home, and you may end up conserving water as well. That is good news no matter what region you live in.

Irrigation systems are the most efficient way to water your lawn and gardens. They are nearly maintenance-free and can reliably save you hours of tedious watering time. Whether you use sprinklers, drip emitters, or a combination of both, you can design a system that is ideal for every plant in your yard.

Chapter 1

5

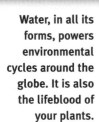

Water, in all its forms, powers environmental cycles around the globe. It is also the lifeblood of your plants.

The water
cycle

The heart of irrigation, whether on a farm or in your backyard, is the modification of nature. Irrigation seeks to create a different environment than the one that naturally exists in a particular area. The result can be as extreme as growing rice in the desert or as simple as misting orchids in a pot. It all comes down to one principle: Plants have unique water needs and grow best when those needs are met in a timely manner. The water available in a plant's native environment shapes its unique water requirements.

The variety of plants we have in our yards results from environmental factors, such as temperature, sun, soil, competition with other plants, and, most of all, the availability of water. The Earth's hydrologic (water) cycle is the driving force behind precipitation, humidity, and groundwater levels. Look at any plant in your yard and see an example of adaptation to these conditions.

But the water cycle is not always predictable. Rain doesn't always fall when we would like it to. Sometimes it doesn't fall at all. As resilient as most plants are to the vagaries of the weather, haphazard or irregular watering results in patchy, uneven growth. Insufficient water weakens plants and makes them much more susceptible to disease and infestation than healthy plants. Irregular watering can cause plants to develop a smaller root system, grow more slowly, and be more susceptible to insect and cold damage than those that receive more even watering. Many insects are actually attracted to wilted, yellowing leaves. Correctly watered landscapes are generally greener and more lush. The hedges, trees, and shrubs in such landscapes are less subject to summer yellowing. Their flowers grow more quickly and remain in peak bloom longer. Irrigated vegetable gardens often yield twice as much produce per square foot as do nonirrigated gardens. The vegetables are larger, better formed, tastier, and stronger.

All this underlines the wisdom of giving your plants the water they need, when they need it. At times this means helping the hydrologic cycle along when it isn't in sync with the plants you are trying to grow.

STEPS IN THE CYCLE

The importance of the hydrologic cycle to life on Earth cannot be overstated. The constant churning of water in one form or another through the entire ecosystem is driven by, and is a driver of, the global environment. In fact, the water that covers two-thirds of our planet is largely the reason we are here. Water, as either ice, liquid, or vapor, makes life possible.

Water is believed initially to have arrived on the Earth's surface through the emissions of ancient volcanoes. Geologic evidence suggests that large amounts of water have likely flowed on Earth for the past 3.8 billion years. Throughout that time the water has continually passed from the ocean to the atmosphere to the land and back to the ocean. There are six distinct steps in this water cycle: evaporation, condensation, precipitation, infiltration and percolation, and runoff.

Evaporation is the process by which liquid water becomes a gas. This happens when water in its liquid state absorbs enough energy that its molecules break free of the force of attraction that wants to hold them together. As a gas, the water rises into the atmosphere, where it **condenses,** the next step in the process. Condensation takes place when the gaseous water cools as it rises into the atmosphere. As the water molecules lose energy and begin to coalesce into water vapor, precipitation, the

Water, water everywhere

- One percent of all the water on Earth is floating overhead at any given moment.
- An acre of corn can add 4,000 gallons of water per day to the atmosphere.
- Ninety-five percent of the freshwater in the United States is underground.
- Every day about 4 trillion gallons of water fall to the Earth as precipitation.

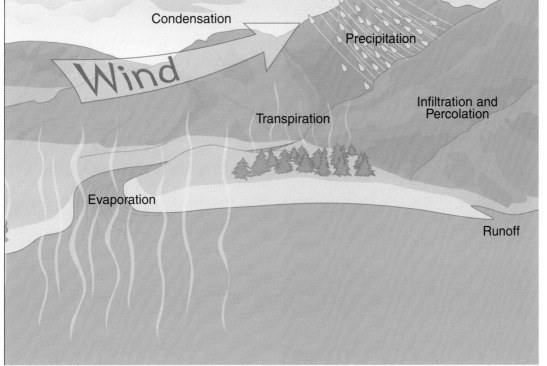

Condensation
Precipitation
Wind
Transpiration
Infiltration and Percolation
Evaporation
Runoff

Water is not just in the oceans and lakes. It literally surrounds you and is constantly moving and changing. Each step in the hydrologic cycle plays an important part in plant life cycles.

The water cycle (left) is a series of interrelated steps that together create an engine to move water constantly around the planet. With time, Siberian ice can become a tropical rainfall.

The water cycle *continued*

Earth truly is a world of water. However, limited freshwater argues for careful use of this precious resource. Carefully planned home irrigation can be a means of doing so.

third stage in the cycle, begins. Precipitation occurs after the water vapor has condensed to a point that it becomes too heavy to be supported by the surrounding air. You typically experience precipitation as rain, snow, or any of the many frozen forms of water such as sleet and hail.

Infiltration and **percolation** are the next steps in the process. Simply put, infiltration and percolation are the movement of water downward through the soil and rock into the groundwater table. This is the main source of water for wells, streams, rivers, and lakes. Some people define infiltration as the phase that occurs at the root zone in the soil and percolation as the phase that occurs in the subsoil and bedrock beneath. The final step is **runoff.** This is the phase that takes all the water that hasn't already evaporated into the atmosphere and conducts it to the ocean, where

it will start the process again. Rivers, streams, creeks—any water that is flowing downhill toward the ocean—can be called runoff.

Another important element to consider is **transpiration,** that is, plants pulling water up from the soil and releasing it out into the atmosphere. Plants, through transpiration, contribute a full 10 percent of the total moisture found in the atmosphere.

THE BIG PICTURE

The Earth's total water content is about 1.39 billion cubic kilometers (331,000,000 cubic miles). About 96.5 percent of that is contained in the world's oceans and seas. A little less than 2 percent is stored in the polar ice caps, glaciers, and permafrost. Just about 1.7 percent is available in groundwater, lakes, rivers, streams, and soil. Because the water cycle functions continuously, with evaporation on a global basis approximately equaling precipitation, the total amount of water vapor in the atmosphere remains constant at around 0.001 percent.

The oceans of the world are being constantly replenished by runoff. Over the past 100 years they have been more than replenished, with the sea level around the globe slowly rising. The sea level rises because of warming of the oceans. The warming has three consequences. First, it causes ocean water to expand, increasing the volume of the seas. Second, a greater mass of water enters the ocean than the amount that leaves it through evaporation or other means. Finally, warming causes the calving or melting of land ice such as ice sheets and glaciers, a primary cause for an increased mass of water entering the ocean.

Throughout the hydrologic cycle, there are endless paths that a water molecule might follow. Water at the bottom of Lake Superior may eventually fall as rain in Massachusetts. Runoff from the Massachusetts rain may drain into the Atlantic Ocean and circulate northeastward toward Iceland, destined to become part of a floe of sea ice or, after evaporation into the atmosphere and precipitation as snow, part of a glacier. Water molecules can take a variety of routes and branching trails that lead them again and again through the three phases of ice, liquid, and water vapor. For instance, the water molecules that fell 100 years ago as rain on your great-grandparents' farmhouse in Iowa might now be falling as snow on your driveway in Vermont. The cycle is endless and respects no national borders.

WEATHER, THE WATER CYCLE, AND PLANT DEVELOPMENT

Genetic evidence suggests that the first plants were created about 700 million years ago. The earliest-known fossil evidence of land plants tells us they are some 420 million to 480 million years old. It was at this time that **vascular** plants (those with internal water transport systems) first developed. This allowed them to migrate out of the oceans and onto dry land. Although these first plants were not very impressive, measuring less than an inch tall, they were the antecedents of all the plants you enjoy in your yard every day.

Before the arrival of plants, the Earth was thought to have been too cold for animal life to exist in a meaningful way. The plants began pumping oxygen into the atmosphere, which allowed for the development of larger, stronger forms of animal life. This explosion of species, among other factors, led to an increase in carbon dioxide in the atmosphere, which warmed the planet. This warmer, wetter world set the water cycle in motion, along with the weather phenomena that have defined the Earth ever since.

The new weather patterns and the environments that developed led to the huge diversity of plant varieties we see today. Of these, the vascular plants predominate. Vascular plants, no matter the species, all share a similar structure based on the transport of water and nutrients within the plant. The vascular tissues move materials within the plant and provide structural support for it as well.

This combination of an advanced vascular system, a self-supporting structure, and the weather it helped create has led to myriad plant varieties throughout the world. Sagebrush, for instance, is adept at living on very little moisture. At the other end of the spectrum, the dwarf monkey flower lives out its entire life during a moist three-week period in spring. Plants are inexorably linked to the weather and the water cycle.

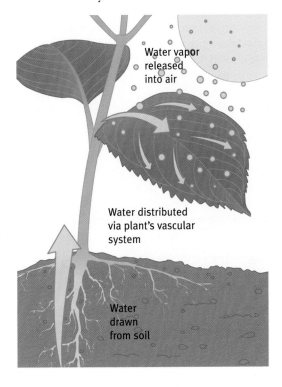

Water vapor released into air

Water distributed via plant's vascular system

Water drawn from soil

Plants are constantly drawing in water from the soil, using it for their needs, and then recycling it into the air, a process known as transpiration. Transpiration accounts for fully 10 percent of the water vapor in the atmosphere.

Foliage for feast and famine

Plants adapt to their environment whether it has too little or too much water. For example, orchids thrive in highly humid climates, where their roots are able to absorb water directly from the air. At the other extreme, a desert dweller such as scorpion weed copes with drought by means of leaves that funnel rain and dew toward its roots.

The plant-water-soil relationship

Plants use water, sunlight, and carbon dioxide to manufacture their food—through a process known as photosynthesis.

Plants evolve in ways that adapt to local conditions. However, no matter where the plant grows, its relationship to water as an integral part of its life processes does not change. Water is the lifeblood of every plant on Earth. Understanding the relationship that exists between plants, water, and the soil they grow in is essential if you want to irrigate your landscape effectively.

Without water, the process by which plants make food, known as photosynthesis, cannot take place. Photosynthesis is a chemical reaction that occurs in the leaves of a plant. The green chlorophyll in the plant's foliage uses water, carbon dioxide, and energy absorbed from the sun to power a reaction that creates simple sugars. These sugars are metabolized by the plant for energy. A by-product of the reaction between water and carbon dioxide is oxygen, which the plant expels through its leaves. Photosynthesis in plants is responsible for virtually all the oxygen in the atmosphere.

Like solar panels, plant leaves must face the sun to function most efficiently. Plants use water to adjust the position of their foliage to maintain correct alignment with the sun. The water pressure in the plant, known as turgor, holds the plant upright and allows the leaves to follow the sun. When plants lack adequate water to carry on their normal life processes, their leaves lose turgidity and they wilt, falling out of alignment with the sun. Once a plant wilts, the root hairs have probably been damaged. These hairs are a specialized part of the root system used to absorb water and nutrients. Each time a plant wilts, more root hairs die, causing plant growth to slow down or stop.

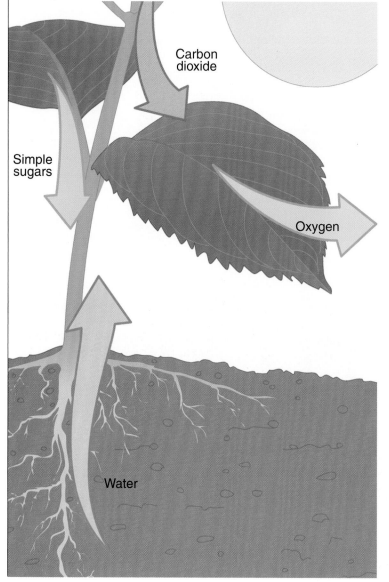

Carbon dioxide

Simple sugars

Oxygen

Water

Mangroves have adapted to life in brackish tidal marshes. Their roots not only absorb the salty water, but also provide protected habitat for many species of fish and other animals.

PLANT PHYSIOLOGY

Plants take in raw materials and energy and convert them into food, in the form of simple sugars, to support their growth. During photosynthesis, plants collect solar energy and combine it with carbon dioxide and water to create simple sugars. The whole process is dependent on water, for the chemical reaction as well as the transport mechanism for the raw materials and the final products.

It all begins in the roots. Virtually all the water a plant uses is drawn into the plant through the roots. Their primary function is to absorb water and minerals from the soil. In addition, the roots anchor the plant in place, produce essential compounds, and store excess food materials. Water absorption happens in the root hairs, the fine, hair-like structures that radiate from the lateral roots within the top layer of the soil, known as the root zone.

From the roots, specialized channels in the stem, known as the xylem, carry the water upward through the plant and out to the branches and leaves. The leaves are the place where photosynthesis occurs and carbohydrates are produced. Getting these nutrients back down to the roots and other areas of the plant is the job of the other specialized channels in the plant stem, called the phloem. Materials can travel in either direction in the phloem. Xylem and phloem work together to form a continuous plant vascular system that reaches out to every leaf and root hair.

Water is the transport medium and the engine that drives this system. A unique property of water molecules is that they have a positive and a negative end. This makes them want to stick together like little magnets. As water evaporates from the leaf surfaces through small pores called stomata, it literally pulls more water up behind it to take its place. This process is repeated down through the plant, drawing water constantly upward through the xylem to the leaves. When water is lacking, this circulation system begins to shut down and the plant's food factory cannot function.

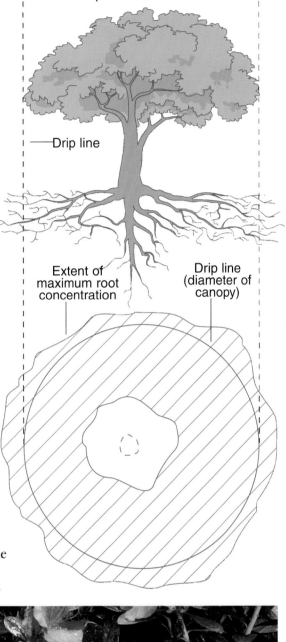

Maximum diameter of plant's branches

Drip line

Extent of maximum root concentration

Drip line (diameter of canopy)

Most water absorption takes place less than 2 feet below grade. In small plants it may occur in just the top few inches of soil. This is known as the root zone of the plant.

A microsprinkler efficiently and unobtrusively gets water to a plant's root system, where it is most needed.

The plant-water-soil relationship *continued*

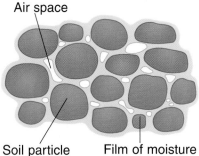

EVENLY MOIST SOIL

Air space
Soil particle
Film of moisture

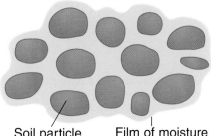

WATERLOGGED SOIL

Soil particle
Film of moisture

THE ROLE OF SOIL

The composition and structure of the soil your plants grow in determines how much water is available to the plant and how much you can water it without waste. This is because different types of soil have varying water-holding characteristics, and because plant root hairs need to be in contact with water to function.

On its face, soil classification can seem complicated. With names such as andisols, gelisols, mollisols, and others that sound just as intimidating, it is no wonder that you may have no idea what type of soil is in your yard. You need to be concerned with only the three basic ingredients of all soils: sand, clay, and silt. Different combinations of these three ingredients create the characteristics that concern most gardeners.

Sand is at one extreme. It drains fast and holds almost no water. Clay is at the other extreme, forming an almost impassible barrier

Great soil is a rich but light blend of organic and mineral ingredients. Its loose structure provides the spaces needed to hold water and air that the plant roots utilize.

The "sticky" nature of water molecules causes them to cling to soil particles, filling the spaces between them. It is this water that is absorbed and used by plants. Too much water can be as harmful as too little water.

to water infiltration, holding water very well. Silt drains faster than clay but still retains water. Soil is a combination of these ingredients plus varying amounts of organic matter.

The preferred garden soil is called loam. It is a mix of these base constituents in a perfect blend that allows for good drainage and water retention. A good loam soil is made up of 45 percent minerals and 5 percent organic matter, with 50 percent pore space between the soil particles. This pore space is vital because water and air fill it. Without the right mix of water and air, plants won't flourish.

Loam is further classified as sand, silt, and clay-loam, depending on which base type predominates. Plant roots grow well in clay-loam. However, pay careful attention to water drainage where this soil predominates. Silt-loam may cause drainage problems if it is more like clay than fine sand. Most plants thrive in silt-loam.

Sandy loam doesn't hold water as well as the others. Keeping it moist is more difficult. (See 'Understanding Soil' on page 34)

Irrigation was first developed to grow food crops. Since then, it has been linked to the progress of civilization. However, agricultural irrigation is not nearly as efficient as it could be.

What is irrigation?

Water accounts for 60 percent to 90 percent of the weight of actively growing plants. Plants use water for everything they do: making food, forming leaves, growing fruits, moving nutrients from the roots to the leaves, and carrying energy from the leaves to the roots. Powered by a process known as transpiration (see page 32), this transport system within every plant cycles through abundant water. It is vital that all this transpired water be replaced every day. Plants that do not receive adequate rainfall will quickly use up whatever moisture is available.

As people settled into towns and villages thousands of years ago, they realized that giving their crop plants a steady supply of water was the only way to grow enough food. Because people could not control when and where it rained, they conceived the practice of irrigation. At its heart, irrigation is simply bringing water to a plant where it is growing. Irrigation compensates for any moisture not provided by a plant's immediate environment.

Whether it takes the form of flooded rice paddies in Asia or drip-irrigated greenhouses in the Middle East, the need for irrigation is more critical today than ever. Natural water patterns are inadequate for the demands of an exploding human population. As a result, the increasing food production in North America is dependent on irrigation. From a homeowner's perspective, irrigation saves more water than hand-watering and protects investments in expensive landscape plantings. Irrigation systems also increase the value of residential property by 5 to 10 percent.

THE WATER CYCLE IMPROVED

Although the natural hydrologic cycle is remarkably efficient and effective at moving water around the planet, there is room for improvement—at least from a human perspective.

Depending on where a plant is growing, you may have to replace all the water it consumes every day. In the case of a mature tree, that could be as much as 100 gallons of water. This is not possible with hand watering where most plants end up either overwatered or underwatered. Poorly watered plants often lose some leaves, abort flower buds, or produce deformed or undersize fruit. Automatic irrigation, on the other hand, can supply the correct water amount before the soil dries out. Properly irrigated plants never lack water and are healthier and more productive.

What is irrigation? *continued*

In general, an irrigation system is designed to keep all parts of the lawn and garden evenly moist throughout the growing season. It is essential for proper plant health that the soil not become too wet or too dry. If it becomes saturated, the excess water must be allowed to drain thoroughly before the next watering. Saturated soil with no air spaces does not allow for proper water absorption. Also, although some roots, especially those of tall trees, grow to great depths, the main job of these roots is to anchor the plants or find water during extreme drought. Normally, all water uptake occurs within the root zone, which is the top 2 feet of the soil for trees and just the top several inches for most landscape plants. An irrigation system allows you to target this zone specifically.

A related issue is fertilizer. For fertilizer to be effective and available to a plant, it requires water. The nutrients in the fertilizer dissolve in the water and are taken up by the plant's roots in the root zone.

In arid regions like this one, the huge evaporative water loss suffered by sprinkler irrigation in arid regions was a primary factor in the development of drip irrigation technology.

THE HISTORY OF IRRIGATION

As people began settling in towns and villages, the need for a stable water supply became imperative. Water was needed for the people to

Water feeds the world

■ It takes 12,000 gallons of water to produce 1 pound of beef. A pound of chicken requires 420 gallons.

■ Rice has been irrigated in Asia for almost 4,000 years. Today, almost half the world's population depends on irrigated rice as its primary source of food.

■ In the United States and Canada, roughly half of all irrigation water is lost before it gets to a plant.

drink, and it was needed to raise the crops to feed the growing populations.

The best-known water managers, but by no means the first, were the Romans. Aside from the Coliseum, nothing evokes images of the great empire like a soaring three-tiered aqueduct, such as the one spanning the Italian countryside (right).

The Roman system is a marvel of engineering, especially considering that the majority of it was built before the first century B.C. At one point, the city of Rome had between 1,200 and 1,300 public fountains, 11 large public baths, 867 smaller baths, and 2 artificial lakes used for mock naval battles, not to mention water used for agricultural purposes. All this water came from hundreds of miles away via 11 aqueducts that delivered 38 million gallons of water every day, without using a single pump. The Romans had so much water that they didn't install shutoff valves on any of the fountains or baths in the city.

Though Rome may represent the pinnacle of ancient water engineering, the Romans did not start the practice. The first known traces of irrigation were found in Mesopotamia and date to almost 4000 B.C. Using a complex system of dikes and levees, aided by human and animal power, the Mesopotamians diverted water many miles from its source and lifted it to great heights, enabling them to create the famous Hanging Gardens of Babylon in about 600 B.C.

Similar irrigation works evolved around the world, driven by the burgeoning population's need for water. For the most part, irrigation was used for agriculture. Only municipalities and the very rich could afford it for decorative landscaping. In the United States, the use of residential sprinkler systems did not become popular until after World War II.

The Roman aqueducts marked the beginning of large-scale water management. Romans were the first people with hot and cold running water in their houses, as well as water gardens in their yards.

Irrigation has often had a decorative aspect. The Hanging Gardens of Babylon, which may have resembled this arid garden, were meant to suggest the look and feel of the mountains of northern Mesopotamia.

Water conservation

Water conservation should be a central principle in your watering system design as well as your overall garden design.

Using an automatic irrigation system may seem wasteful, but it actually wastes less water than hand watering. The average oscillating sprinkler loses almost as much water to the atmosphere as is finally applied to the garden. This happens because the droplets it shoots high into the air begin to evaporate before reaching the plant. Also, water evaporates from the foliage before it reaches the ground, especially in sunny or windy weather.

With hand watering, much of the water is lost. A homeowner may set up a sprinkler and not come back to turn it off until the ground is so saturated that water is running into the street. And because movable sprinklers are hard to adjust to the shapes of individual growing areas, water is wasted on patios and walkways.

Automatic irrigation systems provide a means of watering lawns and gardens without the need to drag a garden hose all over the yard. They allow the application of just the right amount of water at the best possible times. The water that is applied is used efficiently, minimizing waste. The result is the conservation of water resources and the enhancement of plant health.

Irrigation systems are built in sections, called zones. Each zone is designed to water plants with similar water requirements. Turf areas, for example, can be irrigated separately from a grouping of drought-tolerant shrubs or deep-rooted trees. Slopes—notoriously hard to water—require a slow, gentle application that lets the water sink into the soil rather than run off. With sloped areas assigned a separate zone, they can be watered slowly, in short bursts, eliminating typical problems.

Drip irrigation is a newer, even more efficient way to irrigate. It applies water very slowly by dripping it onto the ground or spraying individual plants. If used with an adequate layer of mulch, almost no moisture is lost to direct evaporation. With water applied directly to specific plants, the spaces between them stay dry enough that few weeds can take hold. A carefully planned system can send as much as 80 percent of the water to the plants rather than the atmosphere. With hand watering, that figure can be as low as 20 percent.

THE FRESHWATER CRISIS

Of all the water on Earth, only about 3 percent is freshwater. A bit more than two-thirds of that is frozen in the ice caps and glaciers of the world. That leaves about 0.08 percent available for use. According to the United Nations, over the next 20 years the supply of freshwater available per person will decline by one-third. There are several reasons for this growing water crisis. For instance, the ongoing rise in the population, along with improving standards of living around the world, is creating an escalating demand, especially in the dry areas of the Earth.

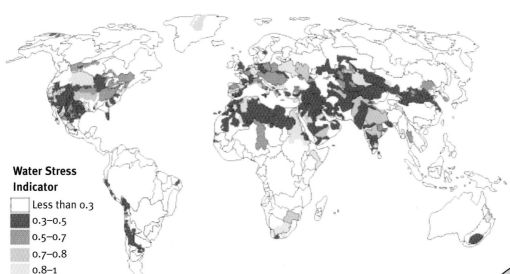

Water Stress Indicator

☐	Less than 0.3
■	0.3–0.5
▦	0.5–0.7
▨	0.7–0.8
▩	0.8–1
■	More than 1
☐	No discharge
⋀⋀	Major river basins

This map shows how water stressed various regions of the world are, that is, how much fresh water is used relative to surface water resources. The red areas show the greatest water stress with an indicator of 1 assigned to them. In these areas, unreplenishable supplies are being tapped to meet demand. Note how many of these red areas are in North America.

Water and wheat

In China it takes 1,000 tons of water to produce 1 ton of wheat.

As a result, freshwater is increasingly recognized as a valuable natural resource rather than an expendable commodity. You may notice this growing shortage in rising municipal water rates or in restrictions placed on your use of water for nonessential purposes. By whatever means this shortage presents itself, one thing is certain: Water conservation is a vitally important issue for everyone.

Another contributing factor is the inefficient water use. Commercial irrigation allows water waste on a prodigious scale, with the water leaking away or simply evaporating before it can do any good. Antiquated public utilities waste millions of gallons of water every year, sending it back into the water table before it reaches a single home or farm.

Water pollution adds enormously to the problem. Pollution makes available water unfit for use, increasing water costs. It also necessitates the search for new water sources. A stronger dedication to conservation is clearly needed in all levels of society to create sustainable water-use practices.

THE ARAL SEA

Even though irrigation systems offer an ideal opportunity to save water by using it more efficiently, poor irrigation practices can cause serious environmental damage when water resources are mismanaged. The Aral Sea in Central Asia is one of the starkest examples of how poor water-management practices can cause devastating damage to crops, jobs, public health, and regional climate.

The Aral Sea, prior to 1960, was the fourth-largest inland lake in the world. Situated in the center of the Central Asian deserts, it functioned as a gigantic evaporator, adding about 60 cubic kilometers of water vapor to the local atmosphere every year. Water from the Aral has always been an important resource for life in the region.

By 1995, the diversion of flows from the Amu Darya and Syr Darya rivers, along with the poorly managed expansion of irrigation in the

Unfortunately, the poor water-use practices of individuals as well as of communities are making depleted reservoirs an increasingly common sight.

Water conservation *continued*

area around the sea, created serious ecological, social, and economic problems. From 1960 to 1995, the sea received less than 1,000 cubic kilometers (454.5 cubic miles) of river water. This caused the water level in the lake to fall by 17 meters (55.7 feet). The shoreline receded approximately 150 kilometers (93.2 miles) from its original position. The once thriving fishery disappeared. The lake split into two parts, the Bolshoi and the Maly (Northern) Aral.

In the past the Aral moderated the cold winds from Siberia and reduced the summer heat. The recent changes led to shorter, drier summers and longer, colder winters. The growing season was reduced to 170 days, and pasture productivity decreased by half. Precipitation around the sea was reduced to an average of approximately 7½ inches (191 mm) yearly. The dust blowing from the old lake bottom is now causing serious health problems and has led to the melting of more than a thousand glaciers downwind of the lake.

At present, steps are just beginning to save and restore the Aral and the environment that millions have depended on for thousands of years. Without proper water-use practices, the same problems are possible in North America. For instance, the Ogallala Aquifer, the biggest in the United States, is under extreme pressure from unchecked demand. Many farmers are rethinking their irrigated agriculture as they become aware of the hazards of overpumping and realize that water is not in endless supply.

DEALING WITH DROUGHT

Parts of North America historically have not been prone to drought conditions. Drought has been associated mostly with the West, where summer heat and lack of rain for long periods are the norm. But in recent years, changes in weather patterns have brought dry conditions to the East on a more frequent and severe basis.

Droughts are not caused just by insufficient rainfall. Surging demand for water has become an important factor as well. This means that the best way to fight drought long term is to change water-use habits. Public education and incentives can make a big difference. For example, in 1995 the city of Albuquerque, New Mexico, launched a program to cut water use by 30 percent over 10 years. After just five years, water use per capita declined 22 percent.

There are many proactive steps to implement in our communities. However, what happens when a drought hits? Here are some suggestions for coping with drought:

Hand watering can waste almost 50 percent of the water applied, compared with a well-designed irrigation system.

Water down the drain

Of all the water on Earth, only about 3 percent is freshwater. Of that 3 percent, more than two-thirds is locked up in ice caps and glaciers.

The Ogallala Aquifer runs underground between the Dakotas and Texas. It has been depleted by 325 billion cubic meters due to overconsumption. That equals 18 times the annual flow of the Colorado River.

Rivers supply the majority of our freshwater but represent only 0.0001 percent (one millionth) of all the water on Earth.

■ *Mulch plants:* Add up to 2 inches of mulch around plants to help conserve soil moisture.

■ *Install windbreaks:* Use an open fence or a hedgerow to slow the wind and reduce drying effects on your yard.

■ *Use native plants:* Take advantage of plants naturally adapted to the local climate.

■ *Wait for wilt:* Hold back on watering until trees and shrubs show signs of stress.

■ *Delay fertilizing:* Withhold nutrients until the watering ban has been lifted or rainfall returns. Fertilizer stimulates new growth, which requires more water.

■ *Mow tall:* Cut grass less often and leave it taller when you do.

■ *Eliminate weeds:* Remove the weeds that compete for scarce water in the soil.

■ *Water accurately:* Avoid watering between plants.

■ *Water appropriately:* Provide trees with one thorough watering in spring and one in summer. In a severe drought, water lawns sparingly. If necessary, allow your lawn to go dormant. Use available water to preserve trees, shrubs, and other high-value plants.

■ *Take advantage of shade:* Move container plants to shaded areas.

■ *Maintain your system:* Check and repair sprinklers to be sure they are not wasting water.

Something as simple as creating a windbreak of trees can significantly reduce the amount of water needed to irrigate your yard.

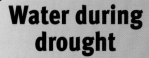

Water during drought

The key to watering during drought restrictions is to wait until just before the point of permanent damage. Learn all you can, and pay attention to the symptoms of thirsty plants:

■ New leaves are smaller than normal.

■ Foliage falls off and branches die back.

■ Leaves wilt.

■ Turfgrass retains a footprint for an hour or more.

Xeriscaping is a relatively new landscape practice that incorporates native and low-water-use plants in landscape designs. These landscapes tend to require much less maintenance as well.

19

Irrigation's
role

I rrigation has been a useful solution to water shortages throughout recorded history. If you needed more water, you simply built a new dam on a river and diverted the water to where you needed it. But today that is not always a practical or affordable solution. The rivers are already dammed, and the population has spread out to the extent that diverting water from one place to another means taking water from people who are already need it, which adds a political dimension to the problem.

New irrigation technology and a much better understanding of plant physiology have fostered the creation of much more efficient systems of irrigation. These modern systems can work for everyone from the farmer to the homeowner.

AUTOMATIC IRRIGATION

Automated and computer-based irrigation timers (above right) are now available that allow homeowners to control precisely the watering time of their plants, adjust for seasonal needs

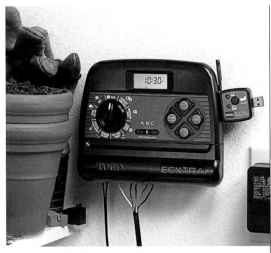

Programmable irrigation timers allow homeowners to adjust for natural rainfall as well as for seasonal and other changes.

throughout the year, shut off the timer if it rains, and adjust to the amount of moisture in the soil. In the near future, timers will be available that can automatically recommend watering schedules and adjust to virtually every aspect of a landscape.

Modern sprinklers are more efficient than ever. There is a sprinkler type for every application. Whether it is a rotor sprinkler covering a large lawn, a spray head watering an area of groundcover, or a bubbler feeding

Up-to-date residential irrigation systems combine several different watering techniques and strategies to minimize water use.

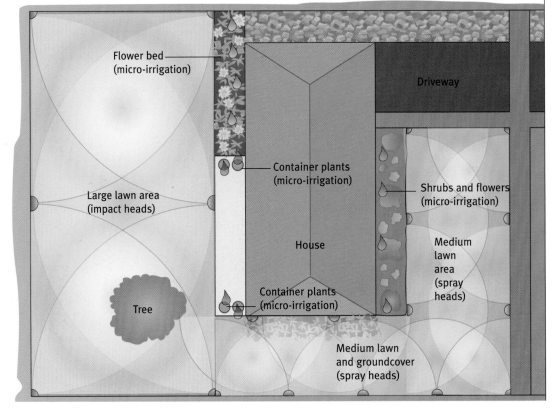

Flower bed (micro-irrigation)

Driveway

Container plants (micro-irrigation)

Shrubs and flowers (micro-irrigation)

Large lawn area (impact heads)

House

Medium lawn area (spray heads)

Container plants (micro-irrigation)

Tree

Medium lawn and groundcover (spray heads)

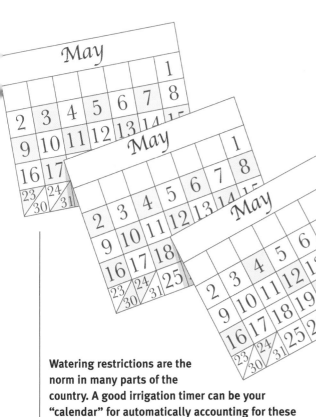

directly on the roots accomplishes several things. First, this eliminated evaporative water losses associated with traditional sprinkler irrigation methods. Second, applying very small amounts of water over long periods of time keeps the soil consistently moist, creating robust plant health even in semiarid conditions. Finally, irrigating just the plants themselves and not the surrounding soil means weed growth greatly diminished, reducing competition for available water.

Drip systems apply water from tubing to the base of the plants using special emitters. These calibrated drip emitters are either preinstalled in the tubing or installed by the user. Different drip rates are available depending on plant needs.

A newer twist on this is micro-irrigation. Micro-irrigation uses miniaturized sprinklers to water very small areas and individual plants without losing excess water to evaporation. This preserves most of the benefits of drip irrigation while extending its usefulness.

Plants in almost any area of your yard can benefit from drip irrigation. About the only place drip systems won't work is on the lawn. Large lawns require the long-range throw of traditional sprinklers. In most other areas, drip irrigation can be used to save substantial amounts of water.

Watering restrictions are the norm in many parts of the country. A good irrigation timer can be your "calendar" for automatically accounting for these watering restrictions.

an individual tree, each can be fine-tuned for any application. Matched Precipitation Rate (MPR) nozzles ensure even, accurate coverage for every corner of a landscape. Irrigation valves are now designed to conserve water, and at the same time protect it from contamination by runoff.

Overwatering and water runoff are major sources of water waste and agricultural pollution in North America. With a well-designed irrigation system, you can be sure you do not add to that problem. In addition, as water rates rise, every drop you save is money in the bank.

DRIP IRRIGATION

The best technologies available today are still drip irrigation and its newer offshoot, micro-irrigation. Both take the concept of even watering and shrink it to the scale of individual plants.

Drip irrigation was first developed in Israel, where water conservation is a high priority. In order to eliminate evaporative water loss, a system was created that dripped water at precise rates, rather than spraying it, from supply tubes onto the ground at the base of plants. Putting the water

Drip emitters are the most water-efficient technology available for irrigating your plants. They enhance plant health while reducing weed growth.

Irrigation's role *continued*

XERISCAPING

Xeriscaping is a relatively new concept in landscape design. Created in 1981 in Colorado as a response to frequent droughts and water shortages, xeriscaping refers to landscape designs that require only minimal irrigation to flourish. The name is derived from the Greek word *xeros,* which means dry. That does not mean that xeriscaped yards need to be dry, barren landscapes. The practice encourages the use of native or well-adapted plants. Nor does it mean maintenance-free. A xeriscape can be as simple or complex as the gardener or designer wishes.

Xeriscaping is applicable to landscapes of any style, including cottage, Japanese, and the Southwestern, among others. They may be formal or natural-looking. The principles used to develop xeriscapes are solid horticultural concepts that work anywhere. Xeriscaping is really about landscaping using native (if possible) drought-tolerant plants and water-saving strategies that create garden and lawn areas that do not consume excessive amounts of irrigation water. Plants well adapted to xeriscaping vary from region to region, so check with your local county extension service for a list of plants that are suited to your area.

Xeriscapes are divided into zones with different water requirements. The **oasis zone** is an area located closest to the house and is where most human activity occurs. Plants in the oasis will have the highest water needs and may also require more maintenance. This is usually the most colorful area of the landscape.

Beyond the oasis is a **transition zone** of moderate water use. This zone contains plants that require infrequent irrigation and usually less maintenance. The outermost zone is a **low-water-use zone,** which requires no supplemental water or very infrequent irrigation only during prolonged dry periods.

By using plants that are well adapted to your area, mulches that suppress weeds and conserve water, and drip irrigation to make the best use of water, xeriscapes can offer color and fragrance with only monthly or seasonal maintenance.

XERISCAPING PRINCIPLES

By applying the following basic principles of xeriscaping to your landscape, you can conserve valuable water resources and create a yard that is less work to maintain and more beautiful to behold.

Xeriscaping can make irrigation-system installation easier and faster. It mandates keeping thirsty plants close to the house, minimizing trenching and extensive plumbing.

Many people assume that xeriscaping is good only for arid desert landscapes, but it can be used anywhere to create a more hardy, water-smart yard.

■ *Group plants:* Design your yard in a way that puts plants with similar water needs in the same area for the greatest irrigation efficiency. This makes maintenance easier and irrigation more efficient.

■ *Practice hydrozoning:* Create irrigation zones that match plant needs so that watering schedules have less built-in waste. (For more on hydrozoning, see page 24.)

■ *Irrigate seasonally:* Adjust your watering schedules to reflect seasonal changes in your plants' water needs. Irrigation requirements change greatly through the course of the year. For instance, spring may bring sufficient rainfall whereas summer may require heavier irrigation.

■ *Practice good irrigation design:* Make sure that irrigated areas are covered uniformly, with no over- or under-watered spots. Good design uses the irrigation technology that is most appropriate to the plants being watered.

■ *Limit turf:* Use turf for function rather than appearance. Turfgrass is ideal for play and high-traffic areas. Other types of plantings may be more appropriate and attractive. Be sure to use grass species compatible with your environment.

■ *Create plant islands:* Arrange water-hungry, high-maintenance plants in accent groupings around the yard rather than in large, difficult-to-water areas.

■ *Choose plants carefully:* Choose plants that are suited to a specific type of environment, such as plants native to your area or ones that come from a similar climate.

■ *Create a patio:* Use hardscape design elements such as patios that enhance your outdoor environment but do not need any water. Choose appropriate materials to complement your plantings as well.

This landscape plan takes advantage of principles of xeriscaping.

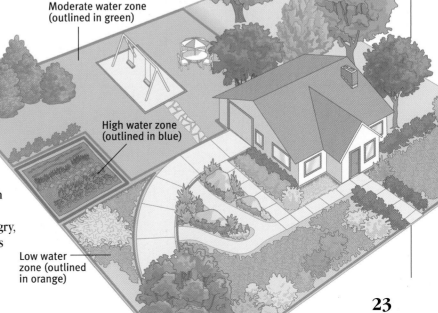

Moderate water zone (outlined in green)

High water zone (outlined in blue)

Low water zone (outlined in orange)

Irrigation's role *continued*

HYDROZONING

Traditionally, irrigation systems have been divided into areas called zones. Zones are sections of an irrigation system that have a number of sprinkler devices sharing the same water lines and a common irrigation valve, with each of the zones controlled independently by the irrigation timer. Zones were first used as a way to maintain proper water pressure in the water pipes feeding the irrigation system, as well as a means of configuring a portion of a watering system for particular crops.

Often the number of sprinkler heads needed to water an area, and the resulting pressure and flow needed by the system to run them, exceeds the pressure and flow that are available from the water source. Each of these independent zones is sized so it won't overtax the irrigation water system. As a result, the optimum water pressure and flow are always maintained.

Hydrozoning extends the zone concept. As the cost of irrigation components has fallen and timers have become more sophisticated, it has become possible to plan and install zones to allow for more specific watering of your plants. For instance, in a traditional layout there might be three or four zones to water the front and back lawns and a few planting beds. In a hydrozoned landscape, you might find as many as 10 zones, each one targeted to a specific plant type. These smaller zones can be set precisely to distribute only the amount of water the plant groupings require.

From a planning perspective, in order for hydrozoning to work correctly and be practical to install, landscapes need to be arranged in such a way that plants with compatible water needs are located on the same zones. This requires a different approach to landscape planning, and often yields surprisingly good results.

A desert oasis is a good example of a natural hydrozone. The plants are grouped close together. All of them have similar water needs that can be met by the available water.

A well-executed hydrozoned yard clusters plants with similar water needs so that each can be irrigated precisely.

PRINCIPLES OF HYDROZONING

Hydrozoning was first used in arid climates, where plants were divided into groupings of high, moderate, and low water use.

■ *High water use:* These are the thirstiest plants, such as lawns, blooming annuals, and vegetables.

■ *Moderate water use:* The plants in this category need more water than nature provides. Usually they need irrigation only while getting established and during long dry spells.

■ *Low water use:* These plants survive with only the water available locally. They are good for planting on slopes, which are difficult to irrigate correctly.

Without hydrozoning, it is almost impossible to correctly water the plants in a large landscape. But by factoring in elements other than water need, such as sun exposure, soil type, and slope, you can create an almost perfect system. For instance, the water requirements of turfgrasses are much different from those of annuals. The water needs of grass located in full sun are different from those of grass that is shaded. Use automatic irrigation controls that allow for multiple run times and start times for each hydrozone. Divide your yard into as many zones as you can. Each area gets the amount of water it needs without any waste.

Take the time to learn about the plants that grow best in your area, and create as many hydrozones in your system as you can afford. The more specific each zone is to the water needs of the plants in it, the more efficient and effective the irrigation will be.

Hydrozoning isn't limited to landscapes with drought-tolerant plants. Even lush landscapes like this one can benefit from precise irrigation.

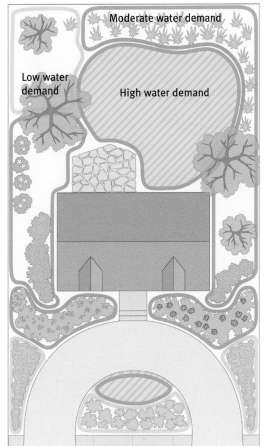

Moderate water demand

Low water demand

High water demand

Hydrozoning is a simple thing to practice. It requires planning the layout of your system and carefully selecting and locating your plants. In this example, turf and flower areas (bordered in blue) are the most water-intensive areas. Bushes and trees (bordered in orange) require less water. Groundcovers (bordered in yellow) demand the least amount of water. Irrigation zones can be planned accordingly.

Irrigation's role *continued*

WATER RESTRICTIONS

Because of droughts and the ever-increasing demand for freshwater, more and more localities are being forced to impose water-use restrictions. Some water authorities limit the days that homeowners can water; others specify the times of the day, usually late evening, when other demands are at their lowest. In some cases, homeowners can be fined for overspray onto walks and driveways. Water rates may also be adjusted to promote long-term conservation. Higher water rates may be imposed during the summer months, or a surcharge may be added to curtail excessive consumption.

Restriction on landscape irrigation is one of the first methods used by localities to reduce consumption when rationing is needed. It is an effective short-term strategy, especially in areas with high water use for irrigation. During an extreme drought, the watering of ornamental plants may be banned outright. Even under such restrictions, automatic irrigation systems allow you to get the most out of the limited water you have available. Such systems can be easily programmed to come on at the time specified by municipal regulations. The sprinklers can be targeted to avoid any water waste. In addition, plants accustomed to proper irrigation have more extensive root systems and a greater chance of survival than non-irrigated plants.

Here are the common types of restrictions that municipalities use to conserve water:

■ *Odd/Even:* This method mandates that certain areas of a water district can water only on odd days of the month, whereas others can water only on the even days.

■ *Interval:* Interval watering means that there is a mandatory amount of time between watering days—for example, every second day or every fourth day.

■ *Day exclusion:* With this method, you would be informed what specific day, or days, of the week watering is not allowed. For example, Monday/Wednesday/Friday or Tuesday/Thursday/Sunday.

Water restrictions do save water, but the practice comes at a price. Local tempers can rise as water use is cut back. Property values are reduced if plantings are allowed to die. And people miss out on the pleasure of growing ornamental plants and vegetables. Educating the community about the wise use of water and adjusting water rates to spur conservation are better long-term strategies.

Online resources for water conservation

Water conservation and good garden management practices go hand in hand. When gathering information, start with the sites listed below.

■ www.irrigation.org
The Irrigation Association is dedicated to fostering efficient water use in irrigation.

■ www.nrcs.usda.gov/partners/for_homeowners.html
The Natural Resources Conservation Service supplies information for commercial as well as residential water users.

■ www.epa.gov
The EPA lists ideas and resources for water conservation as well as a database of native plant species (www.epa.gov/greenscapes/nativeplants/factsht.html).

■ www.garden.org
The National Gardening Association lists practices and resources for saving water in your garden.

■ www.scotts.com
This is a general interest lawn and garden site that gives practices and information on lawn and garden issues.

■ http://www.h2ouse.org
This interactive site explores in-house water conservation.

■ www.awwa.org/waterwiser
This umbrella site give links to all types of water-saving products and references.

■ www.csrees.usda.gov/nea
This site gives links to county extension services and information on many agricultural and irrigation issues.

Conservation tips

- Use native or well-adapted species rather than water-hungry exotics in your landscape.
- Remember to arrange plants with similar water needs into hydrozones.
- Arrange sprinklers to create even coverage to avoid over- and under-watering.
- Water lawns and gardens to keep them consistently moist, not wet.
- Use drip irrigation and micro-irrigation in flower beds to save water and discourage weed growth.
- Install a rain sensor on your automatic irrigation system.
- Practice "grass cycling" (leaving clippings instead of raking them up) to reduce evaporative water loss and to return nutrients to your lawn.
- Remember that shaded areas need less water than sunny areas.
- Aerate your lawn once a year or when thatch is greater than $\frac{1}{2}$-inch thick to enhance water retention and promote deeper root growth and better water absorption.
- Mulch flower beds and trees to retain water and limit competitive plant growth.
- Use a moisture probe to ensure you are watering only the active root zone of your plants.
- If hand-watering, use a hose-end shutoff valve to eliminate overwatering and water waste.
- Create catch basins around trees and shrubs that are hand-watered to allow water to soak into the ground.
- Use multiple, short irrigation run times rather than infrequent long ones to apply the total water needed to reduce runoff and evaporation.
- Water in the early morning rather than the hottest part of the day.
- Use an automatic irrigation system to create the most efficient watering schedule for your yard.
- Adjust your irrigation schedule to account for seasonal variations.
- Prune trees only when needed; pruning enhances new growth, which increases water use.
- Use turf fertilizers that provide a slow release of nutrients to help eliminate surge growth that makes lawns more drought-susceptible.
- Reduce runoff on slopes by watering them for no more than 5 to 10 minutes an hour.

Drip emitters

Lawn aerator

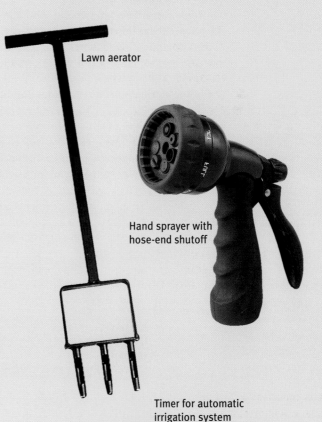

Hand sprayer with hose-end shutoff

Timer for automatic irrigation system

27

Microclimates
in your yard

Most yards do not have one uniform need for a certain amount of water. Instead, each is composed of planting areas that require significantly different amounts of water. These are known collectively as microclimates.

All these microclimates add up to an ecosystem that has a patchwork of irrigation needs. Microclimates can exist in any climate; in fact, two homeowners in two different climates can share similar microclimate characteristics.

For example, a homeowner struggling to maintain a green lawn in hot, dry Southern California does not have the same watering needs as a gardener in New England. But both may have a similar area of their yard that is on a hillside. The water needs of that area will differ from those of the rest of the yard. Slopes or areas under shallow-rooted trees may not receive much water. The plants there may suffer from dehydration even though the rest of the yard is getting adequate water.

The major elements of microclimates interact in different ways in every landscape. The only way to develop a sound irrigation plan is to learn more about each of them and determine how they affect your plants and irrigation plans.

MICROCLIMATE CHARACTERISTICS

Landscape microclimates are created by many different factors. The ones that are most applicable to residential landscapes are rainfall, temperature, wind, humidity, sun exposure, soil, and slope.

■ *Rainfall:* Because rainfall seems to uniformly cover your entire yard—in fact the entire neighborhood—with the same amount of water, it may not seem to be a microevent. However, the effect of rain shadows may drastically alter the amount of water that different areas of your landscape receive. Rain shadows occur in areas that are protected from the prevailing winds by structures, trees, or plantings. By blocking wind-driven rain, these objects can cause a sharp difference in the amount of water the various areas of your yard get from the same storm. As a result, they may need considerably more irrigation than the areas that are more exposed to natural rainfall. Plantings under roof overhangs or sheltered by covered walks may be so dry that they require irrigation, either by hand or from an automatic system, even in an otherwise wet climate.

■ *Temperature:* The hotter the air, the faster water

The different areas of your yard have different needs. These can all be addressed by using the correct water applicator for the plants and microclimate in that section of the landscape.

evaporates, and the sooner the plants will need water again. On a regional basis, areas in the southern United States are hotter than areas to the north. For that reason, more irrigation is required in the South, even though the amount of rainfall may be similar to that of a cooler northern climate. Likewise, when dry spells occur, they tend to cause less damage in cooler northern climates, where there is less evaporative water loss.

Even within your yard, temperature variations can affect your irrigation planning and schedule. Sunny lawns and planting beds are hotter than semishady or shady ones and lose more water to evaporation. The most typical example is a planting bed that is beside a west-facing wall. It picks up substantially more heat than an area on an east- or north-facing wall. If the planting is bounded by a large masonry wall, the mass of the masonry will radiate heat, warming the area long after the sun has gone down.

■ *Wind:* Exposure to the prevailing winds is another factor that affects the microclimates in a landscape. Winds are usually thought of as regional phenomena. In Southern California, for instance, a strong, hot Santa Ana wind occurs seasonally and quickly dries out the landscape, giving rise to the well-known fire seasons in that region. But any area of your yard exposed to strong wind will have accelerated evaporation. Wind carries off moist air, causing plants to transpire water at a higher rate.

Using the correct system in the correct spot in the yard ensures that all your plants get the water they need to flourish. This soaker hose waters plants slowly, putting the water where it is most needed. However, it is a broad-brush approach compared with a well-planned micro-irrigation system. (See pages 79 to 83.)

Microclimates are the small areas of a landscape that have different environmental conditions than other areas in the same yard. These microclimates may have very different water needs.

Microclimates in your yard *continued*

Microconditions can greatly influence the effect of the wind. Putting up windbreaks to protect exposed areas can reduce the wind's drying effect on a landscape. A windbreak can be a fence, a hedgerow, or strategically placed plantings. Whatever you use, be sure it does not completely block the wind. Instead, it should be permeable, slowing the wind down, not blocking it altogether. The reason for this is that on a microlevel, this can create new patterns that affect the areas directly adjacent to the windbreak. Buildings and solid fences can create vortices on their lee side that dry out the plants there at an increased rate. If parts of your garden are exposed to winds on a persistent basis, you should plan to irrigate them on a separate zone.

■ **Humidity:** More water evaporates into dry air than into humid air. In the interior of the continent, away from the coastal areas, the air tends to be drier. It's more humid along the coast and near large bodies of water, such as the Great Lakes. If you live in the interior of the continent, you will need to irrigate more than gardeners in coastal areas. Also, it is important for gardeners in dry climates to use mulch, which reduces evaporative water loss substantially.

■ **Sun:** An area exposed to strong sun for the majority of the day takes up much more water than an area planted with the same material that is shaded for even part of the day. Sunshine fuels photosynthesis, creating an increased demand for water by plants. In addition, the radiant heat from the sun warms the soil and the air, increasing evaporative water loss.

■ **Soil:** Depending on the type of soil you have in your yard, you may need to adjust your irrigation frequency by up to 50 percent. Although soil types are generally uniform throughout a community, it is not uncommon to have more than one type of soil in your yard. If that is the case, you need to create a separate zone for each soil type. For more soil types and classifications, see page 34.

■ **Slope:** An undulating landscape or a hill as a backdrop to your yard can be visually arresting, but watering it correctly can be a bit complex. First of all, hills and slopes are a challenge from a temperature perspective because, depending on their orientation to the sun and the prevailing wind, there can be temperature and evaporation differences from the top of the hill or slope to the bottom. Because cold air is heavier than warm air, slopes tend to be cooler

Wind is a major factor that creates microclimates in your yard, causing exposed plants to transpire more quickly.

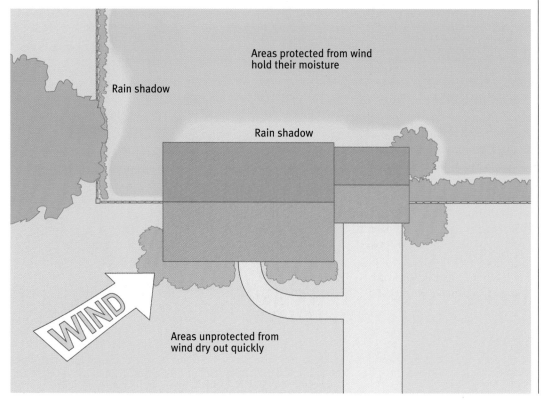

Rain shadow

Areas protected from wind hold their moisture

Rain shadow

WIND

Areas unprotected from wind dry out quickly

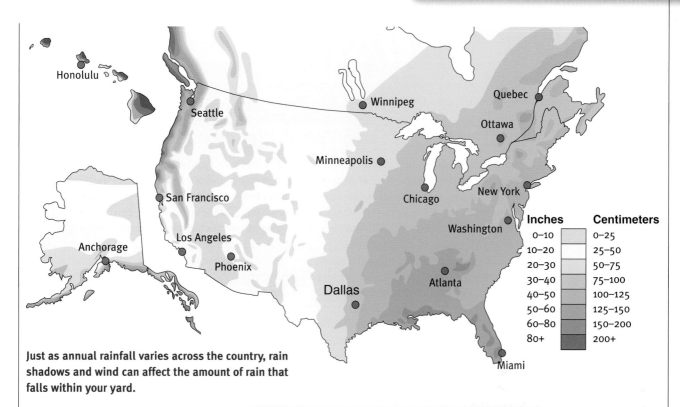

Just as annual rainfall varies across the country, rain shadows and wind can affect the amount of rain that falls within your yard.

Inches		Centimeters
0–10		0–25
10–20		25–50
20–30		50–75
30–40		75–100
40–50		100–125
50–60		125–150
60–80		150–200
80+		200+

at the bottom and collect cold air at night. That is why in certain parts of the country there is frost in the morning at the bottom of a slope and none at the top. The gardener needs to provide a way for cold air to drain off to avoid this. These temperature gradients also affect the amount of moisture needed top to bottom on the slope.

Another consideration when planning irrigation for a slope is the drainage. Because water flows downhill, the top of a hill tends to drain quickly and the bottom collects the water. As a result, if you put the same amount of water on plants at the top of a hill as at the bottom, the plants at the top may not get enough water and the plants at the bottom may get too much. Depending on the degree of the incline, you may also need to adjust the spacing of the sprinklers used on the hill to ensure even coverage. (For more on sprinkler spacing for inclines, see page 127.)

Sun exposure and shade influence transpiration, thus affecting water usage in a lawn or garden.

Understanding
evapotranspiration

Evapotranspiration (ET) rates are a measure of the amount of water that evaporates from the soil, plus the amount of water that is transpired by plants. Evaporation represents water lost to the atmosphere as various factors dry the soil. Transpiration (see page 9) is the water vapor lost through the stomata found on the underside of plant leaves. The sum of the two, usually measured in inches or centimeters per day, is the ET rate for a given plant in a given area.

If you know the evapotranspiration rate for a zone in your yard, you can work out its irrigation needs with this simple equation: Needed irrigation equals evapotranspiration less the precipitation that the zone receives.

If you know how fast the water is being used up by the plants, then you know exactly how much water needs to be applied to compensate for the amount being used. Because the ET rate tells you a plant's water usage on a particular day, using irrigation schedules based on local ET rates is a very precise way to water.

For this reason, it is useful to know the evapotranspiration rate for the area where you

live. ET rates change substantially throughout the year, so homeowners should check them regularly and update their watering accordingly. You might find, for example, that the evapotranspiration rate is 7 to 8 inches per month in July, but only one-third that in November.

New irrigation timers use ET information to create a suggested watering schedule for you. They store historical ET information or access real-time information via the Internet, and then download it to the timer. These devices show great promise in cutting residential irrigation water use.

ET weather stations across the continent track various weather and water patterns. One of the best sources for irrigation-related information is the Irrigation Association (IA). The IA supplies ET information for all 50 states in the United States on its website at www.irrigation.org. You can also obtain local ET information from your county extension service, the weather bureau, and your local water authority.

Originally conceived for agricultural use, ET-based irrigation control was designed for

Evapotranspiration maps show the amount of water being used by plants in any area of the continent on any given day of the year. Knowing that, you know just how much needs to be replaced with irrigation.

raising one type of plant in a uniformly planted field. This made the ET calculations and water applications consistent and fairly simple to compute. Home irrigation based on ET is more complex because it involves various plant types and irregular spacing of those plants. ET rates vary widely from species to species because of many adaptations those plants have made to their native environments. The first residential applications of ET technology were focused on turf watering because lawns are relatively large areas planted with a uniform crop. It is comparable to watering a field of corn.

LANDSCAPE COEFFICIENT

For evapotranspiration-based landscape watering schedules to be any more than estimations, another number is needed. It is called the crop or landscape coefficient (Kc). The Kc is needed because ET information is calculated for only two benchmark plants, grass and mature alfalfa, selected when the ET concept was originally created. These are called the reference ET (ETr) numbers. They do not reflect the unique needs of landscape plants, which vary significantly from the reference ET. For instance, ryegrass needs only about 75 percent of the water that alfalfa does. So the Kc for ryegrass is 0.75 of the reference ET rate for alfalfa. To determine the daily need in inches, you would make the following calculation:

$$ETr \times Kc = \text{plant water requirement (PWR)}$$

It doesn't matter which reference ET number is used, as long as the corresponding Kc is used with it.

Doing this for every type of plant in your yard would be complicated. That is why the new computer- and software-based ET timers are a boon for residential landscape irrigation. Once the basic landscape information is input, the entire process can be automated.

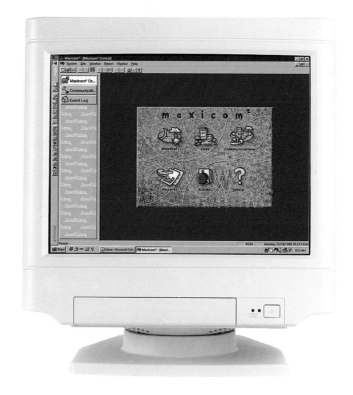

An ET-based irrigation system combines information from moisture sensors with evapotranspiration information to calculate the right amount of water to apply to a landscape.

Simple ET weather stations such as this one have been set up across the country to collect and transmit real-time ET information to farmers as well as gardeners.

Understanding soil

Good soil drains well and holds moisture long enough for plants to absorb what they need. Unfortunately, most of us have to make adjustments for soil that is not quite perfect.

The soil in which your plants grow has an impact on their health and success. It affects the way you water those plants. The soil types in your yard determines water and air availability as well as how fast water penetrates the soil and how long the soil stays wet. All this affects your irrigation needs. To plan an accurate and efficient irrigation system for your home, you need to understand something about the soil that makes up your yard.

All soils are composed of the same ingredients: mineral particles, living and dead organic matter, and pore spaces. A good garden soil is 45 percent minerals, 5 percent organic matter, and 50 percent pore space.

■ *Minerals:* Soils are classified by mineral content based on the type of particles that predominate. The three base particles in all soils are sand, silt, and clay; the difference between them is size and composition. Sand and silt particles are larger, composed mostly of crushed

All soils are derived from three basic components— silt, clay, and sand— in different proportions and with various amounts of organic matter mixed in.

Clay   Silt   Sand

quartz, feldspar, mica, hornblende, and augite. Clay particles are much smaller, needing strong magnification to be seen. They are composed mostly of minerals formed by the chemical breakdown of the minerals in sand and silt.

■ *Organic matter:* This is the part of the soil that is derived from biologic materials. It can include both living organisms as well as decaying animal and plant residues, such as breaking down leaves and plant parts. Combined with organic matter, the particles (also known as separates) form into larger particles, which determine the soil structure. The spaces between the separates are called pore spaces.

■ *Pore space:* This characteristic plays a vital role in soil makeup because an adequate balance of pore sizes is essential. Water is held in the small pores by the attraction of water molecules to themselves. This cohesion is not strong enough to hold the water in the larger spaces, so it drains out, leaving air behind it. Small pore size reduces irrigation requirements; large pore size can require more watering.

SOIL CLASSIFICATIONS

Soil classifications are based on the percentages of sand, silt, and clay contained by a sample. Of all the possible variations, 12 have been defined and are widely accepted. They compose a spectrum of characteristics from very light and dry, as in pure sand, to very heavy and wet, as in pure clay. Everything else falls somewhere in between these extremes. The 12 soils are sand, silt, clay, sandy clays, sandy clay loam, sandy loam, loamy sand, silt loam, silty clay loam, silty clay, clay loam, and loam. (See diagram below.)

About soil pH

Most plants do well in soils with a pH between 5.5 and 7.5. Plant roots can absorb needed soil nutrients best within this pH range. Soil with a high pH can be acidified by adding sulfur. Soil with a low pH can be adjusted upward by adding lime.

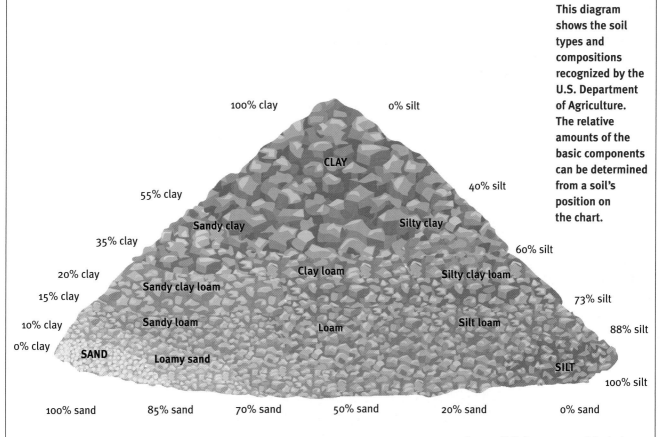

This diagram shows the soil types and compositions recognized by the U.S. Department of Agriculture. The relative amounts of the basic components can be determined from a soil's position on the chart.

Source: U.S. Department of Agriculture

35

Understanding soil *continued*

Loam is the ideal blend and balance of the three basic soil components: sand, silt, and clay. It provides the best possible water retention and drainage characteristics. In well-executed landscapes, loam topsoil is added to help absorb water and prevent the soil from becoming waterlogged by allowing surplus water to drain out quickly. Most landscape soils fall into one of the loam categories.

■ *Clay loam* is characterized by small, platelike particles packed closely together. It has small pore spaces, which makes it drain slowly. Plant roots often grow well in clay loam, but watering is difficult because water puddles up on the surface without sinking in. Most clay loams need little irrigation. Where clay loam predominates, pay careful attention to drainage. If water puddles in the area, mix in organic matter to improve drainage.

■ *Silt loam* has mostly small pores and holds more water than air. A fairly fine-textured soil, silt loam may cause drainage problems if it tends to be more claylike than sandy. It holds minerals and water well, and most plants thrive in it.

■ *Sandy loam* is characterized by large particles providing ample air space and fast drainage. Plant roots grow well in sandy loam, but watering sufficiently can be difficult because the soil drains so well. There is no advantage to heavily watering sandy loam because most of the water will simply drain away. If your soil is sandy, plan an irrigation system that can be turned on frequently and run for short bursts of time. Plants in sandy soils are likely to suffer nutrient deficiencies because minerals are easily washed out. Sandy soils need controlled-release fertilizers.

DETERMINING YOUR SOIL TYPE

Given the importance of soil type to your irrigation and planting plans, soil should be tested to determine exactly what type your property holds. One approach is chemical analysis performed at a soil lab. Lab testing involves collecting samples, sending them to a testing facility, and paying a testing fee. In return you will learn the exact chemical makeup of your soil.

Homeowners may find it cheaper and easier to test their own soil using one of the field tests described on the opposite page.

Either of these tests will give you a good idea of the soil types you have in your yard. Depending on the geology in your area, you may have more than one type of soil. Repeat your testing at various locations if needed. Factor in the characteristics of your soil type(s) when deciding when and how much to water your plants.

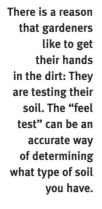

There is a reason that gardeners like to get their hands in the dirt: They are testing their soil. The "feel test" can be an accurate way of determining what type of soil you have.

Jar test

1 A simple way to determine the soil type in your yard is with the jar test.

Fill a glass jar about one-third full with soil from your yard. First remove all rocks and any plant matter, such as stems and roots.

2 Add water to the jar, along with a tablespoon of detergent, and cap it tightly. Shake well and set it aside to settle overnight or until the water is fairly clear. Then evaluate the results.

■ Sandy soil will settle completely and can leave the water looking fairly clear.

■ Clay soil will leave a distinct line of clay at the top of the settled material.

■ Silty loam soil won't settle completely. The water will look dark and have bits of organic matter floating in it.

Feel test

Sandy

Clay

Loam

1 With practice, examining moist soil this way will give you an approximate idea of the soil type you have.

Begin by picking up some dirt from your yard or garden. Rub it back and forth several times in your hands and feel it carefully.

■ A clay soil is slick and smooth, with little or no grittiness. Clay soils are sticky and moldable when wet, and hard and compact when dry.

■ A predominantly sandy soil is gritty and doesn't stick together well. Coarse to fine sand has a moderately gritty feel and doesn't hold together when squeezed.

■ Silt feels smooth and floury when dry, and silky when wet. Organic matter makes a soil feel smoother, as if there were more silt in it.

2 Now, squeeze the dirt in your hand. Does it hold together or fall through your fingers? Does it feel sticky?

■ Clay soil when squeezed feels sticky and forms an impression of your fingers. It can be shaped into a cylinder that holds together well.

■ Sandy soil, when squeezed in your hand, feels gritty and doesn't hold together well. Moist sandy soil can be pressed into a ball, but it will not hold its shape and will break apart with light handling.

■ Silty loam is a good, easy soil to work. A handful of soil can be pressed into a cylinder about a ½ inch long before it breaks.

Understanding soil *continued*

What is beneath the topsoil in your yard can have as much impact on its drainage characteristics as the topsoil itself.

TESTING SOIL DRAINAGE

On a day when the soil is relatively dry, dig a hole about a foot deep and a foot across. Pour a bucket of water into the hole and watch what the water does.

■ If the water drains out almost as fast as you can pour it in, your subsoil is probably sandy and drains too well. You will need to irrigate frequently to keep the soil from drying out.

■ If the hole fills with water, then drains within a few minutes, you have good drainage. Irrigation will not be a problem in such soil.

■ If the water just sits there, you have poor drainage. Improving the soil with soil amendments such as sphagnum peat moss or compost will help. Or consider correcting the drainage of your lot by installing an irrigation system. If you are not ready for such large-scale modifications, consider raised beds filled with good topsoil for vegetable plots and small flower gardens.

SUBSOIL DRAINAGE

Having top-quality, loamy topsoil doesn't always guarantee good drainage. Most lots are covered with a relatively thin layer of topsoil of moderate to good quality. Beneath this lies a layer of subsoil that is generally low in nutrients and either so sandy that it drains too well or so rich in clay that it barely allows root growth. In some areas, the topsoil is directly on top of impervious rock or covers extremely compacted clay called hardpan. Subsoil commonly accumulates materials that leach down from the topsoil. These include clay, iron and aluminum oxides, calcium carbonate, and other materials that can create a very tightly packed layer.

There is little to be gained by installing irrigation in a yard that suffers major drainage problems. Why bring in more water if you're already having trouble getting rid of what you have? Before you invest in irrigation, correct the problem by installing drainage tiles and drains, adding high-quality topsoil, and reinforcing and firming up slopes to ensure that excess water will drain quickly and safely.

Digging a hole, filling it with water, and then observing how well it drains is a good way to determine if you'll have any drainage problems.

Is irrigation right for you?

Manufacturers have vastly improved the controls, valves, tubing, and components needed for a home watering system. Still, extensive installation can be a considerable expense and can disrupt your plantings to the point that it may take several seasons for them to recover. If you spare the budget by doing it yourself, you may find the planning time-consuming. The installation process may take several weekends, with many runs to your irrigation equipment supplier, plus a hefty bill for rental equipment. It is well worth asking yourself whether installing a residential watering system is right for you.

ASSESS THE ALTERNATIVE

Although hand watering can be reasonably effective in some climates, it doesn't approach the precision and water conservation of a carefully planned automated system. Few people have the time to water when their plants most need watering. Nor is it possible for most people to judge accurately how much water is the right amount. Too often, hand-watering wastes water and can damage plants if the water pressure is too forceful.

Convenience is also a compelling reason for installing a system. With an automatic timer, the system will work when you are asleep or at work. It can continue to function while you are out of town, preserving the health of your plants and aiding household security by giving the impression that the house is occupied.

Finally, a watering system can add to the value of your home—sometimes by as much as 10 percent. In addition, the health and attractiveness of your landscaping and the perceived advantages of buying a home with a watering system already installed can speed the sale of your property.

Happy plants mean happy people

A 25-square-foot patch of healthy grass provides enough oxygen for one person for an entire day. That doesn't even include what is added by all the other plants in the yard.

On a block of eight average-size houses, the front lawns have the cumulative cooling effect of 70 tons of air-conditioning. Most whole-house A/C units are rated at 3 to 4 tons.

Designing and installing an irrigation system is not difficult, but it does require good planning and installation technique.

Is irrigation right for you? *continued*

GOOD REASONS TO ADD A WATERING SYSTEM

Only you can decide whether an irrigation system is right for you and your yard. But once you consider the many advantages that automatic irrigation offers, it is hard to say no to it.

■ *DIY friendly:* Any irrigation system takes some installation, but techniques have improved and been simplified greatly since home irrigation first became available. The earlier metal-pipe systems were unwieldy and complicated to install. Modern irrigation systems have piping and heads that simply snap or glue together, and tubing easily cut to the correct length. It is relatively simple to install a modest system in several weekends, especially if the irrigation plans have been carefully prepared. Irrigation equipment suppliers offer a wide range of products to answer almost every need. You can also rent trenching equipment that makes the most laborious part of installation—digging the trenches—fast and painless. The equipment causes so little damage to the lawn and garden that within only a week you can barely see any evidence of the excavation.

■ *Cost-effective:* At one time, the major concern of any homeowner considering installing an irrigation system was the cost. The advent of new lightweight materials has changed all that, bringing the cost of installing a system within the reach of almost every budget. Although prices vary widely according to the size of the property, many homeowners find that an efficient watering system can be installed for less than $2,000, and often less than $1,000. Most systems will pay for themselves in only a few years through reduced water bills. In addition, these systems will let you enjoy the improved health of the lawn and garden, reduced loss of plants to drought, and greatly decreased yard maintenance.

■ *Precise:* Lawn and garden irrigation can be tailored to your specific needs. Hose-end sprinklers are generally imprecise, overwatering

A well-designed, well-maintained irrigation system can add substantial value to your home and make it easier to sell when you put it on the market.

In the final analysis, home irrigation may be worth it just for the time it gives you to enjoy your yard rather than time spent watering it.

slopes and leaving dry areas behind shrubs and trees. On the other hand, irrigation systems are tailored to every space in the yard. Different zones run their own schedules to meet the needs of the plants they are watering. An inground system is laid out to water evenly and only where needed—not on sidewalks or driveways.

■ *Upgradable:* Irrigation systems can be fully manual, fully automated, or something in between. Modern systems are completely adaptable to the changing needs of your yard. Timers can be expanded. Spray nozzles can be changed. Traditional sprinkler zones can be converted to drip or micro-irrigation. Even adding new zones is simple, as long as they are allowed for in your initial plan.

■ *Attractive:* A well-executed irrigation system is barely noticeable. The underground pipes are hidden, and pop-up spray heads disappear into the ground when not in use. Compare that with the look of a hand-watered landscape: hoses and sprinklers all over the yard. They are unsightly, and present a real tripping hazard as well.

■ *Long lasting:* New irrigation system components are built of weather-resistant plastics, which are not subject to rust or decomposition. They can be expected to last for decades. Some even carry lifetime guarantees. Individual parts—such as sprinkler heads—that may be stepped on or nipped by the lawn mower can easily be repaired or replaced. In fact, the only routine maintenance needed in most climates is the occasional cleaning of exposed parts and the flushing of drip emitters to prevent the buildup of deposits.

■ *Easier gardening:* Many homeowners dream of a beautiful landscape that takes care of itself. An automatic irrigation system comes close to achieving that dream, letting you enjoy the pleasurable aspects of gardening while avoiding much of the drudgery. The use of a moisture sensor or rain shutoff with your timer means the system requires the least possible human intervention.

■ *Mulch friendly:* Automatic irrigation is also well-suited to a process that is central to low-maintenance gardening—mulching. Mulch is the perfect cover for the unattractive tubing of many drip systems. And using mulch prevents weed germination, keeps the ground cooler, slows down evaporation, and generally decreases yard upkeep.

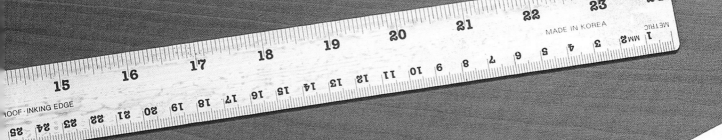

Planning your system

Careful planning is the key to success when adding an irrigation system. Each landscape is unique and requires its own unique plan. The starting point is a map of your landscape and an understanding of its watering needs. The map should be as detailed as possible, dividing the landscape into zones and describing the particular needs of each zone. If you are moving into a new home, it's important to wait until the landscape plan is completed on paper before planning a watering system.

Explore your water supply options. You'll want to confirm the water capacity of your home and find out whether there are any municipal water restrictions. You might also want to explore alternate or supplemental sources of water, such as a well or a pond.

Once you've established your water source, you have a few basic decisions to make: Do you want a sprinkler system, a micro-irrigation system, or both? Each has advantages, so you'll want to learn about the products available before you decide which is best for your landscape and your budget.

If in the end you have any doubts or areas of concern, consult a professional. It's far better to uncover a mistake at the planning stage than to discover a major flaw after the system is installed.

You will also need to decide whether you want to do the work yourself or hire a professional. The following pages will help you draw up a plan that is right for your landscape and help you decide how to implement it.

SCALE: ☒ 1" = 10' ☐ 1" = 20' ☐ 1" = 3...

Planning your system

DIGEST

Q&A

Q What sprinkler heads are the most effective?

A *Bubblers* get the bronze medal. They can water areas up to about 5 feet in diameter. They flood water onto the ground and do a good job of watering trees and shrubs.

Fixed-spray sprinklers win the silver medal with a range of about 5 to 15 feet. They are available in many different preset and adjustable patterns, making them versatile for watering.

Rotor sprinklers win the gold medal—they are good for distances from about 15 to 45 feet. They come in two varieties—impact sprinklers and gear-drive sprinklers. Impact rotors are ideal for large lawn areas. Gear-drive rotors water more slowly and are well-suited to slow-draining soils, slopes, and lawns. (For information on these sprinkler heads, see page 49.)

To do

✓ Find out local code requirements.

✓ Draw a scale diagram of the property and all buildings and plantings. Also indicate any microclimates.

✓ Have all buried utilities in the yard marked, and add them to the drawing.

✓ Measure the water system flow capacity and pressure.

✓ Plot in the needed sprinklers, using head-to-head coverage.

✓ Define the final irrigation zones based on the total flow of the sprinklers and the available water supply.

✓ Plot in the irrigation lines, zone valves, and timer positions.

A DROP AT A TIME

Drip emitters, as the name implies, drip water onto the soil at the base of a plant. They water slowly, at about 1 to 4 gallons per hour. Drip emitters are either in-line emitters or punch-in emitters. This means they are directly in the water flow (in-line) or are connected to the outside of the drip tubing (punch-in) emitters.

Micro-irrigation uses miniaturized versions of normal sprinklers to water individual plants or small areas of plants. They water at a higher rate than drip emitters, anywhere from 10 to 15 gallons per hour. They are available with flow rates ranging from ½ to 4 gallons per hour.

TOOLS OF THE TRADE

To measure and record the dimensions and layout of your property, you'll need the following to take measurements:
- 50-foot tape measure
- Carpenter's level
- String
- Stakes

To make the initial drawing, you'll need:
- Plain and graph paper on a clipboard
- Pencils and erasers
- Drawing compass
- Ruler

TIMERS ON YOUR SIDE

A timer, also called a controller, is the brains of an irrigation system. Without a timer, you might as well be hand-watering. Timers are either mechanical or programmable.
- Mechanical timers, although simple to use, have limited capabilities and cannot be programmed for municipal water restrictions. They are not useful in many areas of North America.
- Automatic programmable timers can be set to run your irrigation system indefinitely.
- Advanced programmable timers can accommodate water restrictions as well as rain and seasonal changes to your irrigation schedule.

But that's not all. New technology will soon make it possible to program a timer from a personal computer using weather information from the Internet to create a watering schedule.

FINDING FREE WATER

Irrigation systems can be connected to water sources other than your home's water supply.

- You may be able to dig or tap into a well to supply water for your irrigation system.
- Consider installing a system for collecting and storing rainwater for irrigation use.
- It is possible to recycle water from your home ("gray water") to use for irrigation.

Whether you use your home's water supply or an alternate source, you'll need to install a backflow prevention device to protect your home's drinking water from accidental contamination.

TRY THE "CATCH-CAN" TEST

Got a system you think might need an upgrade? All it takes is an hour and some empty cans to find out how much water your sprinklers apply and where they apply it. See page 144.

Professional
versus DIY

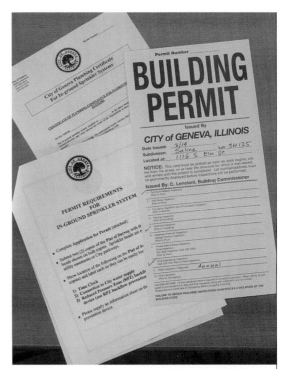

Before starting any irrigation project, check with your local municipality to see what regulations apply and what permits are needed.

Do-it-yourself (DIY) irrigation is becoming easier and less expensive every year. New components and materials make installing an irrigation system a job that can be done by a capable homeowner in a few days. But the process of digging trenches, installing the plumbing, and meeting all the building codes is still involved. Carefully evaluate your desire to DIY before you dig in.

Installing a system requires little in the way of specialized equipment. You can rent any items you do need. Doing the job yourself usually costs about half as much as having the system professionally installed. However, a poorly installed system can require extensive revisions, thereby negating any savings you may have accrued doing it yourself. So plan your system thoroughly before you begin. And carefully consider whether it is a project you want to take on yourself.

A system that requires extensive trenching may best be handled by the pros. However, a homeowner can rent several trenching and digging machines.

NEED HELP?

Don't hesitate to consult with an irrigation system specialist. Many irrigation dealers will draw a plan without charge if you buy the parts from them. See the section "Design Services" (opposite) for more information

In a few cases, it is best to leave the installation work to a qualified dealer: if you have severe erosion problems, very rocky soil, steep slopes, or delicate plantings that need protection. One advantage of consulting a professional in the planning stage is the advice you can obtain concerning problem areas.

Many municipalities require that a licensed plumber install at least some parts of an irrigation system—for instance, a copper pipe from the city water main to the main irrigation system shutoff or to the backflow prevention device. If so, you can still save money by preparing the work site beforehand. Determine the proper placement of the components, dig the trenches and holes, and have the needed parts on hand before the plumber gets there. If your municipality has no such restrictions, you are free to do the entire installation yourself.

Planning
aids

A little assistance from a landscape architect, an irrigation dealer, or a planning service can save time. The better ones will design your system and create a master list of all the parts and fittings you will need—a list you can forward to a local home center in order to pick up all the parts in one trip. Some design companies charge a small fee; some will assist you at no charge—a service they offer to potential customers. There are several advantages to consulting with the pros:

■ They provide exact spray patterns (which are hard to plot), ensuring even water coverage— a detail that's important for efficient operation.

■ A pro may be aware of specialized sprinklers and emitters for specific needs.

■ Professionals can recommend the newest solutions for your landscape. Irrigation systems are constantly being improved and updated. It's a retailer's job to keep up with developments.

FINDING A DESIGN SERVICE

Check whether there are irrigation dealers or landscape architects in your area that offer design services. If there are several, it's a good idea to check out more than one. Some are better than others, whether free or not.

Make sure the service will supply a complete parts list for the system they have designed. This is a task where firsthand knowledge of irrigation components and fittings is important—and often baffling to the newcomer. Also, if you are considering a do-it-yourself service, be sure it requires precise measurements of your yard. If it does not, you cannot be sure the result will be as accurate as it needs to be.

If you choose to use a free online or mail-in planning service from a manufacturer or supplier, you will still have to supply all the basic measurements discussed in this chapter. You can complete the entire site map in a few hours. When you are done measuring and drawing your yard, just mail or upload your information to the manufacturer, and your plan will soon be on its way back to you.

A free design usually includes a completed design and a list of parts for the system. Such a service saves you time and provides a more accurate plan than you could do yourself.

Design services

The major irrigation equipment suppliers offer design services. Irrigation dealers may also be a good source for design expertise.

■ **LAWN GENIE** www.lawngenie.com
Lawn Genie is a well-known brand that offers a no-cost irrigation design service.

■ **ORBIT** www.orbitonline.com
Orbit offers an online interactive design program that helps you draw and submit your plan.

■ **RAIN BIRD** www.rainbird.com
Rain Bird offers a comprehensive design service but charges a modest fee, which is refunded if you purchase any Rain Bird products (no minimum dollar amount).

■ **TORO** www.toro.com
Toro is a major player in irrigation and offers a free design service with e-mail notification to let you know when your design is ready.

Understanding
irrigation systems

In addition to watering your lawn, the irrigation system you install should be flexible enough to handle the many plants and environments in your yard.

The three basic irrigation systems—sprinkler-based, micro and drip, and hose-end—each have advantages. Which system is best for you depends on the water needs of your particular landscape.

A sprinkler-based system is the most popular method of irrigating residential landscapes but the most work to install. It delivers water through underground pipes to individual sprinklers (or heads) and uses your home's water pressure to release it with enough force to produce a spray. Many different spray heads and nozzles are available. By varying heads in different zones of a landscape, you will meet most water needs.

Drip and micro-irrigation systems deliver smaller amounts of water more frequently to a landscape's root zone. These microsprayer or drip systems use much less water than other systems but do not work well for expansive areas. They are ideal for smaller gardens and potted plants.

Hose-end systems deliver water via a garden hose attached to an outdoor spigot. More sophisticated hose attachments and timers have improved the ease and effectiveness of these systems. You can set up hose-end systems as either sprinkler systems or drip systems. They are easy to install, requiring no digging, but hoses can be a tripping hazard and must be taken up at the end of each season.

Most likely, you will combine two or more of these systems to create an overall system that addresses all your irrigation needs.

SPRINKLER-BASED SYSTEMS

When people think of sprinkler systems, they typically envision either large arcs of water produced by fixed-head sprinklers or the

Where to soak up useful info

Many irrigation specialists offer free or low-cost clinics or workshops. These may be sponsored by retailers or local horticultural societies. Attending a clinic or workshop is a good way to learn about the basics of irrigation, both planning and installing, and an opportunity to ask questions of an expert. Check with your local home center or irrigation dealer.

expansive lawns that are not often dug up and replanted.

Three types of sprinkler heads used in these systems are made for different watering needs.

■ *Impact rotors* are best for large lawn and garden areas because they have the longest range and generally the highest precipitation rate. They deliver sweeping streams of water in circular areas up to 90 feet in diameter (a 45-foot radius).

■ *Gear-drive rotors* also deliver sweeping streams of water that can cover a large area, but the precipitation rate is generally lower. These heads are well suited to watering slopes where runoff is a problem.

■ *Fan sprays and bubblers* are stationary spray heads with a shorter range than impact rotors or gear-driven rotors. They do not rotate or move but emit a fan of water that covers an area less than 15 feet in diameter. They are commonly used for small areas of turf and flower beds.

unmistakable *tick-tick-tick* of an impact sprinkler. They are picturing a traditional automatic sprinkler system.

If you need to irrigate a large lawn, this is definitely the best system. It uses underground plumbing to send water under pressure to large sprinkler heads. The heads are usually the only visible components; pop-up heads recede underground when not in use.

Because these systems require considerable trenching, they are more expensive to install than aboveground systems. However, inground sprinkler systems require little maintenance. Usually all they need are minor adjustments and, in cold climates, seasonal draining. As an investment, an inground, high-pressure sprinkler system can add considerably to the resale value of a home.

Sprinkler systems use more water than micro-irrigation systems but much less than hand-watering. Because they deliver water quickly and efficiently, they are a good choice for

An impact rotor is ideal for watering large grassy areas but may not be the best choice for flowers, ornamentals, and shrubs.

49

Understanding irrigation systems *continued*

Drip irrigation was developed to save water in arid environments, but also promotes more robust plant growth when properly used.

DRIP AND MICRO-IRRIGATION SYSTEMS

Drip and micro-irrigation systems are the water-saving champions of the irrigation world. They apply water, either by dripping or spraying, directly to individual plants or small areas of plants.

■ *Drip:* These systems use small emitters installed in water lines to drip water at a slow, constant rate directly at the base of a plant. Because the water is delivered directly to the surface of the soil, it does not evaporate and soil beyond the drip area stays dry. The ability to withhold water from certain areas of the landscape is an advantage because dry soil prevents weed seeds from germinating. Homeowners can keep areas such as the spaces between rows in a vegetable garden or gravel walks and driveways virtually free of unwanted vegetation by not irrigating them.

Drip irrigation also keeps leaves dry, thereby avoiding plant diseases. With hand-watering and sprinkler irrigation, diseases tend to spread to susceptible leaves via drops of water bouncing from the soil. Diseases also may be promoted since the leaves often stay wet, inviting fungal diseases. Keeping foliage dry inhibits the spread of disease.

■ *Micro-irrigation:* Micro-irrigation systems use miniaturized sprinklers installed in small water lines to apply water. The aboveground spray does result in some evaporation, but these systems are nearly as efficient as drip systems and have a broader range of applications.

Drip and microsystems are usually installed on the surface, so no digging is necessary. This makes them easy to install, so you can adapt to changing plant layouts. Some hardware stores and garden centers carry inexpensive drip irrigation kits that can be installed in a day. Installing a new emitter takes only seconds. You can also take up a drip irrigation system in minutes to rototill a bed or to store the system for the winter.

Adding a layer of mulch over your drip or microsystem is a fast and easy way to hide whatever is not already hidden behind or under plantings. More important, the mulch prevents evaporation, which would otherwise happen quickly because water is delivered at such slow rates.

Drip emitters and microsprays are available in many sizes and shapes.

New hose-end systems can handle a wider range of irrigation needs than earlier systems. This setup includes several timers and controls that allow you to preprogram four separate irrigation zones.

HOSE-END IRRIGATION SYSTEMS

Hose-end systems are just what they sound like—irrigation systems that deliver water by means of a garden hose. For years this meant a sprinkler set in the middle of the yard, and then the water turned on or off at the garden spigot. Most people tended to turn on their system and forget about it, which led to overwatering. Because of this, hose-end systems have been regarded as the "poor relation" of the irrigation world. But recent improvements to timers and other features have made this water delivery system easier to use and more versatile, particularly for small planting areas.

One advantage of a hose-end system is its portability. Because it is a surface system attached to an outdoor spigot, it is easy to roll up and put away when garden work needs to be done or winter is coming.

In the past, most gardeners didn't use timers with their hose-end setups. Those that did used a simple battery-operated box that would control only one zone. A hose-end setup could water a small lawn well, but not much more.

Today, several manufacturers produce systems with multiple zones and controls that mount beside your spigot and can be run on house current or batteries. Hose-end systems give you much of the functionality of inground irrigation. In addition, you can use either sprinklers or drip and microcomponents—whatever works for your yard.

Like the tubing used for drip systems, hoses can be quickly covered with mulch. Also, like drip systems, sprinklers can be added or taken away easily.

If you have a small garden to water or if you cannot justify installing a permanent inground system, a simpler hose-end layout may fit your needs.

Hose-end timers are available in mechanical or programmable models. Often, several different zones can be watered with one timer.

51

Water sources

The first thing to consider as you begin to draw up plans for your irrigation system is the source of your water. Most homeowners rely on their household water supply; however, in many regions it has become an increasingly costly and complicated source.

For instance, more and more areas are adopting progressive water-rate pricing structures, which means that the more water you use, the more you pay. In addition, water-use restrictions are increasingly imposed by states or communities, limiting both when and for how long irrigation can be done. Also, in many communities water used for landscaping is not subtracted from sewer fees, even though water used in a sprinkler system does not drain into the sewer system. Some municipalities allow a separate meter for the watering system, but excessive installation fees discourage many homeowners. All these measures are intended to conserve potable drinking water supplies. As a result, you may be able to save money if you can tap into another source of water for your irrigation needs.

GOING "OFF THE GRID"

Some alternative water sources can be used alone or as a supplement to the municipal water supply to meet irrigation needs. These include irrigation wells, ponds and other surface water, rainwater catchment systems, and reused "gray water" (bathing, dishwashing, and laundry wastewater) from your home.

Wells, ponds, and other surface-water sources are the easiest to use and set up. Rainwater retrieval systems are more involved. Gray-water systems require by far the most work to install properly and safely.

Each of these systems has requirements that are best discussed with a licensed irrigation planner or master plumber. If your system will require a pump, it's critical that the pump has the proper pressure and flow for the job. It's best to consult with a qualified pump dealer to determine the pump type and size to use for your system. (See photo on opposite page.) Take along a copy of your irrigation plan.

WELLS, PONDS, AND OTHER SURFACE WATER

Irrigation wells, ponds, and other surface water are fairly simple to tap into. Basically, a pump extracts water from the source, adds pressure, and sends the water into a line that delivers it where it is needed. Choosing the right pump for the job is the challenging part.

There are two pump types—deep-well and shallow-well. As a general rule, a well that is more than 75 feet deep calls for a deep-well pump. A shallow-well pump is fine for shallower wells and surface water.

■ *Deep-well pump:* The most common deep-well pump is a jet pump. It is a self-contained unit that is dropped into the well, with just a power cord, a water line, and sometimes a separate tether coming up out of the well. This pump is virtually silent because it operates underwater far beneath the surface—a feature you may appreciate at four in the morning when your sprinkler system comes on.

■ *Shallow-well pump:* A shallow-well jet pump works the same way, for wells or other shallow water sources, and is also fairly quiet.

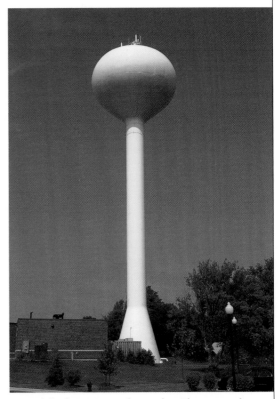

A municipal water supply need not be your only source of irrigation water. Wells, ponds, and roof runoff systems are sources that can supply water at little cost.

Suction pumps are another option for shallow water sources, but they are not as quiet. They sit at ground level and use a hose to draw up the water. The pumps are portable and can be used for other jobs if need be. They're also easy to service if there are problems.

Jet pumps and suction pumps do the job well, provided they are big enough to handle the demand.

If a pump is used only to feed an irrigation system, a holding tank may not be needed, provided the output from the pump is high enough to meet the pressure and flow needs of your most demanding irrigation zones. If your irrigation plan calls for the use of a water pump, buy the pump only after you have completed your irrigation design.

Backflow prevention (see page 73) is a key element in any irrigation system. It is especially important when you are pumping nonpotable water. Even if your irrigation system will be completely separate from your household water, some regulations may require that backflow prevention be installed. Contact your building department to find out which backflow prevention meets local codes.

USING RAINWATER

In some areas of the country, it may be possible to use rainwater as the sole source or as a supplement to a freshwater municipal supply.

The simplest rainwater systems collect runoff from a building's gutters and redirect it to a sealed storage tank, sometimes referred to as a cistern, for later use. In some circumstances, diverters may be installed that send the excess water back to the storm drains when the tank is full. To keep leaves and other debris out of the water storage tank, "sweepers" are used. These work by flushing the first several gallons of water to come off the roof into the normal storm drain, then allowing the rest to be collected and stored for later use. Systems such as this are surprisingly simple to create, and most homeowners can benefit from their use.

As with a well or pond system, you need a pump to move and pressurize the water for your irrigation system. Because rainwater is usually used as a supplement to your normal water supply, you will need to tie into that system. Backflow prevention (see page 73) is mandatory. As always, check the local codes before you embark on a project of this nature.

Ponds are a good source of irrigation water. Using any type of surface water requires the use of a special pump to get the water to your irrigation system at the right pressure.

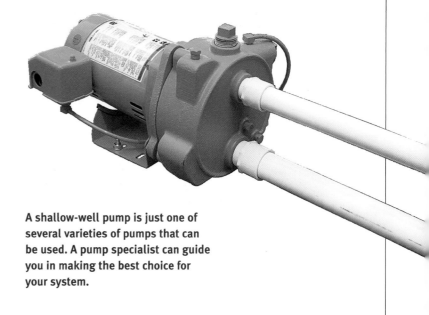

A shallow-well pump is just one of several varieties of pumps that can be used. A pump specialist can guide you in making the best choice for your system.

Water sources

continued

A rain barrel is a simple way of solving an age-old problem: how to capture water during times of plenty and save it for times of need.

RECLAIMED WATER

Using reclaimed residential water, or gray water, to irrigate lawns and ornamentals is gaining in popularity in many localities. Reclaimed water is water that has been used for household tasks such as washing dishes or clothes. It has not been used in toilets and has not had toxic substances added to it. Several municipalities now supply treated reclaimed water to homes through a separate delivery system and require that it be used for all landscape irrigation.

Reclaiming your home's gray water without municipal assistance requires extensive replumbing and constant vigilance that toxic substances are not poured down sink drains. The plumbing work is much easier in new construction but is possible in an older home if you are committed to its success.

You can route runoff from your roof to a planting area and hold it in a gravel-filled catch basin. More sophisticated systems are available that capture and even filter rainwater for other uses.

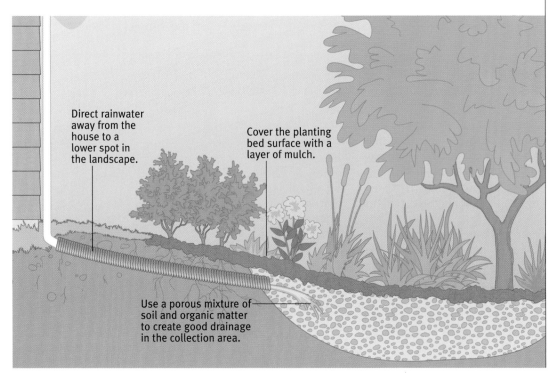

Direct rainwater away from the house to a lower spot in the landscape.

Cover the planting bed surface with a layer of mulch.

Use a porous mixture of soil and organic matter to create good drainage in the collection area.

Pumps
and master valves

If you install an irrigation pump or a master valve, it will require a special connection to your timer. This connection is needed because both of these devices must be running at all times while the irrigation system is functioning—in the case of a pump, even before the irrigation system is activated. If you are using a pump or master valve, your timer should have a pump start relay terminal. This allows you to coordinate the use of your pump with the rest of your irrigation system.

■ *Pump start relay:* This electrical device lets your irrigation timer communicate with the pump. Because an irrigation timer operates on low voltage, and pumps are built to use normal house current, the relay acts as a go-between, changing the irrigation timer voltage—usually 24 volts—to standard household voltage.

The pump start relay should be connected to the master valve (MV)/pump relay terminal and to the COM terminal on the timer (see page 141), using normal irrigation valve wire. The pump is then connected to the relay, using

wiring appropriate to your pump.

The pump start relay must be mounted at least 15 feet from the timer and from the pump to avoid electrical interference that may cause it to malfunction.

■ *Master valve:* This valve opens and shuts the water supply every time the irrigation system is used and ensures that water will not be wasted when the system is off. A master valve is cheap insurance against a major plumbing failure.

Unlike the main shutoff for the house water supply, the master valve opens and closes every time the system is used. For instance, if a primary connection on the supply side of an irrigation valve fails for any reason and the system is not running, no water will be lost.

The master valve should be installed in a protected location between the main shutoff and the irrigation valves. Like the pump start relay, the master valve is attached to the MV terminal and the normal COM terminal on your irrigation timer using normal irrigation wiring. You do not need a relay for the master valve.

Master valves are the same valves you would use as automatic zone control valves. They are installed on the main irrigation supply line to turn the water off when the system is not active.

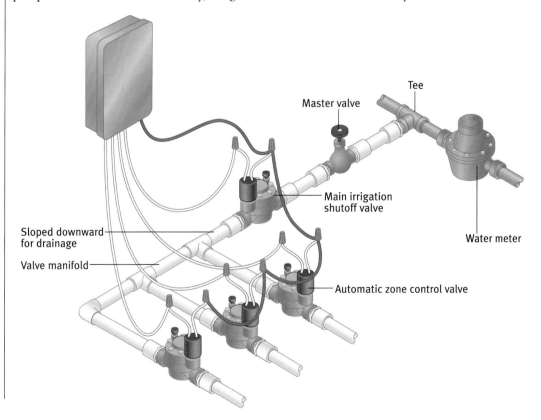

Tee

Master valve

Main irrigation shutoff valve

Sloped downward for drainage

Valve manifold

Water meter

Automatic zone control valve

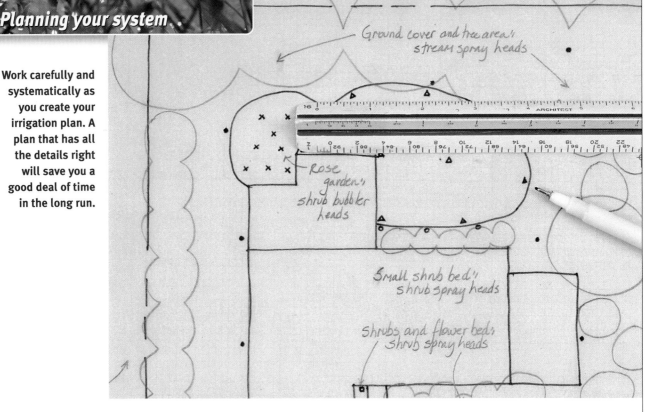

Ground cover and tree area's
stream spray heads

Rose
garden:
shrub bubbler
heads

ARCHITECT

Small shrub bed:
shrub spray heads

Shrubs and flower beds:
shrub spray heads

Work carefully and systematically as you create your irrigation plan. A plan that has all the details right will save you a good deal of time in the long run.

Measuring
and mapping

Planning is in many ways the most important step in creating an irrigation system. A well-planned job will proceed smoothly, with few last-minute changes or extra trips to the store. Each irrigation job is unique because each depends on a wide range of factors, all closely tied to the property to be irrigated.

An effective irrigation plan is tailor-fit to the contours and quirks of the yard.

If someone else creates the actual irrigation specifications for you, they will need accurate and clear information about your property and the existing water source.

Unless you plan to contract out the entire process to an irrigation dealer, clear off some desk space, gather some simple drafting tools, and think through the project on paper. Give yourself sufficient time to get your measurements right. If possible, have someone help you; two sets of eyes decreases the possibility of mistakes.

In this section, you'll learn how to determine the water capacity of your home, how to measure and draw your property on a grid, and how to choose and plot the components for your system.

Tools you will need

To draw your new irrigation system, you will need only a modest collection of drafting tools. In addition to the landscape drawing you have been working on, you will need a scale ruler, a drawing compass, a calculator, colored thin-tip markers, and the parts list or catalog from the manufacturer.

Take all measurements carefully. Then measure again to ensure accuracy.

PLOTTING YOUR PROPERTY

Whether you design an irrigation system yourself or use a service, you will need to make a scale drawing of your yard. Since this drawing will be the basis of your system plan, it is important that it be precise and accurate. You will need plain and graph paper, pencils, erasers, a 50-foot or longer tape measure, a ruler, a compass, and stakes for marking the landscape.

■ *A basic sketch:* If an existing landscape or real estate drawing is available, you can use it to get started. However, it is important to double check all measurements. If no previous layout drawing is available, begin by making a rough sketch of your property on plain white paper. Then take the measurements.

Start by measuring the outside dimensions of the house. Then measure in both directions from the corners of the house to the property lines. Have someone hold one end of the tape measure for you, or stake it through the loop at the end of the tape to hold it in place. Pull the tape taut for an accurate measurement.

■ *A scale drawing:* Once you are sure of the house and lot measurements, transfer them to graph paper. Unless your yard is very large, an 11×17-inch sheet will provide adequate space

Property sketch

Begin by making a rough sketch of the layout of your property without concern for the exact scale of the drawing. Include the following in your drawing, then record your measurements:

■ Property outline
■ House and other structures
■ Driveways and walkways
■ Gardens and flower beds
■ Trees and shrubs
■ Future plantings
■ Lawn areas
■ Slopes
■ Sun, shade, and wind direction

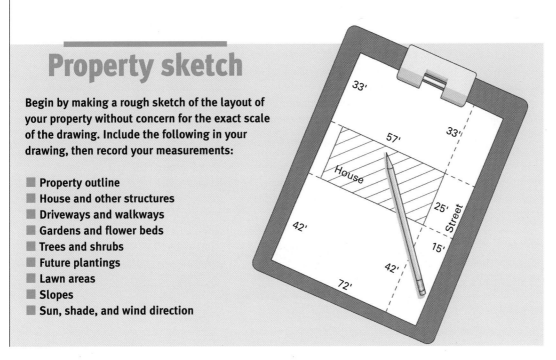

57

Measuring and mapping *continued*

to work with. If you are using a manufacturer's design kit, use the paper in it. Decide on a convenient and easy-to-remember scale, such as 1 square = 1 foot. (Use your largest property dimension to check that the scale you've chosen suits your paper size.) Using a pencil and ruler, transfer your measurements to the graph paper. Draw all elements precisely to scale. Don't be surprised if the property lines are not perfectly rectangular; few lots have 90-degree angles at each corner. Redraw the plan if needed; a reliable plan is well worth the extra labor.

■ *Adding permanent features:* Once you have plotted the lot and house to your satisfaction, add the other permanent features, such as patios, decks, driveways, toolsheds, walkways, and retaining walls. Use the corners of the house as reference points for correctly locating these

features on the plan. Also, indicate any low windows because you won't want them constantly soaked by sprinklers.

If you are careful to draw to scale, you don't need to put every measurement on the plan. Omitting some measurements will keep the plan uncluttered and easy to read.

Your plot should include all permanent plantings, such as trees, shrubs, flower beds, and vegetable gardens. Mark them by name if you can, and take special note of any trees with low-hanging branches that might block spray patterns.

Draw with an eye to the future. For example, indicate the current height and spread of trees as well as their approximate size at maturity. As tree trunks grow, they may block sprinklers from reaching parts of the yard. It is best to position sprinklers with these changes in mind. Also include any future plantings.

Basic hydraulics

To maintain good water flow and water pressure, an effective irrigation system must be designed in accordance with sound hydraulic principles.

There are two types of water pressure: *static pressure* and *dynamic pressure*. Static pressure refers to the pressure exerted on pipes and fittings when no water is flowing. It indicates the amount of water pressure that is potentially available to the system. Dynamic pressure is the force exerted by water when a spigot or faucet is open. In technical terms, it is the static pressure minus the losses caused by the pipe friction and any elevation changes in the system. Because the dynamic pressure is dependent on where you measure it, it is important to measure it as close as possible to the point where your irrigation system will connect to the water supply.

Dynamic water pressure is affected by friction and elevation. *Frictional loss* occurs whenever water flows through any sort of pipe, valve, fitting, or fixture. All of these create a drag on the water flow that is cumulative and can cause significant pressure loss. The best way to reduce friction loss is to use the fewest fittings and connections you can. Right-angle elbows are particularly frictional; substituting two 45-degree elbows will result in less loss of pressure. If possible, use larger pipes than called for leading up to the irrigation valves—for example ¾ inch rather than ½ inch. It's best to determine pipe sizes for your irrigation system after you have determined the minimum pressure and flow needed for the system.

Elevation changes can add or subtract pressure too. If the water flow is

downhill, the elevation change will add pressure; if it runs uphill, the change will reduce the pressure. For the sake of calculations, this loss is defined as 0.433 pounds per square inch (psi) per foot of elevation change. This would be a positive or negative amount depending on whether the slope is up or down relative to the water flow.

You will need to calculate your system's gallons per minute (GPM) rate, which measures the rate at which water flows through the system. Again, measure it at a point as close as possible to where your irrigation system will be connected to the home supply line.

Pages 60 and 61 explain how to measure water pressure as well as GPM.

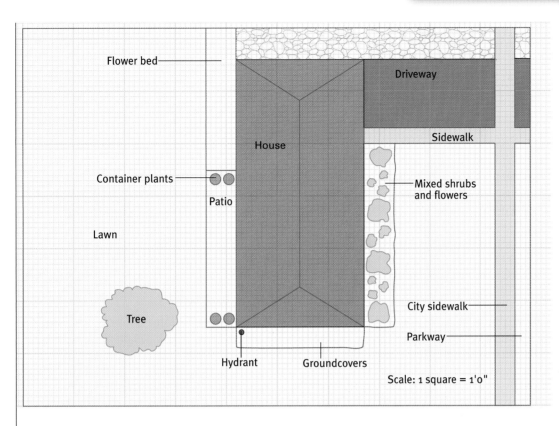

Flower bed

Driveway

House

Sidewalk

Container plants

Mixed shrubs and flowers

Patio

Lawn

City sidewalk

Tree

Parkway

Hydrant

Groundcovers

Scale: 1 square = 1'0"

Once all the structures and hard surfaces have been included, draw in the plants. Pay attention to every area of the yard, and include elements that are planned but not yet installed or planted.

Mark the locations of the water supply line, water meter, and spigots as well as any pumps and wells.

■ *Factoring wind and slope:* Add the compass points—N, S, E, and W—and indicate the direction of prevailing winds that may affect sprinkler placement. Mark the position of all underground utilities as well. Call the utility companies for help with this.

Because water flow and pressure are affected by slope, it's important to indicate any slopes in the landscape that exceed 10 percent. To measure slope, use a spirit level or a line level, a long string with a weight attached to one end, a tape measure, and a helper. Make a loop at one end of the string and attach it to the highest point, using a marking stake. Have your assistant stand at the bottom of the slope and raise the string, holding it taut, until it is even with the higher ground. Check it with the level. Then your assistant can feed out the weighted end

of the string until it just reaches the ground and forms a 90-degree angle.

Measure both the string's horizontal stretch (the run), and the vertical distance to the ground (the rise). To find the slope, simply divide the rise by the run and multiply the result by 100. For example, if the rise is 2 feet and the run is 12 feet, the slope would be 17 percent (2 ÷ 12 = 0.166). Sketch the slope on the plan, and record the incline you measured.

With a helper and a few basic tools, you can take the necessary measurements to determine the slope of various areas of your yard.

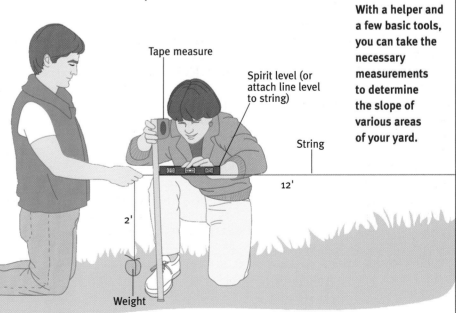

Tape measure

Spirit level (or attach line level to string)

String

12'

2'

Weight

Measuring and mapping *continued*

PRESSURE AND FLOW

If you are planning a whole-yard system with more than just a few sprinklers, it is vital to determine the correct water pressure and flow of your home's water supply

Some experts advocate measuring the system at the same time of day that you will be watering. Because your watering times may change (or be at 4 a.m.), it is best to measure it several times over the course of a day. Use only the lowest readings in your planning. If possible, take readings in summer, when municipal water levels are at their lowest and demand for irrigation water is at its highest.

You will need to determine the static and the dynamic pressure as well as the water flow, measured in GPM.

■ *Determining static pressure:* Borrow or rent a water pressure gauge from an irrigation equipment supplier or home center. To take a reading, find the spigot (Faucet 1) that is closest to your main water supply line where you plan to attach your irrigation system. Attach the pressure gauge. Select a different faucet (Faucet 2) inside the house. For the tests to be accurate, use faucets that are close together and, if possible, on the same water line. Open Faucet 1 all the way to activate the gauge. Record the pressure reading that appears on the gauge dial. This is the static water pressure.

■ *Determining the dynamic pressure:* Open Faucet 2 all the way so the water is flowing at full force. Check and record the dynamic pressure reading on the gauge at Faucet 1. Note: If your water pressure is above 80 psi, you will need to install a pressure regulator/reducer when installing your irrigation system.

■ *Determining the flow:* If the dynamic pressure reading is less than 40 psi, adjust the water flow from Faucet 2 until the pressure gauge reads 40 psi. Place a 5-gallon bucket under Faucet 2 and time how long it takes to fill. Use the chart below to determine the water system's flow rate in GPM. This will be the flow at 40 psi. Repeat this procedure at 45 psi and 50 psi and record the results.

If you don't have a 5-gallon bucket, time how long it takes to fill your bucket. Then figure out the flow in GPM using the formula:

$60 \div$ Fill time (seconds) $\times$ Bucket size (gallons) = Flow (GPM)

For example, a 2-gallon bucket that fills in 15 seconds indicates an available flow of 8 GPM ($60 \div 15 \times 2 = 8$ GPM).

You will need to measure the water pressure and flow in your home's water system. A combination flow and pressure gauge simplifies this task. If one is not available, follow the directions given on the following pages.

Quick gallon-per-minute test

Use this quick method to get a fairly accurate assessment of your water supply's flow. Use a sports watch or stopwatch to time how long it takes to fill a 5-gallon bucket. Then use the chart below to estimate your system's flow.

TIME TO FILL BUCKET	GALLONS PER MINUTE
15 seconds	20
20 seconds	15
25 seconds	12
30 seconds	10
40 seconds	7.5

This is a typical outdoor water meter installation. It is usually found near the street or close to the point where the main water line enters the building.

MEASURING YOUR HOME'S WATER SERVICE

First locate the water meter. If you live in a cold climate, it is probably in the basement. In nonfreezing climates, it may be near the street or just outside the house. If you don't know where it is, look it up on the property plan you received when you bought the house, or call the local water company or municipality.

■ *What size is the water meter?* Water meters usually come in three sizes: ⅝ inch, ¾ inch, or 1 inch.

The size should be stamped on the meter. If it is not, contact the water company. Write down the water meter size next to the static water pressure. If your municipality does not use water meters, or if you use a well or pressure tank, you don't need to worry about the meter size.

■ *What size is the main service line?* The service line is the main water supply pipe running from the street to your house. You need its inside diameter (i.d.) to determine your home's water capacity. Your local water

company or municipality may have this information, especially if your home is new. If not, it is easy to measure it yourself.

The service line measurement should be taken immediately in front of the water meter, on the supply (street) side. If you don't have a meter, measure the pipe running from the street into the house. Wrap a piece of string or tape once around the pipe. The length of the string is the outside circumference of the pipe. The diameter of the interior of the pipe is less than its outside circumference and varies depending on the material the pipe is made of. Copper pipe, for example, is thinner than galvanized steel or schedule 40 PVC pipe. It is easy to tell the pipes apart: copper pipe is metallic and reddish bronze; galvanized pipe is a grayish metal; PVC pipe is plastic.

To determine the inside diameter of the service line, use the Service Line Dimensions chart on the top of page 62. Record this measurement along with the static water pressure and the water meter size.

To measure the inside diameter (i.d.) of your home's main water line, wrap a string around the pipe just after the meter and measure the length of the string needed. Then use the chart on the top of page 62 to find its i.d.

Measuring and mapping

continued

SERVICE LINE DIMENSIONS

Use this chart to find your supply line size, based on the length of a string wrapped around the pipe. For example, if your service line is galvanized steel pipe and it takes 4 inches of string to encircle it, the size of your line is 1 inch.

Length of String	2 ¾"	3¼"	3½"	4"	4⅜"	5"
Size of copper service line	¾"	*	1"	*	1¼"	*
Size of galvanized service line	*	¾"	*	1"	*	1¼"
Size of PVC (schedule 40) service line	*	¾"	*	1"	*	1¼"

* This dimension in this material not manufactured.

CALCULATING SYSTEM CAPACITY

Calculating your home's water capacity tells you the maximum amount of water you can expect to be able to use at any one time. This information helps you determine how many sprinklers or emitters you can run at the same time in your irrigation system.

If your system will be professionally designed, submit the water capacity measurements and your site plan to the irrigation design service. If you are designing the system yourself, use the water capacity chart below to double check your flow readings. Table 1 applies if you have a water meter, Table 2 if you do not.

■ *Using the flow tables:* Find your water meter and service line sizes in the left columns. Then find the static water pressure along the top. Read over and down to find the approximate water capacity for your home's water system. For example, if the water meter measures 1 inch, your service line measures ¾ inch in diameter, and the static water pressure is 55 psi, the table indicates that you will have a maximum flow of 13 GPM available for your irrigation system.

WATER CAPACITY IN GALLONS PER MINUTE (GPM)

Table 1: For systems with a water meter (75-foot copper service line or less)

Size of Water Meter	Size of Service Line	30	35	40	45	50	55	60	65	70	76	80
⅝"	½"	2.0	3.5	5.0	6.0	6.5	7.0	7.5	8.0	9.0		
⅝"	¾"	3.5	5.0	7.0	8.5	9.5	10.0	11.0	11.5	13.0		
⅝"	¾"	6.0	7.5	9.0	10.0	12.0	13.0	14.0	15.0	16.0	17.5	18.5
⅝"	1"	7.5	10.0	11.5	13.5	15.0	16.0	17.5	18.5	20.0	21.0	22.0
¾"	1¼"	10.0	12.0	13.0	15.0	17.0	18.0	19.0	21.0	23.0	24.5	26.0
1"	¾"	6.0	7.5	9.0	10.0	12.0	13.0	14.0	15.0	16.0	17.5	18.5
1"	1"	10.0	12.0	13.5	17.0	19.5	22.0	23.5	25.0	26.0	28.0	29.0
1"	1¼"	12.0	15.5	17.5	21.0	23.5	26.0	28.5	30.5	32.5	34.0	35.0

Static Water Pressure (psi)

Table 2: For systems without a water meter (75-foot copper service line or less)

Size of Service Line	30	35	40	45	50	55	60	65	70	76	80
½"	2.0	3.5	5.0	6.0	6.5	7.0	7.5	8.0	9.0		
¾"	6.0	7.5	9.0	10.0	12.0	13.0	14.0	15.0	16.0	17.5	18.5
1"	10.0	12.0	13.5	17.0	19.5	22.0	23.5	25.0	26.0	28.0	29.0
1¼"	12.0	15.5	17.5	21.0	23.5	26.0	28.5	30.5	32.5	34.0	35.0

Static Water Pressure (psi)

Note: The tables assume a 75-foot copper service line—that is, the line running from the street to the house. If your line is PVC, add 2 GPM. If the line is galvanized, subtract 5 GPM. If the service line is significantly longer than 75 feet, contact an irrigation equipment supplier to determine a more specific calculation.

If the service line is longer than 75 feet or if it is old and corroded, the flow could be limited—which would result in considerable loss of pressure.

The values given in the water capacity tables assume a static water pressure that is the same as the dynamic, or working, pressure of the system. But if the dynamic pressure that is actually available when the water is running is much less than your static pressure reading, you should ignore the tables and use the water-flow test reading on page 60 for your planning.

DIVIDING YOUR YARD

If your yard is extremely small and you are watering only one type of plant such as grass, you might be able to water it all at once. More likely, you will need to water in stages. This requires that you divide your yard into areas with different watering needs.

Using colored pencils or markers, first divide your yard according to the plantings in it. Lawns, flower beds, trees, and patio planters all have different needs and should be watered separately. Outline the different plant areas on your property plan.

Next, look at the microclimates on your property. Mark any areas that receive heavy sun or shade, and include areas that get substantial reflected solar heat. Also mark areas exposed to frequent wind.

Lawns should be divided into separate areas, because they usually require more frequent watering than most other plants. To keep the irrigation piping design simple, it is usually easier to designate the front, back, and side lawns as separate areas, even if they are small.

Plants that need infrequent, deep watering, such as trees and shrubs, should be watered separately from plants that require frequent, shallow watering, such as annuals and vegetables.

Trees and shrubs planted individually in a lawn can be watered using the lawn system, but

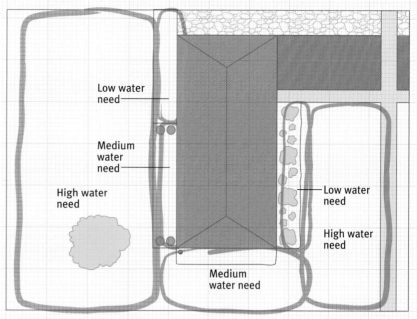

Begin creating irrigation zones by using colored pencil or markers to divide your yard plan into large areas based on plant types and water needs.

Yard divisions

Divide your yard according to:
- **Water needs**
- **Turfgrass areas**
- **Trees and shrubs**
- **Patio and container plants**
- **Slopes that exceed 10 percent**
- **Specialty plants with unique needs**
- **Shade vs sun**
- **Wind exposure**

check to be sure they receive adequate moisture from all sides and don't block spray patterns.

Container plants dry out more quickly than plants in the ground and need separate watering. Keep plantings with special needs separate too. Roses, for example, should not have their leaves moistened. It's a good idea to provide a separate micro-irrigation or bubbler zone for a rose bed.

Problem areas, such as slopes, should be watered separately as well.

Taking these factors into account, divide the yard into areas with similar needs. It often helps to group the areas into large squares or rectangles first. Then subdivide these until you have all individual needs identified. Label the areas according to the predominant vegetation: lawn, shrubs, groundcover, and so on. Later on, you will designate these areas as actual irrigation zones.

Irrigation
components

It is no longer the case that metal components are superior to plastic ones. New plastics are not subject to corrosion and have good resistance to damage and ruptures. They are also less expensive.

For many years, the inground sprinkler system was the major player in the irrigation world. But horizons have broadened. Today, irrigation options include drip irrigation; its offshoot, micro-irrigation; and even an updated hose-end system. An effective irrigation system typically incorporates elements from more than one of these watering methods to achieve the most efficient result.

Once you've identified your watering requirements, you're ready to choose the irrigation components that will best meet the unique needs of your landscape.

Understanding how sprinkler systems and components operate will help you avoid expensive mistakes, even if you are not installing your own system. With literally hundreds of options—for instance, some companies offer dozens of different spray-head nozzles—it is important to understand a few basic concepts and applications.

As you survey the products available, seek advice from an irrigation dealer. Even if you plan to design and install the system yourself, a supplier with a thorough knowledge of the product line can help you avoid pitfalls.

Whenever possible, purchase products from the same manufacturer, particularly sprinkler heads and nozzles. This is especially important within a given zone—to ensure that parts will be compatible, that flow rates will match, and that later you will have no trouble finding replacement parts. Many sprinkler nozzles are now color-coded for easy identification. This is a big help when you are installing for the first time or changing coverage patterns later. The coding is specific to the maker. If you mix and match, you risk making a mistake. As you install the system, keep a record of which components you used and where you used them. Then if you need a replacement part, you can simply refer to your list.

UNDERSTANDING TIMERS

The brains behind an irrigation system is the irrigation timer. An irrigation timer is essentially a clock that tells the irrigation control valves to open and close at preset times for a preset number of minutes. Though composed of only a clock and a few circuits, this device can do amazing things. It is possible to install an irrigation system without a timer, but the advantages of having one make up for the modest additional cost. A manual system requires a person to be there to turn it off and on, and this system cannot deliver water as efficiently as a system run by even a basic mechanical timer.

■ *Mechanical timers:* The first timers were simple mechanical devices consisting of a mechanical clock and a few mechanical switches for starting/stopping a system at a specific time. Because they can manage only a limited number of zones, they are inconvenient and inefficient for more complex irrigation systems. Mechanical timers are still produced, but their popularity is fading as new devices with improved convenience features are added to the market.

■ *Hose-end timers:* Hose-end timers, as their name suggests, mount directly to a hose fitting—normally a garden spigot. They have traditionally been controlled by a simple mechanical timer, and their popularity has been declining as homeowners have opted for the latest programmable, inground products. However, the hose-end method of irrigation offers a

unique advantage to people with small urban yards: Because the basic components are above ground and removable, the entire system can be picked up and stored for the winter. In addition, it's easy to add on to a hose-end system—by attaching a garden hose or sprinkler. Because the hose-end system is so easy, flexible, and well suited for small urban yards, its popularity has rebounded in certain areas in recent years. Manufacturers have responded by simple offering programmable hose-end timers that can control multiple irrigation zones. If you have limited space and a modest budget, a hose-end timer and irrigation system is worth considering. (For information on hose-end systems, see page 51.)

Simple hose-end mechanical timers such as this one let you set a basic irrigation schedule for a single zone. This is good for watering a small lawn or one type of plant material.

A mechanical timer such as this one is useful for small, simple irrigation plans. However, much more sophisticated programmable models have supplanted this simple timer.

Irrigation components *continued*

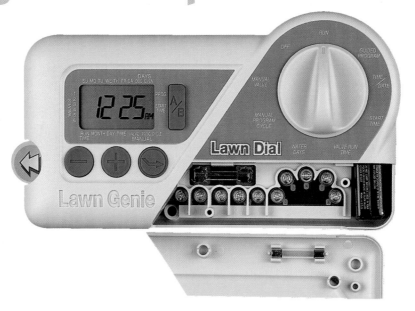

Programmable timers allow you to create and save complex, calendar-based watering schedules. Programmable timers even let you adjust for seasonal changes in water needs, among many other features.

■ *Programmable timers:* Programmable timers have become the norm for residential irrigation systems. Most have similar capabilities and functions. Multizone programmable timers are the most widely available.

Programmable timers are designed to be as autonomous as possible. Once you've entered the irrigation scheduling information, you've done your part and the timer will do the rest. Programmable timers are a huge step forward from mechanical models because they can "remember" complex scheduling information and deliver water according to daily, weekly, or monthly cycles. The newest models even have 365-day calendars built into them, making it possible for them to deliver water in accordance with complex municipal watering schedules.

The timer interacts with the zone control valves the same way a mechanical timer would, sending an electrical signal to the valves and telling them when to open and close. Most programmable timers will also start irrigation pumps and open master valves. Many can make automatic adjustments based on information from rain and moisture sensors.

Be sure the timer you choose has the capacity to cover the number of zones you've planned. It's a good idea to buy a timer that exceeds your current needs; an unused station or two makes it easy to add new zones later.

Programmable timers are fully electronic, with digital or liquid crystal screens to display your irrigation program information. Begin by entering the time, the date, and the day of the week. Then manually enter the watering schedule for each zone.

Look for a timer that can run multiple programs, will allow you to put all your zones or any combination of them on different schedules, depending on plant needs, time of year, and other watering factors. With multiple programs, you can also have one set of zones watered three times a week, another set watered once a week, and another watered on a different day. In any case, remember that only one zone can run at any given moment.

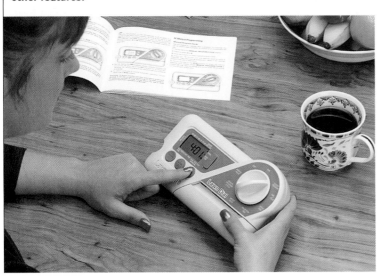

SOFTWARE-BASED TIMERS

Software-based timers are the "next big thing" in residential irrigation. Like Palm Pilots, software-based timers will let you download information from a personal computer into the memory of your irrigation system timer—information that can be used to manage all the details of your watering system. These timers promise to improve dramatically the convenience (no more standing in the garage to set your irrigation timer) and functionality of watering.

Currently, software-based systems are available only with expensive and sophisticated commercial irrigation timers (usually referred to as "controllers" when used for large-scale installations). These controllers manage myriad watering schedules for huge landscapes, and automatically adjust each schedule—sometimes one sprinkler at a time—using information fed to the controller from the Internet and even from a satellite (which provides real-time evapotranspiration data). These capabilities are far beyond what is needed by a homeowner.

However, this kind of technology is on the horizon for homeowners. When it arrives, software for your home computer will interactively guide you through the process of creating a multizone watering schedule for your

Advanced programmable timers such as this one can be set up using a personal computer. The irrigation schedule is then loaded into the timer's memory to be run.

yard, which you can download into a timer. You'll be able to fine-tune the data you enter concerning zone parameters or watering needs as easily as you make corrections to a word processing document. You'll also be able to save as many programs as you like for future use.

Advances in wireless technology include the introduction of wireless rain sensors for home use. Soon, you can expect to see "smart" sprinklers, each in its own zone and activated based on information from moisture sensors positioned nearby. This will provide substantial water savings and improved plant health, compared with current programmable systems.

At the high end of the timer spectrum are units equipped with software that help you program your system. Taking its cue from systems that have long been used in commercial applications such as golf courses, it can even recommend a watering schedule based on your landscape.

Programmable *features*

When you shop for a programmable multizone timer, you'll encounter a baffling number of possible features from which to choose. Each feature not only addresses a specific irrigation need, but also increases the cost of the timer. So assess your needs realistically before you take the plunge. And remember: The most important feature is ease of use. You should be able to read the controls easily and even figure out some of them without having to read the instructions. Several popular features are available.

■ **Run times:** Check the timer's minimum and maximum run times to be sure these will suit your needs. If you are using drip irrigation, for instance, you may need to run that zone for an hour. At the other extreme, sprinklers watering clay soil may need to run only a minute or so at a time so the water can soak in. Your timer should be able to handle both situations.

■ **Multiple start times:** Some timers offer only one start time per zone per day. This may be acceptable if you are watering only one kind of plant (turfgrass, for example), but it will not do for most yards. Variables such as the plant type, sloping lawns, or slow-draining soil may demand several short waterings during the same day. This requires several start times. Look for a timer with three or more start times.

■ **Watering schedules:** There are dozens of possibilities: seven-day, odd-even day, and interval watering are just a few.

With the advent of municipal watering restrictions across the country, variable scheduling has become important. Because restrictions can change with the water conditions, your timer needs to adjust to current and future standards. You can find timers that allow an almost infinite combination of schedules. The best even allow 365-day scheduling.

■ **Battery backup:** This feature ensures your programming isn't erased during a power failure. It also allows you to disconnect the timer for the winter and plug it back in during the spring; the timer will have the program, current time, and date stored in memory, ready for action.

■ **Rain delay:** A rain delay feature allows you to cancel watering when it rains. Some even allow

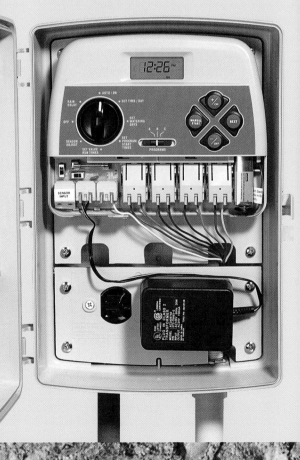

68

you to program several days without irrigation—ideal when enough rain falls in one day to keep plantings watered for a week.

■ *Sensor functions:* These features allow the timer to override the programmed irrigation schedule when a moisture sensor is attached and it determines that no water is needed.

■ *Manual override:* This common feature allows you to water outside the normally programmed hours. It is useful for spot watering and for adjusting your spray patterns.

■ *Pump start/master valve control:* This feature allows the timer to control an irrigation pump or the irrigation master valve, if you use one. Some even allow the pump to start several minutes before the sprinklers do, in order to build system pressure.

■ *Multiple programs:* This feature lets you create more than one watering program to run from the same irrigation timer. It allows different combinations of zones, start times, and run times, on the watering days you select.

CHOOSING A TIMER

Choosing a timer may seem a daunting task, given the number of available features described above. However, if you ask yourself the following four questions, the answers will likely narrow the options considerably.

■ *How many zones should the timer cover?* This is the easiest question to answer. Always select a timer with more zones than your irrigation plan calls for. That gives you room for easy expansion later on. So once you have figured out the number of zones you will need to install in your yard, just add one or two to that total.

■ *How many different programs do you need?* Look for a timer with three or more programs. Multiple programs allow you to separately water the different areas of your landscape (lawn, flower beds, vegetable gardens, for example) at different intervals. Having only one program requires that you run all your zones every time you water. Even in the simplest landscapes, this is not efficient.

■ *How many start times do you need?* By having more than one start time per day, you increase your ability to tailor your watering schedule to the unique conditions in your yard. With multiple start times, you could decide to

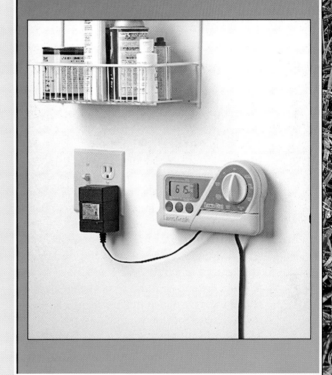

irrigate at 6 a.m., 4 p.m., and 9 p.m instead of only at 6 a.m. The correct number of applications per day depends on the needs of your yard and the plants you are watering, not what the timer can do. So save water and money by using multiple start times whenever you can.

■ *Do you need an indoor or an outdoor timer?* Make this choice based on where your valves will be located, as well as the most convenient location for you. In a city, or if children wander through your yard, you may want to keep the timer inside. There are models available for indoor and outdoor use, as well as weatherproof cabinets to accommodate any model.

Irrigation components *continued*

Manual angle shutoff valve

Automatic shutoff valve

UNDERSTANDING VALVES

Depending on the type of irrigation system you have, you will use either manual valves, automatic valves, or both. Because most systems today are automatic, they use mostly automatic irrigation valves to control the flow of water to the sprinklers or drip emitters.

■ *Manual irrigation valves* are essentially the same as any other shutoff valve in your home. They consist of a valve body and a valve stem that you operate by turning the handle on the end of the stem. When the handle of a *gate valve* is turned, it slowly raises and lowers a metal flange inside the valve that resembles a gate and controls the flow of water through the valve. Gate valves are good for preventing water hammer effects because their slow operation—it typically takes six or seven twists to turn one on or off—allows time for excess pressure to be normalized. *Ball valves,* on the other hand, are convenient because they work fast. A quarter turn is usually all that is needed to fully open or close one of these valves. But this fast operation can cause pressure surges in the pipes. Systems need to be designed with that in mind.

■ *Automatic valves* operate without direct human contact. Anytime you use an irrigation timer, you must use automatic irrigation valves to control the water flow to the sprinklers. If your timer also controls master valves, these will also be automatic valves.

Most automatic valves operate using a solenoid controlled by the timer, a plunger, and a rubber diaphragm to start and stop the water flow. In the closed position, the solenoid pushes the plunger down, blocking a tiny port in the diaphragm. This allows a small chamber to fill with water. The pressure from the water keeps the diaphragm pressed against the valve seat so no water can pass through the valve. When the timer tells the valve to open, the solenoid pulls the plunger up, letting the water escape through the port, emptying the chamber and flowing through the lines. This lowers the pressure on the diaphragm, which then lifts off the valve seat, letting water flow freely through the valve.

Automatic valves must be installed in the proper orientation to the flow, and care should be taken to size them correctly. These valves can

The antisiphon valve protects your home's water supply from contamination from water that could be sucked from your watering system. This type opens when there is outbound pressure. When the system is turned off, a valve shuts and air is allowed in to drain the system.

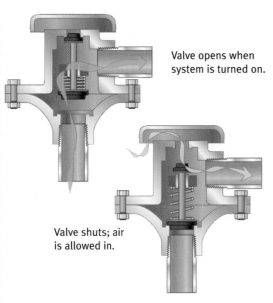

Valve opens when system is turned on.

Valve shuts; air is allowed in.

also be operated manually by use of a small bleed valve located on the main valve body.

IN-LINE AND ANGLE VALVES

The valves used in your irrigation system will be one of two configurations—in-line or angle. This nomenclature refers to the path in which the water flows when the valve is open.

■ *In-line valves:* Most of the valves used in irrigation systems are of the in-line type. This means the pipes or hoses are attached in a straight line so that water flows straight through the valve body from the inlet to the outlet. Shutoff valves, zone control valves, and master valves are usually configured this way to minimize water pressure losses to the valve body. Manual in-line valves are ball valve or gate

In-line valves, such as this automatic valve, have a water path that is straight through the valve body, minimizing pressure losses.

valve configurations. Most automatic zone valves, other than antisiphon valves, are in-line as well.

■ *Angle valves:* Angle valves, unlike in-line valves, do not have a straight water path through the valve body. The water is forced to make at least one turn to get from the inlet to the outlet.

If you live in a cold climate and opt to use angle valves, you should bury the main irrigation line below the frost line, but not necessarily the lateral lines that feed the sprinklers. In that case, an angle valve can be used as a system shutoff connecting the deeply buried water supply line to the more shallowly buried irrigation pipes. While the abrupt angle of the valve creates friction that reduces water pressure, cobbling together other fittings to accomplish the same end can be even more obstructive.

■ *Antisiphon valves:* For the most part, the only angle valves used in building your system will be antisiphon valves, which prevent water from backflowing into the house. (See page 73.) Install them at the highest point in your system. That way, water flows up into them from the supply lines, then down out of them to the irrigation zone's lateral lines, which supply the sprinklers.

Finally, you should remember when selecting either an in-line or angle valve that you will operate it frequently if it is a manual valve. You may want to select a metal valve and use PVC adapters to attach it to the plastic pipes. Plastic valves work fine but have a less precise feel to them when they are opened or closed. Metal valves hold up better under frequent use, and it is easy to tell when they are fully opened or closed.

An antisiphon valve (above) is angled so it can be easily installed at the correct height above the sprinklers.

Angle valves, such as a zone control valve (left) are useful when the layout of your system calls for an abrupt turn.

Irrigation components *continued*

VALVE FEATURES

Automatic irrigation valves come in many configurations depending on the maker, but typically share common features.

■ *Bleeds:* To operate automatic valves manually, you will use a bleed, where the diaphragm inside the automatic valve is allowed to open, letting water flow freely through the valve. Bleeds are useful for flushing debris from the valve and for operating from the valve manifold.

There are two types of bleeds: internal and external. With internal bleed, no water is vented out of the valve body onto the ground, making it the slightly more water-efficient method of the two. In either case, it is a small amount of water. Both bleed types are useful at different times.

■ *Connections:* Residential irrigation may use any of three common connections: *slip, threaded,* and *barbed.*

Slip connections are the easiest to put together but require some type of adhesive to seal and hold them. For example, unthreaded PVC components are joined with a special two-part cement that actually welds the plastic together. **Threaded** fittings and pipes, which may be PVC or (less commonly) galvanized, are a good choice where components may need to be taken apart and reassembled later. Teflon plumbing tape should be applied to the male threads before the parts are joined. Barbed connections are used with polyethylene (poly) pipe, which is softer than other materials.

The fittings have several rows of ridges around each end, which lock to the poly pipe when it is pushed over them. This type of connection can be reused as often as needed. However, valves with barb fittings, while convenient, are not always easy to find.

■ *Sizing:* Many irrigation texts make valve selection sound like a job for a rocket scientist. This may be the case for large commercial installations. However, for residential use you will probably be using either ¾- or 1-inch valves, depending on the flow you need. For flows of less than 15 gallons per minute, use a ¾-inch valve; for flows of more than that, use a 1-inch valve.

Keep the following general rules in mind when choosing valves:
■ The valve should not produce a pressure loss greater than 10 percent of the static pressure available in the supply line. This data should be available in the manufacturer's catalog.
■ The valve should be the same size as or no less than one size smaller than the pipe supplying it.
■ The valve should not be larger than the lateral line that it is attached to.

BACKFLOW PREVENTION

Backflow is the unwanted flow of water in an irrigation system back into the household water supply. Most health departments consider the water in an irrigation system to be contaminated. Because your irrigation system is connected to the freshwater supply for your house and the community, backflow represents a real contamination concern to you and your neighbors. For that reason, virtually every community requires a backflow prevention device (BPD) on all systems connected to the general water supply. Each community has its own standards. Check with local building codes to find out what you need to use.

Backflow can contaminate the freshwater supply in several ways. For example, if you were to use a hose to apply fertilizer and a drop in pressure occurred in the city water main, the fertilizer could well be siphoned back into your home's supply pipes, where it could end up coming out of a kitchen or bathroom faucet. Or if the irrigation system suddenly shut off, dirt, bacteria, pesticides, and other contaminants

Automatic valves make a programmable irrigation system possible. They are available in sizes that work with any home irrigation system and are required if you plan to use an irrigation timer.

from around the sprinkler heads could be pulled into the irrigation pipes and into your home's water system. If sprinkler heads are located at a higher elevation than the manifolds, this danger is increased.

COMMON BACKFLOW PREVENTION DEVICES

Your irrigation system should include a backflow prevention device recommended by local codes. Understanding the different backflow prevention devices ensures your buying the right device for your system.

■ *Atmospheric vacuum breaker (AVB):* This device is most often used with automatic zone control valves rather than as a stand-alone unit. Because atmospheric vacuum breakers cannot have continuous water pressure on the supply side and still work properly, they are installed on each zone just past the zone valves. For that reason, the combined AVB and zone control valve, known as an antisiphon valve, will greatly simplify installation for the homeowner—if this type of backflow prevention is allowed by local codes. These devices need to be installed 6 to 12 inches above the surrounding ground in order to function properly.

■ *Pressure vacuum breaker (PVB):* Only one PVB is needed for an entire system, making it easy to conceal in the yard. It costs more than an atmospheric pressure breaker but can be less expensive overall, depending on your system, because only one is needed. A PVB doesn't rely on gravity to work, so it can have pressure on the inlet and outlet sides at all times and still function properly—which means that you can install one on the main line in front of the zone valves. It needs to be 12 inches above the highest lawn sprinkler head, which can make installation difficult in some hilly applications.

■ *Double-check valve (DCV):* A double-check valve assembly is installed on the main irrigation supply line before the zone valves. It is expensive, but only one is needed for the entire system. Because it is not affected by elevation differences, it is used most often in hilly

Backflow prevention devices

Antisiphon valves combine a backflow preventer with an automatic valve to simplify installation. This antisiphon valve protects zones but is not recommended for use on a main line.

A pressure vacuum breaker is a common type of backflow preventer that is available as a stand-alone device or as part of an antisiphon valve.

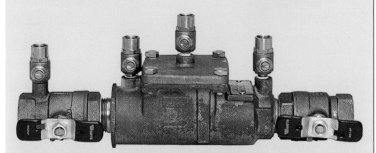

A double-check valve assembly is more expensive and sophisticated than other backflow preventers. It is usually mounted on the main irrigation line, and only one is needed for an entire system.

73

Irrigation components *continued*

applications and can be installed out of sight, below the surface of the ground. The main drawback is that there is no way to know if the unit has failed. Many municipal codes don't allow its use. Also, these devices are not easily drained at the end of the season, which may make them impractical for use in cold climates.

■ *Reduced-pressure backflow preventer:* Similar to the double-check valve is the reduced-pressure principle device (RPD). One of these will protect the whole system, although other backflow preventers may be required as well. An RPD must be installed above ground and is best suited to an irrigation system that draws water from a lake or other reservoir but is also connected to municipal water as a supplemental supply. An RPD reduces water pressure more than the other backflow prevention devices.

■ *Air gap:* Like an RPD, an air gap is used when water supplies come from both municipal and nonpotable water sources. A small holding tank acts as a buffer between the pump and the municipal water. A 6-inch air gap must be maintained between the top of the nonpotable water in the tank and the end of the municipal water line. The supplemental gap isolates the two water sources from each other, preventing contamination. You need expert knowledge to build an air gap system correctly.

SPRINKLER BASICS

Sprinklers make the final delivery of water to the ground. It is important to choose sprinkler heads that send the right amount of water to the areas that need coverage. The major sprinkler types are *fixed sprays, bubblers,* and *rotary sprays.* Choosing the best sprinkler is a matter of deciding which of the available options best suits your needs. Choose among these variables:

■ *Patterns:* The spray pattern, or arc, of a sprinkler is the portion of a circle that it covers. It is described as a specific angle (for example 90 degrees) or as a fraction of a circle (quarter-circle). These refer to the same pattern. You can usually fine-tune a pattern by adjusting the head or changing the nozzle.

■ *Trajectory:* The trajectory of a given sprinkler or sprinkler nozzle refers to the angle above the horizon of the spray that it throws. This can be an important consideration if you plan to install sprinklers in windy locations because the wind

An effective watering system is the result of considering pattern, trajectory, spray radius, and the water pressure available.

Each type of sprinkler has strengths and weaknesses. That is why different types are used for different applications. Carefully matching the sprinkler to the watering task will assure the healthy, lush landscape you want.

affects the trajectory of the water. That has a big impact on the pattern and the amount of water lost to evaporation. In windy locations, a lower trajectory is needed. The trajectory is typically adjusted by replacing the standard nozzles on the sprinkler or by placing the heads closer together.

■ *Radius:* The radius of a sprinkler is the distance it throws water. This determines how closely spaced the sprinklers must be to achieve proper water coverage. For instance, a sprinkler with a radius of 45 feet will cover 90 feet if it is a full-circle pattern but must be placed no more than 45 feet from other sprinkler heads. You will learn more about how to lay out your sprinkler heads correctly on pages 91–93. The radius of some sprinklers is somewhat adjustable but can be reduced by no more than 25 percent.

■ *Matching the sprinkler to the water pressure:* Most sprinklers are designed for normal water pressure. Low-flow heads are intended for areas where water pressure is low (less than 40 psi static pressure) or where water conservation is a priority. Because these heads apply water at a slower rate, they are ideal where the soil is mostly clay and subject to runoff.

PRECIPITATION RATE

The amount of water a sprinkler applies to the ground in a given amount of time is its precipitation rate, usually expressed as inches of water per hour. For instance, sprinkler heads in a front yard that deliver 1 inch of water over the entire yard after running 1 hour have a precipitation rate of 1 inch per hour. Each plant has a water requirement that can be expressed in inches per week. Knowing the precipitation rate of your sprinklers enables you to figure out how long to run them to supply the right amount of water.

■ *Matched precipitation rate (MPR):* In a given irrigation zone, all sprinkler heads need to run at the same precipitation rate, regardless of the pattern, to achieve even water distribution within the zone.

Manufacturers have addressed this need by creating MPR nozzles. These ensure that no matter which pattern you are using, each nozzle will produce the same precipitation rate as any other MPR sprinkler nozzle produced by that manufacturer.

For instance, if you are using half-circle fan spray sprinklers alongside full-circle fan spray sprinklers made by the same manufacturer, you know that the half-circle sprinklers will produce

Irrigation components *continued*

the same number of inches per hour of water as the full-circle sprinklers. With MPR nozzles, the precipitation rate is the same for any pattern within that zone. Before MPR nozzles were introduced, the only way to get even coverage was to measure and adjust the flow from each sprinkler head. The MPR feature allows you to mix quarter, half, three-quarter, and other patterns with the assurance that you will get even distribution of water on all plants. A few high-end makers are now offering adjustable-pattern MPR heads.

Although patterns can be mixed using MPR heads, different types of sprinklers such as spray or rotary heads cannot be mixed because they have different precipitation rates. Spray heads have precipitation rates ranging from about 1 to 2 inches per hour, whereas rotary heads have precipitation rates ranging from 0.25 to 0.83 inch per hour. Mixing them would result in uneven coverage, with some areas underwatered and some overwatered.

SPRINKLER TYPES

Sprinklers come in two basic heads—fixed spray and rotary.

■ *Fixed spray heads,* called sprays or fan sprays, are easy to recognize. They have no moving parts and emit a stationary spray of water that covers an entire area—for example, a half or full circle—at one time. The radius of the spray is usually 5 to 15 feet, making these heads well suited to medium-size areas. A large area, such as a lawn, would require too many spray heads to be practical.

These heads can be pop-up or stationary. Pop-up heads are the most versatile and account for the majority of sales in new systems. This is because pop-up heads retract when not in use, then rise when the water is switched on. Pop-up heads are available in various heights ranging from about 2 to 12 inches to accommodate various plant heights. Some spray heads are flush mounted, meaning they are low to the ground; these work only if there is no neighboring foliage or if they are set in a lawn with short grass. For short-mown lawns, 2- or 3-inch pop-up heads are perfect; for the typical lawn, 3- or 4-inch heads are appropriate; for taller, water-saving grass, a 6-inch pop-up head can be used.

■ *Shrub heads* are stationary heads set on risers that elevate them permanently above the foliage they are watering. Their height prevents foliage from blocking the spray pattern but can create problems with foot traffic. To reduce the danger of tripping, use a flexible joint at the base of the riser. Place shrub heads in

MAXIMUM PRECIPITATION RATES

This chart lists the maximum amount of water that can be applied to different soils before runoff occurs.

SOIL TEXTURE ("Cover" means groundcover growing in place; "Bare" refers to bare soil.)	MAXIMUM PRECIPITATION RATE (INCHES PER HOUR)							
	0– 5 percent Slope		5–8 percent Slope		8–12 percent Slope		12+ percent Slope	
	Cover	Bare	Cover	Bare	Cover	Bare	Cover	Bare
Coarse sandy soil	2.40	2.00	2.00	1.50	1.50	1.00	1.00	0.50
Coarse sandy soil								
Over compact subsoil	1.75	1.56	1.25	1.00	1.00	0.75	0.75	0.40
Uniform light sandy loam	1.75	1.00	1.25	0.80	1.00	0.60	0.75	0.40
Light sandy loam								
Over compact subsoil	1.25	0.75	1.05	0.50	0.75	0.40	0.50	0.30
Uniform silt loam	1.00	0.50	0.80	0.40	0.60	0.35	0.40	1.0
Uniform silt loam								
Over compact subsoil	0.60	0.40	0.50	0.25	0.40	0.15	0.30	0.10
Heavy clay or clay loam	2.00	0.15	2.00	0.10	0.12	0.08	0.10	0.06

Source: U.S. Department of Agriculture

Color-coded heads make it easy to find the radius and pattern you need.

unobtrusive spots away from traffic to make them less susceptible to breakage.

■ **Bubblers** are considered fixed-spray sprinklers, though they don't actually spray. They flood water onto the ground around it. Bubblers are available in patterns to suit any planting bed shape. Bubblers are ideal for watering trees and groundcover areas up to 5 feet in diameter.

■ **Rotary heads,** also known as stream heads or rotary sprinklers, cover the largest area of any sprinkler. Rather than irrigating the entire pattern at once, rotary heads send out a high-velocity stream of water in one or more directions while rotating slowly to cover a pattern. Most rotary heads cover a minimum radius of about 20 feet and a maximum of about 45 feet.

Rotary heads apply water more slowly than spray heads, which makes them suitable for slow-to-drain clay soils. However, this means they need to run longer than spray heads and may lose more water to evaporation. If your area is subject to strong winds, rotors are a good choice. The large spray droplets they produce are not as prone to pattern deformation as are

Spray heads (or fan sprays) produce their entire pattern at the same time. There is no rotation and no moving parts. They throw a spray as far as 15 feet.

Bubblers are fixed sprays that don't spray—they flood. They pour water onto the ground to irrigate shrubs, trees, and ground cover. Bubblers cover areas up to 10 feet in diameter.

CHOOSING THE BEST SPRINKLER FOR YOUR NEEDS

There are sprinkler heads for every part of your yard. It is important to match the correct head to the area being watered. This chart will help you narrow the choices and make a better decision.

| | Spray Heads | | Rotary Heads | | |
	Fixed	Shrub Head	Impact or Gear	Multistream	Bubblers
Small lawns	Yes	No	No	No	No
Medium lawns	Yes	No	Yes	Yes	No
Large lawns	Sometimes	No	Yes	Sometimes	No
Flower beds	No	Yes	No	No	Yes
Groundcovers	Sometimes	Yes	Sometimes	Sometimes	Yes
Shrubs	No	Yes	No	No	Yes
Isolated areas	No	No	No	No	Yes
Slopes	Low gallonage	Low gallonage	Yes	Yes	No

Irrigation components *continued*

Multistream rotor sprinklers have a slower watering rate than other sprinklers. This makes them perfect for watering slopes and clay soils.

Impact rotors use a spring-loaded arm to create their rotation, giving them a distinctive sound. They are well-suited to large lawns.

fan sprays. Another benefit is that you will need fewer sprinklers, and therefore less trenching and plumbing, to cover a given space.

The best-known rotary head is the impact rotor sprinkler, also known as the impulse sprinkler. It uses a spring-loaded drive arm that, when pulled into the stream of water by the spring, is deflected sideways, giving a broken rotational movement and the familiar sh-sh-sh sound. Impact sprinklers are fully adjustable and can cover a full circle or any part of a circle.

For part-circle use, look for impact heads with a built-in antibacksplash device to keep them from watering the area you want kept dry. Metal impact heads generally require a minimum static water pressure of 40 psi to

operate efficiently. If your system has a static water pressure of 40 psi or less, use plastic impact heads.

Gear-driven rotary heads are becoming popular. They use a water-powered gear drive to turn the rotary stream in a smooth, nearly noiseless pattern. Choose one with a closed-case design, which keeps out dirt. Most gear drives are fully adjustable from full- to part-circle patterns and cover about the same area as impact heads. They also work well when spraying dirty or muddy water.

Multistream rotors produce several jets that rotate slowly to water their entire trajectory. They cover a smaller area than that covered by other rotary heads—16 to 35 feet is typical. However, they are well suited to watering slopes and slow-draining soils. They are available as pop-up or fixed-shrub sprinklers.

Fixed-Spray patterns

Fixed-spray heads are available in different patterns. By mixing and matching patterns, you can create complete coverage with almost no overspray. Check manufacturers' literature to see which patterns they offer. This will help when drawing your irrigation system.

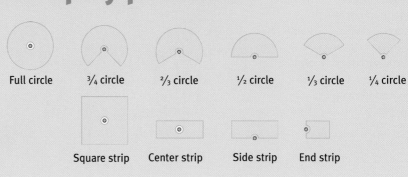

Full circle   ¾ circle   ⅔ circle   ½ circle   ⅓ circle   ¼ circle

Square strip   Center strip   Side strip   End strip

A drip emitter hose has emitters preinstalled in the hose. It works well for areas with evenly spaced rows, such as vegetable gardens.

DRIP AND MICRO-IRRIGATION

Drip irrigation has revolutionized commercial and home watering systems. Older drip systems, invented to maximize scarce irrigation water in arid areas, proved to be water efficient and beneficial to plants. Micro-irrigation, a recent variation, expands the range of the water-saving concept to a much broader spectrum of settings and plants.

■ *How they work:* Both types use a special pressure reducer/filter to maintain a consistent, lower water pressure. This allows them to apply water slowly over longer periods of time. Traditional drip irrigation uses drip emitters, which apply water drop by drop directly to the ground at the plant base. Because there is no water spray, the problem of evaporation loss is nearly eliminated.

Micro-irrigation uses miniature sprayers to water more like a sprinkler but to apply water slowly to small areas.

Both systems are designed to keep the root-zone soil consistently moist. As a result, drip and microsystems reduce plant stress and promote solid, healthy growth.

You need not choose between traditional sprinklers or drip/micro-irrigation; modern irrigation designs combine the two. For instance, a typical design includes sprinklers for lawn and garden areas and drip/microcomponents for planting beds and smaller gardens (because each emitter covers only a small area).

Every irrigation dealer has a full range of drip emitters, sprinklers, and misters—as well as pipes, stakes, and fittings. Often these parts, though they look alike, are not compatible. For this reason, it is best to purchase all components from the same manufacturer.

Drip irrigation puts water directly on the ground at the plant base. This reduces weed growth between plants while giving the root zone its needed water supply.

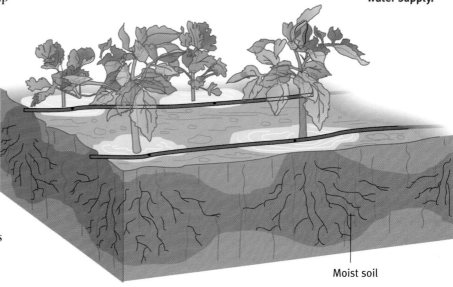

Moist soil

Irrigation components

continued

Drip and microcomponents are available in hundreds of varieties. There is a drip/microemitter designed for almost any plant or irrigation environment. Be sure to use components from the same company to ensure compatibility.

■ *Microtubing:* The choice here is easy. Micro-irrigation systems all use ½-inch poly landscape hose for the supply lines and sometimes for all the lines. For lateral lines, ¼-inch or, more rarely, ⅛-inch vinyl tubing may be used, especially for container gardens and microsprinkler systems. To connect the supply line to the water system, elementary aboveground drip systems often use garden hose. More permanent installations may use buried PVC or poly pipe for the main line.

Drip and micro-irrigation components use easy-to-assemble barbed fittings. In most cases, you simply poke a fitting or an emitter into the ½-inch hose or ¼-inch tubing. The resulting connections are surprisingly solid and watertight.

As always, it's a good idea to buy all components from one manufacturer. Tubing sizes vary slightly from one manufacturer to the next; when fittings are mixed and matched, a leak may result. There are fittings available that alleviate this problem by using threaded collars along with the barbed fitting. Once the fitting is in place, the collar threads tightly over the outside of the tubing, crimping it onto the barbs of the fitting, eliminating any play in the connection. Although these work, it is better to buy matched components.

Purchase ½-inch supply hose, which can be used for supply and lateral lines with emitters, jets, and microsprays. If the hose will be exposed to the sun, be sure it has good UV resistance (it should contain at least 2 percent carbon black).

Use ¼-inch tubing to connect emitters and microsprays to the ½-inch hose. Tubing is available as plain hose or emitter tubing that has the emitters preinstalled. The latter arrangement speeds the installation and minimizes leaks.

■ *Emitter Tubing:* Sold in rolls, ½ inch and ¼ inch emitter tubing can be cut to length and connected

Kits are available that contain all the needed components to connect a drip/microsystem to any standard garden faucet. They take only a few minutes to put together and connect.

Dual shutoff Y-connector (one outlet left free for hose use)

Faucet-type antisiphon vacuum breaker (backflow preventer)

Coupling

Washable filter

Pressure regulator

Line connection

Drip manifolds allow you to run individual emitter lines to separate plants and control the water flow to each. They are easily hidden by foliage or even mulch and can run off the spigot. In this instance, the pressure regulator and filter are integrated into the manifold.

to the main line or lateral lines in the same way as any other poly pipe. These practical and durable watering devices are worth looking for because their results are so good, especially in flower beds and vegetable gardens, under hedges, around large trees, and in mass plantings. On the downside, regularly spaced emitters don't permit as much flexibility or precision as individual emitters.

■ *Manifolds:* Multiple outlet emission devices are more commonly known as drip/micromanifolds. They are often used with underground irrigation systems but can be easily retrofitted to hose-end systems as well. These manifolds are a useful new addition to the drip/micro family because they allow quick connections to new or existing irrigation systems, and they allow you to water different plants differently in the same flower bed.

When connecting any low-flow system, you need a pressure regulator and mesh filter. The filter and regulator usually end up installed in the valve box with the zone valves. This can be cramped and awkward. However, with the right drip/micromanifold this is not a problem, because the filter and regulator are built into

the manifold itself. The manifold can be connected the same as any other sprinkler.

The other advantage of manifolds is that the many tubing lines are much easier to install. Normally, you would need to connect a ½-inch tee to the riser where your drip system would connect, then run ½-inch tubing throughout the area, attaching emitters and ¼-inch tubing where needed. Then you would run the ½-inch tubing back to the other side of the tee to complete the circuit or clamp off the end on shorter runs. A manifold eliminates some of this work. It can sit in the center of the area where it is being used, on a stake or the riser, whichever gives the best location. Then up to twelve ¼-inch lines can run from the manifold to the areas or plants that need water. Because ¼-inch tubing is much easier to handle than ½-inch tubing, the installation goes much faster. Also, some manifolds allow you to adjust the flow to each of the ¼-inch lines individually. This ensures that each emitter line will have the correct water flow and pressure to operate at its greatest efficiency.

To reduce maintenance, keep your runs of ¼-inch tubing no longer than 5 to 10 feet long.

Irrigation components *continued*

■ **Drip emitters** deliver water drop by drop, keeping root zones moist and the surrounding soil dry. They may be installed in the irrigation line (in-line) or punched into the line (punch-in). Emitters are available in a range of flow rates from 0.5 to 4 gallons per hour (GPH). Some new designs have pressure-compensating abilities to counter the effects of slopes in the landscape and dips in the lines.

Clogged emitters were once a serious concern; because little water flows from their outlets, flushing them is next to impossible. This problem was solved with a turbulent-flow design, which keeps dirt particles in continuous motion so they are flushed through the emitter. All emitters and emitter tubing manufactured today are designed to keep from clogging.

Punch-in emitters can be poked into ½-inch hose. Or they can be inserted into the ends of ¼-inch tubing to water individual plants. Some manufacturers produce drip emitters combined with hold-down stakes to make installation easier.

In-line emitters fit into the end of tubing; then you attach tubing to the other end of the emitter and continue the line. Like punch-in emitters, they can be placed wherever needed by simply cutting the tubing, inserting the emitter, and pushing the tubing back together. The emitter is protected and won't get knocked off accidentally. In-line emitters are also available preinstalled in emitter tubing. In-line emitters are ideal for watering small plants in short rows.

■ **Microsprays and bubblers** are low-volume devices like drip emitters, but they apply water in a fanlike spray pattern, like a fixed-spray sprinkler. They can spray in full- and partial-circle patterns with flows from 6 to 10 GPH and can cover a radius of 6 to 11 feet. They are ideal for small areas such as flower beds and groundcovers.

■ **Misters** are commonly used in greenhouses and work well with plants that have high-humidity needs, such as ferns and bromeliads, and with hanging plants. Misters are available in flows from 1 to 5 GPH. Misting a plant also waters its roots, because droplets fall from the leaves to the soil. To be effective, misters should be run in a separate zone.

Emitters are available in several flow rates, from 0.5 gallon per hour (GPH) up to several gallons per hour. This allows for wide-ranging applications.

A turbulent-flow in-line emitter (top) solves the problem of clogging. Any sediment in the water is kept moving by the chaotic flow until flushed out. A standard in-line emitter (bottom) pokes into ¼" tubing at either end.

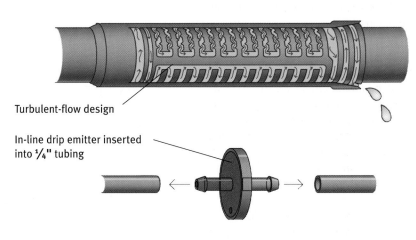

Turbulent-flow design

In-line drip emitter inserted into ¼" tubing

■ *Hookups and conversions* make it possible to convert traditional high-pressure zones in your present sprinkler system to micro-irrigation without digging or removing pipes. Retrofit kits allow you to convert a single sprinkler riser to a micro-irrigation drip zone. Because it is not possible to have a zone that contains both sprinklers and micro-irrigation, an entire zone would need to be dedicated to drip/micro use.

The kit includes a filter, a pressure regulator and riser adapter, and the converter itself. From a sprinkler riser, you can convert to a single low-pressure line, or you can install a manifold, which will provide six or more outlets for attaching ¼-inch poly tubing. If all the outlets are not needed, as is often the case, leave the unused outlets capped and keep them for future use. For exact installation details, follow the manufacturer's instructions.

In the case of pop-up sprinklers, it may be possible to use the housing as an adapter rather than removing it. You can buy a retrofit kit designed for this purpose. These kits are not universal, so make sure the kit you choose is compatible with your sprinkler. To install, remove the nozzle mechanism from the sprinkler housing and replace it with the retrofit components: a pressure regulator, filter, and threaded riser.

You will have to attach a filter and pressure regulator to the riser. (Some manifolds have these parts integrated into them.) The fine mesh filter is used in all drip/microapplications to trap sediment coming through the pipes before it can clog the emitters. The better manufacturers combine the filter, the pressure regulator, and the manifold into a single unit that screws directly to the sprinkler plumbing, greatly simplifying installation.

The conversion process may leave you with a number of unused spray heads, which must

be capped. To do so, replace the sprinkler with a ½-inch threaded cap on each unused riser. Special caps are also available to cover unused pop-up sprinkler housings.

Whether connected to a garden hose or a dedicated irrigation system, microsprays such as this one are perfect for watering flowers and groundcover areas.

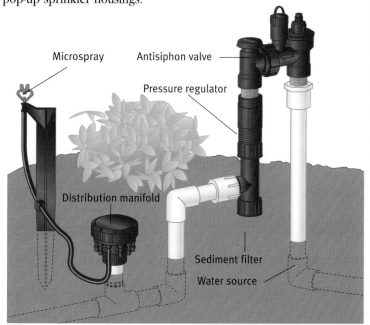

This typical connection to a zone control valve uses a separate pressure regulator and sediment filter.

Irrigation plumbing

Plumbing forms the veins and arteries of an irrigation system. The more clog-free the pipes and the stronger the joints, the less maintenance the system requires.

Early systems used galvanized steel pipe, which is strong but prone to clogging. Copper pipe resists such clogging and is still the choice material for interior plumbing. However, for irrigation purposes, copper has been replaced by cheaper and more durable plastic materials—PVC (polyvinylchloride) pipe and poly (polyethylene) tubing. Some plumbing codes still mandate the use of metal fittings and components. Check local codes first.

Here are a few plumbing terms you should know when dealing with pipe.

■ **Nominal size:** A comparative reference for different sizes of pipe and tubing, rather than being the actual size.

■ **Wall:** The thickness of the pipe walls, expressed as a decimal number. This is an indication of the pipe's strength.

■ **Outside diameter (OD):** A pipe's actual outside diameter, useful in determining a nominal size (typically a pipe's inside diameter; see pages 61-62).

■ **Inside diameter (ID):** The diameter of the inside of a pipe. This is the measurement that matters when you are matching different pipes and fittings. Most pipe size is described by its inside diameter.

At the easy end of the plumbing scale are drip emitters that use a flexible supply line. To install an emitter, you need only puncture the tubing and press in the emitter.

■ **Working pressure:** The maximum water pressure the pipe can handle before failing. For safety reasons, the working pressure provides a buffer in the rating.

■ **Schedule:** A pressure and strength rating. Standard pipe for general plumbing is most commonly schedule 40.

■ **Sweat fitting:** A nonthreaded copper fitting that is secured and sealed using melted solder.

■ **Galvanized steel pipe:** Also called "iron" and rarely used in irrigation anymore. But you may run into it if you are repairing or expanding an old system.

Steel pipe is easy to assemble and take apart because it has threaded connections, which allow fittings and pipe to be reused if they are still sound. Steel pipe collects mineral deposits on the inside that worsen with age, resulting in an average flow loss of 50 percent in 15 years. These deposits may also flake off and clog sprinklers after only a few years. Whenever possible, replace steel with plastic or copper.

Combining steel pipe with fittings of another type of metal can lead to corrosion. The combination of steel and, for instance, copper creates a weak current known as electrolysis, which causes corrosion at the connection. To prevent corrosion, use a dielectric fitting whenever connecting steel to copper. When connecting to plastic, use a transition fitting made for the purpose.

■ **Copper:** A material used only occasionally for large commercial irrigation jobs and where local codes require it. Copper also works well for shrub head risers because it tarnishes to a green color that blends with foliage.

Copper pipe comes in three types—K, L, and M. The differences are the thickness of the walls. Type M, with the thinnest wall, is most commonly used in irrigation systems.

Copper fittings are almost exclusively sweat fittings, meaning they are soldered together. A soft solder, containing 50 percent tin and 50 percent lead, is usually used. Solder with more than 50 percent lead should be avoided for health reasons. Areas to be soldered must be clean and dry. Transition fittings that have a threaded end as well as a sweat or slip-on fitting are used to connect copper pipe to plastic or steel pipe.

Flared and compression fittings also are available for copper pipe. These fittings can be taken apart easily and reassembled, making them usable when wet, which is not possible with solder. However, these fittings are much more expensive.

PIPE FITTINGS

Pipe fittings for irrigation systems include a sometimes bewildering array of small parts. Here are the common ones.

Poly Pipe

•**Insert Coupling:**
Connects two lengths of poly pipe

•**Insert Tee:**
Connects three lengths of poly pipe

•**Combination Tee:**
Attaches threaded riser between poly pipe and sprinkler

•**Stainless-steel Clamp:**
Clamps insert fittings

•**Insert Elbow:**
Forms 90-degree angle using two pieces of poly pipe

•**Combination Elbow:**
Forms 90-degree angle using poly pipe and PVC pipe

•**Insert Adapter:**
Adapts threaded outlet to insert fitting for poly pipe

PVC Pipe

•**Threaded Coupling:**
Connects sprinklers to ½" riser

•**Slip or Socket Coupling:**
Connects two lengths of same-size PVC pipe

•**Reducer Bushing:**
Connects two lengths of different-size pipe

•**Slip or Socket Tee:**
Connects same size PVC pipe at 90 degrees from main line

•**Reducer Tee:**
Attaches threaded riser between PVC pipe and sprinkler

•**90-degree Slip or Socket Elbow:**
Forms 90-degree angle with same-size PVC pipe

•**45-degree Slip or Socket Elbow:**
Forms 45-degree angle with same-size PVC pipe

•**Reducer Elbow:**
Forms 90-degree angle and provides threads for threaded riser

•**Male Adapter:**
Adapts threaded outlet to socket joint for PVC pipe

Both Poly and PVC Pipe

•**Manifold Tee:**
Connects control valves together into manifold

•**Drain Cap:**
Caps draining system

•**Drain Valve:**
Automatically drains system when pressure is off

•**Slip-Type Compression Tee:**
Connects irrigation system to main service line

•**Threaded Riser:**
Rises from pipe to sprinkler

•**Cutoff Riser:**
Rises from pipe to sprinkler; can be cut to desired height

•**Flexible Riser:**
Rises from pipe to sprinkler in high-traffic areas; flexible

•**Adjustable Riser:**
Rises from pipe to sprinkler; height can be adjusted

Irrigation plumbing *continued*

USING PLASTIC PIPE

In the overwhelming majority of cases, irrigation pipe is now plastic, for several good reasons. Unlike metal, plastic does not corrode or collect deposits that reduce water flow. It is also less expensive and easier to install. (However, in very cold climates metal can better withstand temperature extremes.) The two types most widely used are rigid PVC pipe and flexible polyethylene (poly) tubing.

■ *Polyvinyl chloride (PVC)* lasts virtually forever if it is not cracked or cut. Landscape-quality PVC is rated to 160 psi, making it resistant to bursting. It is unlikely to be damaged by temperature changes in all but the coldest climates when buried at an appropriate depth. PVC is rigid, like copper, and usually less expensive than poly tubing. Like copper, each joint must be welded individually using a solvent/cement combination. PVC pipe is available in various lengths, but 20 feet is standard. Schedule 40 PVC is usually recommended for outdoor irrigation. Be sure to use PVC approved for irrigation systems.

Throughout North America, even the colder regions, PVC and poly pipe are used for the majority of new irrigation installations.

■ *Polyethylene (PE)*, often just called poly, is flexible enough to make 90-degree turns and bend around obstacles to eliminate cutting pipe and gluing in fittings. It is also available as long rolls that are easily cut to length, which potentially reduces the number of fittings needed in your system. Any needed connections are easily made using press-together barbed fittings.

Poly's major drawback is its weakness. It can burst under high pressure, especially during pressure surges. These occur mostly in the main line when the water flow in the line is abruptly halted, such as when a valve is shut. Over time, pressure surges can weaken and crack poorly manufactured pipe. For your protection, and to be sure that your poly pipe meets its stated pressure ratings and all standards, use landscape-quality pipe marked NSF. This pipe has been pressure, temperature, and construction certified.

■ *Using both PVC and Poly:* Is PVC or poly the better choice? Increasingly, the two pipes are being used together, notably in colder areas. Pressure surges are likely to occur only in the main pipes, so PVC is still recommended for the main supply lines. Use poly pipe for the lateral lines to the sprinklers. In areas where freezing occurs, some experts recommend using metal pipe rather than PVC in the main supply lines, and running loosely-installed poly pipe inside larger-diameter PVC pipe. The loose installation allows the poly pipe to contract in cold weather, and the PVC protects it from compression damage.

PRESSURE RATINGS FOR PVC PIPE

The most commonly available PVC pipe for residential irrigation use is called schedule 40. Note that as the pipe dimension increases, its maximum working pressure decreases. However, schedule 40 is well within the pressure tolerances required for most home installations.

Nominal size	o. d. (inches)	i. d. (inches)	Wall thickness (inches)	Maximum working pressure (psi)
1/2"	0.840	0.622	0.109	590
3/4"	1.050	0.824	0.113	480
1"	1.315	1.049	0.133	450
1 1/4"	1.660	1.380	0.140	365
1 1/2"	1.900	1.610	0.145	330
2"	2.375	2.069	0.154	275

Source: British Columbia Ministry of Agriculture and Food

Your completed irrigation plan is the road map you will use to guide you through the entire installation. Take the time to draw it as accurately as you can.

Drawing
the plan

Now that you've sketched a simple plan and gathered basic information about your home, your yard, and your home's water system, and the components best suited to your needs, it's time to put it all together into a plan of action.

GETTING GOOD ADVICE

Ideally, you should take to an expert the information you've gathered and the plot plan you've drawn. This person can draw a precise irrigation plan that is perfect for you. Obtain advice from an irrigation designer, an irrigation dealer, or manufacturer services (see pages 46 and 47).

Making the plan entirely by yourself is not hard but can be risky. If you plot the plan yourself, at least have a specialist look it over once you have finished. A specialist can point out errors and things you may have overlooked. It is better to ask a specialist's advice during the

Getting the pipe sizes right

Landscape-quality PVC and polyethylene pipes are available in various sizes; the most common are $3/4$ inch, 1 inch, and $1^1/4$ inch. Valves also come with variously sized openings, such as $3/4$ inch and 1 inch. Be sure to get pipes and valves large enough for your needs. If you don't, your sprinklers will not be able to do their job.

When choosing pipe size, take into account the total number of gallons used by the sprinkler heads, the total length of your pipes, the type of pipe, the number of elbows used, and elevation changes.

Your best bet is to take the plans to a qualified irrigation dealer, who can tell you which size pipe to use.

planning stage, even if you have to pay for it, than to spend hundreds of dollars later to fix mistakes caused by a faulty plan. In particular, it is important to get the pipe sizes right.

■*DIY:* To plot the plan yourself, you'll need a calculator, a lead pencil, colored pencils, an eraser, the manufacturer's parts catalog or list, a drawing compass, a ruler, and your site plan.

87

Drawing the plan *continued*

It is important to have the manufacturer's parts list on hand as you work. This will help you determine the minimum and maximum spacing of heads, the flow in gallons per minute, and the spray pattern for each sprinkler. A parts list is typically arranged according to the type of sprinkler (spray head, rotary, or bubbler) and includes a list of valves, fittings, timers, and other parts.

Your plan should already show the buildings, plantings, walkways, and other landscape elements (see pages 56 to 63). It should also show basic delineations between planting areas (the squares and rectangles based on plant types and microclimate factors, page 63). These areas will help you determine your final irrigation zones.

Irrigation design symbols

Using these standard symbols will make your plan easier to read—both by you and your irrigation equipment supplier. You may find that manufacturer's have their own sets of symbols, often with model numbers included.

- Stream bubbler, half pattern
- Stream bubbler, opposite streams
- Pop-up sprinkler, rectangular pattern
- Pop-up sprinkler, 90-degree arc, 9' radius
- Pop-up sprinkler, 9×18' rectangular pattern
- Pop-up sprinkler, 90-degree arc, 12' radius
- Pop-up sprinkler, 180-degree arc, 12' radius
- Low-angle shrub spray, 90 degrees
- Low-angle shrub spray, 180 degrees
- Stream rotor, 24' radius
- Stream rotor, 180 degrees
- Stream rotor, 90 degrees
- Stream rotor, 112 degrees
- Stream rotor, 202 degrees
- Automatic globe valve
- Timer
- Antisiphon valve
- PVC pipe, schedule 40, ¾"
- PVC pipe, class 200, ½" and ¾"

USING SYMBOLS

Whether you plan to do the installation work yourself or hire a contractor to do it, your design needs to convey to the installer exactly what needs to be done. It helps to use standard graphic symbols and accepted conventions that convey your ideas clearly and simply. A confusing drawing is an open invitation to costly mistakes by you or an installer. Why risk that?

Use simple graphic symbols in your irrigation design, preferably symbols well-known in the industry. Be sure every component graphed is easy to understand. That way, if you need advice on your plan, you will not have to waste time explaining yourself to every consultant who looks at it. Remember, you are communicating ideas, so keep it clear and simple. No matter which symbols you decide to use, be sure to include a legend—in the lower right-hand corner of the plan—that defines each.

Buying all irrigation components from one manufacturer will simplify the graphing process because you won't have to keep track of which part came from which company.

PLOTTING THE VALVES

Having roughed out the location of your valves in your plan, it is time to determine a path for bringing in water to supply the sprinkler heads. Start by plotting the water meter and the main service line on the plan.

■ *Main and master valves:* Determine where you'll be installing the main irrigation shutoff valve and the connection to the house water supply. This manual valve, used to turn the entire irrigation system on and off, should be installed on the house side of the water meter, as close to the meter as possible to ensure the best pressure and flow. It will be in the basement or outdoors, located at some point between the meter and the house. In nonfreezing climates and under certain circumstances, you may be able to connect the main irrigation shutoff valve to an outside faucet supply line. Mark the planned main irrigation shutoff and system connection location on your irrigation plan.

A master valve, not to be confused with the main irrigation shutoff, is an automatic irrigation valve just like the ones controlling your irrigation zones. It opens and closes every time the irrigation system is activated so the water supply to the zone valves is turned off when the system is not in use. It is not usually mandatory but is an inexpensive fail-safe in the event of an unseen zone valve failure. If you are going to use a master valve, locate it between the main irrigation shutoff valve and the first zone manifold, or tee, in the irrigation supply line. Remember, the master valve needs to control water to the entire system.

■ *Zone control valves:* Each zone will be operated by a separate zone control valve. To simplify the installation, zone control valves are installed together in groups called manifolds. Place each manifold in an accessible outdoor location, such as near a door or patio, but away from heavy foot traffic. Locating each grouping of valves in the area of the yard that the valves

will be watering makes maintenance and manual operation easier and is a logical approach. There is no limit to how many manifolds you can have. Strive for simplicity, using as few as you can, and keep them close to the main service line. Be sure to mark the manifold locations and control valves on your plan.

This automatic in-line control valve and its wiring are installed inside a protective plastic valve box.

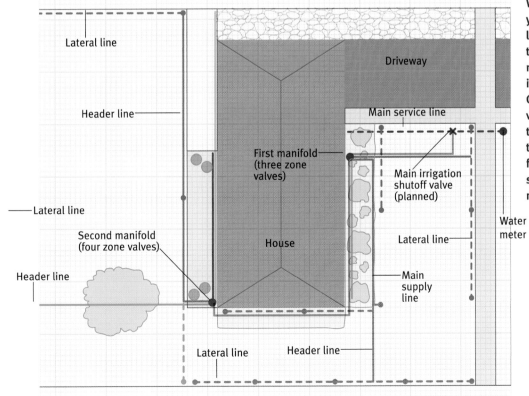

When plotting your manifold locations, be sure to show the total number of valves in each manifold. Group together valves watering the same area of the yard, and aim for no more than six valves per manifold.

Drawing the plan *continued*

PLOTTING WATER LINES

The house's main service line usually follows a straight line from the water meter to the street if the water meter is indoors, or between the water meter and the point where the water line enters the house if the meter is located near the street. Indicate the main service line on the plan as a dotted line (see page 89).

Next, determine the path of the irrigation supply line that will connect the manifolds to the main irrigation supply line at the irrigation system shutoff. Mark this line on your plan. If your main irrigation shutoff valve is located indoors, run the line outdoors first. Then split the line into header lines to feed your valve manifolds. Keep your irrigation map simple and clean; the fewer turns and connections

you make, the better your pressure and flow will be. If the shutoff is near the street, first run the main supply line toward the house, and then toward the manifolds.

Because each zone is independent and has its own control valve, you need a separate pipe system for each. Start by drawing one header line per zone, using a different colored pencil for each zone. This line carries water to the lateral lines, so be sure not to connect sprinkler heads to it. Add lateral lines to each header line as needed to connect the sprinkler heads on that zone. The following tips will help you plan.

■ Avoid forcing water to make too many turns to minimize loss of pressure.

■ Avoid running lines under established driveways and sidewalks, if possible.

■ Run more than one header line in a trench whenever possible to reduce digging.

■ Place lines 1 to 2 feet outside established flower beds and shrub plantings to avoid damaging roots when digging the trenches.

■ Place lines no less than 3 feet from the house and other structures to avoid construction backfill and inadvertent damage to pipes.

One of these three connection methods will work for your system. Choose the method that is most convenient, secure, and appropriate for your house and climate.

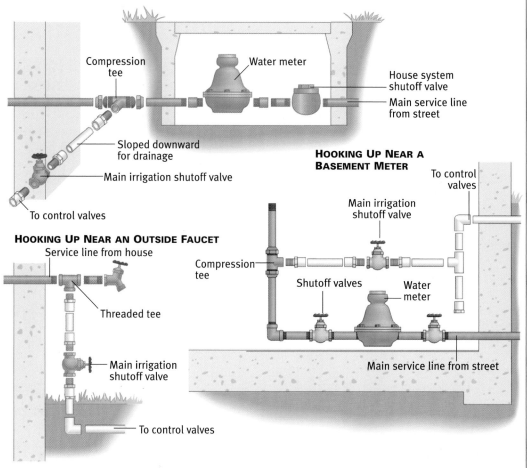

HOOKING UP NEAR AN OUTSIDE METER

Compression tee

Water meter

House system shutoff valve

Main service line from street

Sloped downward for drainage

Main irrigation shutoff valve

To control valves

HOOKING UP NEAR AN OUTSIDE FAUCET

Service line from house

Threaded tee

Main irrigation shutoff valve

To control valves

HOOKING UP NEAR A BASEMENT METER

To control valves

Main irrigation shutoff valve

Compression tee

Shutoff valves

Water meter

Main service line from street

Most landscapes are a combination of turf, shrub areas, flower beds, and planters. Each requires different sprinkler or micro-irrigation layouts.

SPRINKLER HEAD PLACEMENT

Plot sprinkler head placement using a drawing compass to indicate the pattern each head will cover. For example, if your drawing scale is 1 foot equals one square on your graph paper and the sprinkler you're drawing has a throw radius of 10 feet, adjust the compass so its radius is equivalent to 10 squares on the graph paper (10 feet). To cover the most surface with the fewest sprinklers, use the maximum recommended spacing for the water pressure available to your sprinklers. To compensate for wind or low water pressure, move the sprinklers closer together.

Begin placing sprinklers in the corners of the squares and rectangles you have drawn on your plan (see page 63) using a quarter-circle pattern in each one. Use head-to-head coverage (see page 92), in which the spray from every sprinkler just touches each sprinkler head adjacent to it. Position sprinklers evenly along the sides, drawing a half circle around each. If this doesn't cover the entire area, place sprinklers in the center and draw a full circle around each. This will give you equidistant, or square, spacing. (For more information about triangular and square spacing, see page 93.)

■ *Step-by-step planning:* Start with the largest of the squares or rectangles on your plan, leaving the smaller and odd-shaped sections for last. When you've completed the larger rectangles, begin positioning heads in small lawn areas, such as parking strips. These are usually watered by one or two rows of partial circles. Narrow spaces can be watered with strip nozzles or drip irrigation. Finally, add sufficient shrub spray heads and bubblers to irrigate shrub areas, flower beds, and planters. Mark riser locations for drip/micro areas as well. Where possible, set the sprinklers at the back of the bed or along the periphery. As you position sprinklers, jot down the details you'll need later to finalize your zones: Use your symbols to indicate the pattern, and write in the GPM rating for each sprinkler. You can find GPM ratings on the manufacturer's chart.

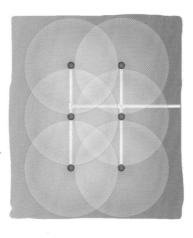

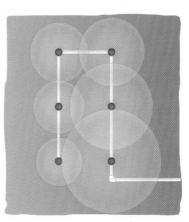

A branch layout (left) produces even pressure. The zone on the immediate right is not well laid out. Pressure losses will be evident in the sprinklers at the end of the long, turning run.

These impact-rotor sprinklers are placed using proper head-to-head coverage. The spray from each just touches the heads of adjacent sprinklers in the same zone.

Drawing the plan *continued*

■ *Head-to-head coverage:* The heart and soul of efficient sprinkler layout and watering is head-to-head coverage. The concept is simple: Position sprinklers so the spray from every head touches all the adjacent sprinkler heads.

   To irrigate adequately, spray patterns must overlap. When they overlap, they compensate

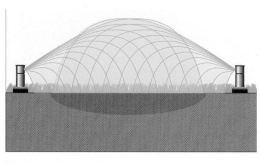

Incorrect spacing creates areas that are over- and underwatered.

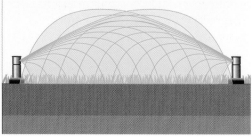

Proper head-to-head coverage ensures even water distribution within each zone.

for coverage problems that often arise along the edges of a coverage area. For instance, because water naturally loses force as it leaves a sprinkler head, it may not always reach the outer edges of its assigned spray pattern. The wind or the sprinkler's placement on a slope may distort the sprinkler pattern edges. When a sprinkler pattern includes a steep trajectory, the sprinkler head may throw water beyond the pattern edges and leave the area near the sprinkler head itself dry. Head-to-head coverage takes care of all these problems.

   The distance a sprinkler can propel water is called the radius, or throw. For example, a full-circle fan spray that produces a spray diameter of 30 feet has a radius of 15 feet. To create correct coverage, it should be placed 15 feet (50 percent of 30 feet) to 18 feet (60 percent of 30 feet) from the heads adjacent to it on the same zone. Heads on different zones may end up beside each other.

   If your static water pressure is lower than normal (40 psi or less), the radius of your sprinklers' spray pattern may be shorter than expected. The sprinkler manufacturers supply pressure versus radius information with the sprinklers. To create proper head-to-head coverage, use the pressure reading you took of your home's water system and the manufacturer's information to determine the correct spacing for your sprinklers

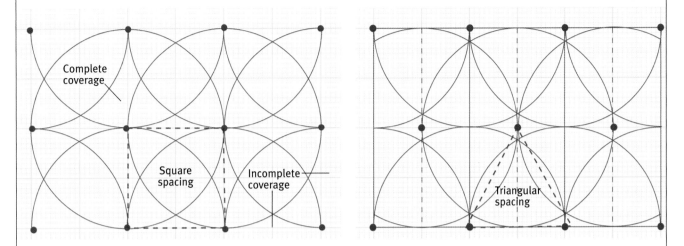

Complete coverage

Square spacing

Incomplete coverage

Triangular spacing

Coverage basics

- Most fan spray heads cover a radius of 10 to 15 feet.
- Rotary sprinklers can cover a radius of 25 to 45 feet.
- Bubblers reach 1 to 5 feet.

Square spacing: Irrigation plans are usually drawn using square spacing or triangular (staggered) spacing. Square spacing, with heads located at each of the four corners, is the easiest to plot. However, it does result in excessive overlap, because some spots inevitably are watered by four sprinklers. Also, because sprinklers have to be placed relatively close together (usually at 50 percent of their spray diameter), more sprinkler heads are needed.

Triangular spacing: Triangular spacing is hard to fit into the house lot edges but easy in open spaces such as large lawns. In triangular spacing, heads are located at each of the three points formed by a triangle. This means that you need fewer heads because more surface is covered with less overlap. You can place them farther apart (usually at 80 percent of the diameter, or throw, or even slightly more) using fewer heads. For example, spray heads are typically placed at 16 feet or less in square spacing, and 18 feet in triangular spacing.

To plot triangular spacing, first choose one side of a rectangular or square area as a baseline, then plot the two corner quarter-circle sprinklers, followed by equidistant half-circle sprinklers in between them as needed.

Triangular spacing of heads (above) is more efficient than square spacing (above left), needing fewer heads to provide proper coverage. However, it is hard to achieve in small yards because of overspray on walkways and drives.

A bubbler head (left) delivers a concentration of water at the base of plants.

(So far, this is the same as square spacing.) Next, draw lines from the midpoints between the sprinklers. Place the next row of sprinklers on these midpoint lines. Continue to alternate the sprinkler heads between half-space and full-space lines. This will give you a triangular spacing.

While triangular spacing can save you installation costs, local codes may prohibit overshoot on the outside edges. Check with your local building permit department.

Special situations

I t's rare when the zones of a home landscape fall into neat, square packages just right for symmetrical sprinkler patterns. Planting beds are usually organically curved—and lawns often have angles and shapes to fit around lot lines and buildings. So there are usually a few areas that call for special planning. Here are some ideas for coping with the inevitable nonstandard yard elements.

■ *Adjustable pattern heads:* Rotary heads are generally fully adjustable, but most fan spray heads have fixed static spray patterns such as full circle, three-quarter circle, or half circle. If you have an awkward angle to cover, you may be able to find a fan spray head that will work— there are myriad patterns available. You can also take a look at adjustable pattern nozzles, called variable arc nozzles (VANs). These can be adjusted to cover anything from a sliver of a circle to nearly a complete circle.

■ *Fill-in heads:* When an irrigation layout has equally spaced heads, a few spots are often under watered. Rather than struggling to modify the layout to achieve a perfect match, it's easier to add a fill-in head. This is a sprinkler that is not located in the same symmetrical pattern as the others or has a coverage area that is smaller or greater than the others. Sometimes such heads cause significant overlap, but this is better than leaving a dry spot in a corner of the lawn.

■ *Undesirable overthrow:* There are always areas that you want to keep dry, such as patios and public sidewalks. Some overthrow is inevitable, especially with triangular spacing. But you can plan where the overthrow will occur. To keep an area spray-free, use it as the baseline for a triangular or square pattern. With a combination of quarter- and half-circle heads, you can usually design an area so that two or more sides have no overspray. If an area has two or more lines that need to be spray-free (for instance, an intersection of two sidewalks),

Although some overspray is inevitable, watch your system while it is running and adjust sprinkler heads to avoid a wasteful pattern.

you may need to add some fill-in heads and part-circle nozzles. Rotary heads are also available with spray deflectors that shield the spray from an unwanted area.

■ *Obstacles:* Water must reach all parts of the garden in spite of obstacles. Even a flagpole can block enough spray to leave a dry area on its far side.

To solve this problem, use triangular spacing of sprinkler heads placed so the obstacle is at the approximate center of the spray throw. Sometimes this is not possible because the tree or other obstacle may not be situated at a point that is easily watered by an otherwise symmetrical spray area. Try adjusting the plotting. You will probably need fill-in heads with smaller ranges to cover everything evenly. Always remember to plot your sprinkler locations to allow for future growth so plants don't become obstacles a few years down the road.

Plant groupings, such as clusters of shrubs, can be watered by outside heads positioned around them in a triangular pattern. Make sure at least part of the trajectory reaches all spots. Trees and shrubs need less water than grass, so you might want to put them on a separate zone and provide them with micro-irrigation.

■ *Rounded corners and curves:* It is difficult to avoid overthrow at a rounded corner, such as the curved entrance to a driveway. You can reduce this with careful placement of sprinkler heads or use of adjustable heads. Creating correct coverage is difficult, but a little too much overlap is preferable to leaving dry spots.

■ *Hedges and borders:* You should water shrubs, flower beds, and hedges on their own zones with bubblers, shrub heads, or micro-irrigation. It is also possible to include these plants on the lawn's zone—by installing flush-mounted heads at the periphery of the lawn. If the hedge or planting is dense enough, water will not pass through it to soak the wall behind or the property next door.

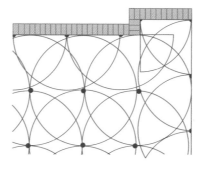
Working around a building

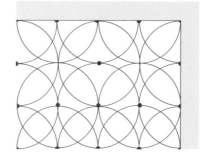
Avoiding watering a public sidewalk

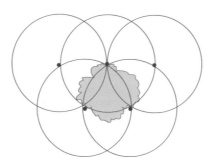
Using triangular spacing to work around an obstacle

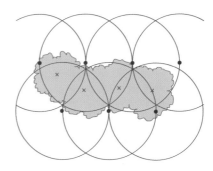
Using triangular spacing for an irregular group planting

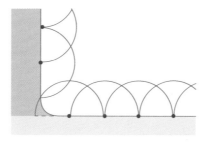
Reducing water loss at a rounded corner

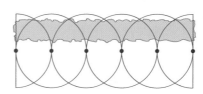
Watering hedges and lawns with a sprinkler on a riser

Irrigating around inside and outside corners

Special situations *continued*

FINISHING YOUR ZONES

Once your landscape plan has all the sprinklers and spray patterns drawn in and you are satisfied that all your plant areas will receive adequate coverage, it's time to divide the plan into finalized zones. Remember, a single control valve controls the sprinkler heads in each zone, and all heads must be of the same type (rotary, fan spray, bubbler, or drip/microsprinkler).

■ *Calculating and dividing:* Unless you have a very small yard, the normal operating water pressure for your home's water system will not allow you to run all of your irrigation components at the same time. Even if it did, you probably wouldn't want to. You don't want a shady lawn that stays relatively moist to be watered as often as a planter box in full sun,

for instance. So as you divide your irrigation plan into individual zones, make sure each has a total operating pressure no greater than the water supply can support. Now you need to evaluate each of the preliminary zones or areas you created earlier (see page 63), based on plant type and environmental factors, to see that the total water demand for the area does not exceed the limits of the water supply.

Using a calculator, add up the total gallons per minute (GPM) for each zone. Add the GPM needs of each sprinkler of the same type, then add 10 percent to compensate for pressure loss to the pipes and fittings. If an area's total GPM does not exceed the total flow available from the water supply (see page 62), that area can remain on a single zone. For instance, if the GPM of all sprinkler heads in a proposed zone adds up to 9, you would add 0.9 GPM (or 10

After drawing in all your sprinkler patterns, establish your zones. Define the final zones by adding up the GPM rates for each area. Then divide them so that none will require more water than is available from the water system. Keep each zone's flow small enough to allow for future expansion.

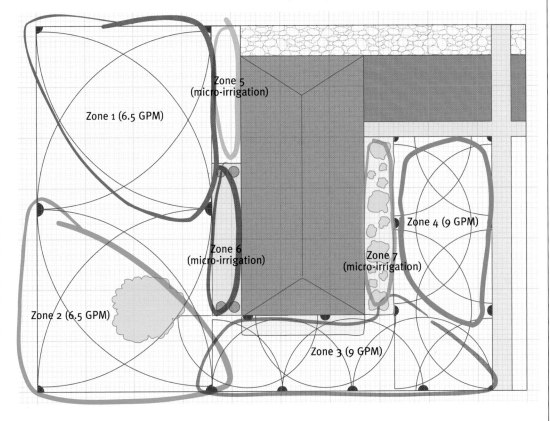

Zone 1 (6.5 GPM)

Zone 5 (micro-irrigation)

Zone 4 (9 GPM)

Zone 6 (micro-irrigation)

Zone 7 (micro-irrigation)

Zone 2 (6.5 GPM)

Zone 3 (9 GPM)

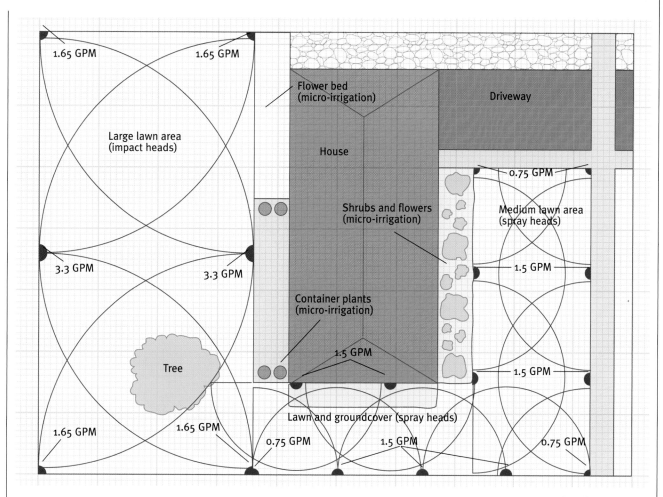

1.65 GPM   1.65 GPM

Flower bed
(micro-irrigation)

Driveway

Large lawn area
(impact heads)

House

0.75 GPM

Shrubs and flowers
(micro-irrigation)

Medium lawn area
(spray heads)

3.3 GPM   3.3 GPM

1.5 GPM

Container plants
(micro-irrigation)

Tree

1.5 GPM

1.5 GPM

1.65 GPM   1.65 GPM

Lawn and groundcover (spray heads)

0.75 GPM   1.5 GPM   0.75 GPM

The plan now has all the required sprinklers plotted. Write the GPM rating for each sprinkler on the plan beside each sprinkler head.

percent), to get a total of 9.9 GPM for the area. If the water supply's maximum GPM were 12, the zone would be fine. However, if the total sprinkler GPM is close to 12 or exceeds it, you need to divide the zone to leave a little breathing room.

Once you have the zones broken up into sizes that the water system can handle and that serve the needs of the plants being watered, go back and add the needed valves and plumbing parts to your plan.

■ *Planning tips:* If you have to subdivide a proposed zone, consider the following factors.
■ Take into account any future expansion you might need for future planting areas.
■ Look for the simplest, most clear-cut places to break up a zone. You want each zone to be as inclusive as possible, not scattered around the yard.
■ Leave extra capacity in each zone so a sprinkler head or two can be added without causing overload.

■ Create zones for plants with similar water needs.
■ Give parts of the lawn that may be shadier and need less irrigation a separate zone.
■ Group sprinklers together according to elevation. If your yard is hilly, group together sprinklers that are at about the same elevation. Otherwise, the water in the system will drain out through the lowest sprinkler each time the sprinkler is turned off, possibly causing flooding and overwatering.

When you are done laying out all the sprinklers and valves, count up the number of zone control valves you have plotted. This will equal your final zone count, a number you will need when selecting a timer.

Your working landscape plan is now complete; it's time to prepare for the installation.

Planning
for cold weather

If you live in a cold climate, you will have to prepare your irrigation system for the winter months before the temperatures fall. Planning for winter early makes dealing with it much easier later.

For those living in cold climates, there is one more thing to consider: winter. Before the cold weather comes, you must completely drain irrigation systems to prevent damage caused by the expansion of freezing water within pipes and components. There are two ways to get your system ready for winter: Pay someone to do it for you or do it yourself. One method of draining requires that you install additional valves in the system. Do this along with the rest of the installation work. It is important to consider draining options during the planning phase.

■ *The contractor approach:* If you hire an irrigation contractor to come to your home and drain the system, expect to pay about $100 per year. When contractors winterize a system, they install a fitting downward from the anti-siphon device outside the house. After shutting off water to the system, they attach a compressed air line to the fitting and blow out the water from each zone. After the system is blown out, all that is left to do is drain the line between the backflow prevention device and the shutoff valve.

■ *The DIY approach:* Draining the system yourself will save you that $100 and won't take much time. There are two basic options: Blow out the system with compressed air or drain the system using drain valves. In areas where the frost line extends more than a foot down, the compressed-air method is recommended. If you don't own or don't want to rent a compressor and live where winters are not as severe, you can use the drain valves.

You must install drain valves at the low spots in each zone. Use at least one drain per zone. In poorly drained soil, you may need to dig a dry well below each drain valve to ensure that no water collects and freezes there. To make a dry well, dig a hole about 16 inches in diameter and 3 feet deep. Then fill it with gravel or pebbles.

■ *Manual drain valves:* If your system will include drain valves, you can choose either manual or automatic valves. Place manual drain valves at the low point of each zone and the main irrigation line. Install drain valves in valve boxes, so at the end of the season you can remove the valve box cover and open the drain valve. Be sure to turn off the water supply before opening the drains. Leave the valves open for a few hours or even a couple of days to let all the water escape from the pipes and the valves. After the water has drained, shut the valves to keep insects from getting into the system.

You'll also need to drain water from the main supply line. Do this by opening the drain valve that's ahead of your zone valves. Even if this line is in your basement, it should be drained, because it more than likely runs through the foundation wall of your home and is exposed to outside temperatures.

■ *Automatic drain valves:* Install automatic drain valves, like manual valves, at the low point of each zone. You must dig a small (about 1 cubic foot) gravel-filled dry well beneath each one to disperse the water. When the zones are running, the valves close automatically. When the zones have completed watering, the valves open and drain the lines. At the end of the season, when you shut off water to the system, the system will drain itself. To be safe, check that the drains are working properly by manually removing a sprinkler from a zone to see whether water remains in the pipes.

You will still need a manual drain ahead of the automatic valves to allow drainage of the plumbing that runs between the main shutoff and the valve manifolds.

■ *Compressed air:* If you live in an area with deep freezes, you can use compressed air to blow out the system. You will need a 25 cubic foot per minute (cfm) or larger compressor, with pressure regulator.

Caution: Do not exceed 50 psi (3.52 kg/cm^2) of air pressure. Exceeding 50 psi can result in severe equipment damage.

You'll also need to install a pressure fitting for the compressor hose located down from the main irrigation water shutoff valve. Once this is in place, you can use the compressor and irrigation timer to blow out each zone.

For your own safety, avoid standing over or near the heads and valves when air is being blown into the irrigation system.

If you observe proper safety precautions, you can blow out your system for winter preparation. Blowing out residual water with air ensures that no water is trapped in the pipes to freeze later on.

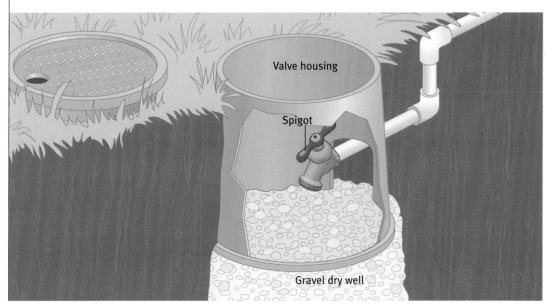

Valve housing

Spigot

Gravel dry well

Manual and automatic drain valves can drain an entire zone. Place them at all the low points within each zone. Notice the gravel-filled dry well in the bottom of the drain valve housing.

Installing your system

With a detailed plan in hand, you're ready to begin the multistep process of installing your watering system. First the preliminary work: You will need to create a comprehensive parts list, gather tools and materials, and stake out and mark your yard based on the dimensions from your drawing.

As you mark the yard, you are marking the foundation for the watering system, so work slowly and carefully to get it just right.

If your system calls for trenching, pace the digging so it does not get too far ahead of the pipe installation. Trenches left unfilled are hazardous and can fill with water, which will complicate the installation when the next weekend arrives. It's better to rent a trencher twice, if need be.

To begin with, you'll turn off the main shutoff valve for your house; this valve is usually near the water meter. With the water turned off, install a main irrigation shutoff valve. Once that's done, you can turn the water on for your house and use the main irrigation shutoff valve to control water running to the irrigation pipes.

Carefully follow the plumbing techniques outlined on pages 108 and 109. Because it may be difficult for you to get to buried system connections if they spring a leak, you want to make sure your joints are solid. Take some time to practice the techniques needed for installing the pipe you have chosen for your system. If you do, the installation will proceed more quickly, and the final results will be more reliable.

Chapter 3

The installation of your
watering system requires
careful planning and
attention to detail,
but is not difficult.

Installing your system

DIGEST

To do

✓ Check for buried utilities.

✓ Buy parts and then some— you can always return extras.

✓ Gather your tools.

✓ Set aside ample time to deal with the main hookup— often the toughest step.

THE IMPORTANCE OF BEING FLEXIBLE

Sprinklers, no matter what type, are installed on some sort of riser. The riser can be a straight pipe many inches in length or a flexible pipe that allows the sprinkler to be moved after it is connected.

A "swing-joint" connection allows a sprinkler to flex slightly in the ground when stepped on or struck, which makes it less vulnerable to breakage.

TRENCHING 101

■ To soften the soil, water the ground approximately two days before you begin digging.
■ Dig trenches by hand with a square-bladed garden spade, or rent a power trencher.
■ Cut out the sod first and set it to one side of the trench.
■ Dig the trench the same width as the spade blade.
■ Dig trenches at least 6 inches deep. Set the dirt on a tarp if possible, on the opposite side of the trench from the sod.
■ Dig drainage pits under all valves, and fill them with 8 inches of gravel.

It's a Wrap

Pipe-thread tape, indispensable for joining threaded pipe, seals the joint and makes it easier to twist on the fitting. Wrap the tape clockwise around the threads, pulling it tight and completely covering all the threads with two layers of tape.

PLASTIC IS KING

Over the years, steel, copper, and even cement have been used for irrigation system plumbing. Today plastic is king. Two plastic pipe types, serving different purposes, are commonly used.

PVC (polyvinyl chloride) is used for main supply lines because it is strong. It may also be used for the lateral lines that supply water to sprinklers.

Polyethylene (PE), often referred to as poly pipe, is more flexible than PVC but not as strong. It works well for low-pressure lines—for instance, lateral lines that supply sprinklers—and for tubing used in drip/micro-irrigation systems (shown).

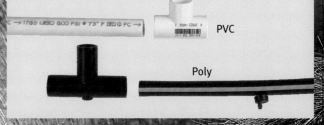

PVC

Poly

Q How do I join various types of pipe for my irrigation system?

A **PVC** pipe is joined using a solvent-welding process. First brush primer onto the areas to be joined, to clean away dirt and soften the surface of the plastic. Apply the cement to the same areas, and the two pieces are pushed together. The cement welds the plastic parts together; once made, joints cannot be wrested apart.

Poly, or PE, pipe is even easier to work with. It can be cut to length with pipe shears or a saw. A joint is made by pushing the end of the poly pipe onto a barbed fitting. Barbs dig into the soft plastic to hold it in place, and a hose clamp secures the fitting permanently.

Copper is joined by sweat connections, made by melting metal solder onto joints using a propane or butane torch. The name comes from the appearance of drops of melted flux at the joint after it has been heated enough to melt the solder. The joint looks as though it is sweating from the heat. This method takes practice.

Galvanized steel, with its threaded fittings, looks easy to join: Simply twist the parts together. But there is a catch. Because the ends must be threaded, steel pipe cannot be cut to size. Thus, you must have myriad sizes of pipe on hand.

MYTHS, FACTS AND GOOD ADVICE

Myth: Just bury the pipe.
Fact: Slope your pipe toward drains built into the system or debris may accumulate and clog emitters and sprinklers. In cold climates, undrained water will freeze and rupture pipes.
Good advice: When installing any pipe, give it a constant pitch— 1/8 inch per foot—so water will flow toward a system drain when not under pressure.

VALVE SAVVY

■ *Master valves* and *main system shutoff valves* are installed on the main line, just after it tees off the house water service line.

■ *Drain valves* are always installed at the lowest point in the zone they are intended to drain excess water, otherwise standing water may be trapped in the pipes.

■ *Antisiphon* valves and in-line valves are used for zone control.

■ Drain and antisiphon valves are installed in groupings called *manifolds* (see page 119).

Each manifold waters a particular part of the property—for instance, the front yard or a flower bed.

■ When building a valve manifold, always leave extra space so you'll have the option of adding new valves in the future.

Materials
and tools

Having a complete list of parts, including part numbers and quantities, will cut down on trips to the home center in the middle of your installation.

One of the benefits of using a design service is that a complete shopping list, including all parts and fittings, comes with the drawing.

If you have created your own design, it's possible to obtain an effortless shopping list by bringing your plans to an irrigation equipment specialist, who can calculate your needs. There may be a modest fee.

If you'd rather list the parts on your own, go over your plan carefully, measuring the length of all metal, PVC, and/or poly pipe being used. Note both the number and sizes of heads, couplings, tees, elbows, clamps, and other fittings that you

will need. Remember to include the parts needed for making the main connection to the irrigation line. Many suppliers offer parts lists with blank spaces that you can fill in to indicate the number of each of the items you need. Use a pencil—you'll inevitably make changes.

TOOLS

The tools you'll need depend on the type of pipe you'll be using. Shown on the page opposite are tools for laying out and installing a PVC- and poly-based system; for tools needed for copper or galvanized steel pipe, see page 109.

Materials you will need

Most installations call for sand and gravel to line valve boxes and drainage dry walls. If you need to run a line through your house's foundation, you'll need caulking compound or hydraulic cement to seal the hole. If you're installing PVC and poly pipe, have primer and cement on hand. Electrical tape and wire ties tidy up pump and valve wiring.

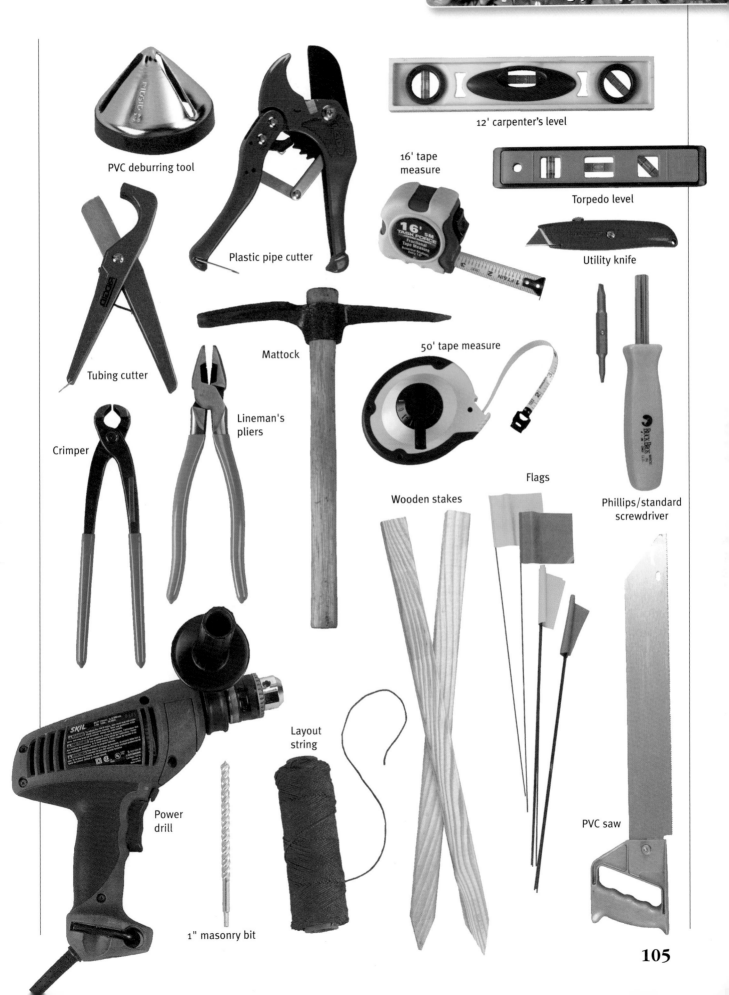

PVC deburring tool

Plastic pipe cutter

12' carpenter's level

16' tape measure

Torpedo level

Utility knife

Tubing cutter

Mattock

50' tape measure

Crimper

Lineman's pliers

Flags

Wooden stakes

Phillips/standard screwdriver

Power drill

Layout string

1" masonry bit

PVC saw

105

Trenching
the yard

Even if you plan to use a power trencher, you will have to do some digging by hand around buildings, flower beds, and other obstacles. The work will be easier if you soften the soil by moderately watering the area for a few days before using the shovel.

Before any digging begins, mark all buried utilities. Striking gas or water lines can be hazardous. Hitting underground phone or cable lines is more likely because these are often near the surface.

Renting a power trencher will save time and spare your back. This machine, which looks like a big chain saw, piles soil neatly to one side of the trench. Use it only on lawns—not flower beds, groundcover, or steep slopes. Dig at a pace that parallels the plumbing installation. Empty trenches are dangerous. The rental company will provide instructions for using the machine.

To dig trenches by hand, use a sharp straight-edged garden spade and dig trenches to the required depth—typically 6 to 12 inches. Dig the trenches as wide as the spade blade. In lawn areas, first remove the sod and put it to one side of the trench. As you dig, place the soil on a tarp

on the other side. Replacing soil is then a simple matter of raking it back into the trench and setting the sod on top.

If it is necessary to run pipe under a sidewalk or driveway, there are two methods for digging. Force a length of 1-inch metal pipe through the soil under the walkway by driving it with a hammer or even a small sledgehammer. Protect the pipe threads by adding a coupler fitting, a 6-inch piece of pipe, and a cap to both ends.

Another technique lets water pressure do the work. Use a garden hose and a length of pipe with a hose adapter attached. The pipe must be at least 12 inches longer than the width of the pavement. Dig a trench on both sides of the spot where the tunnel will be, making sure there is enough room to maneuver the length of pipe. Put on safety goggles and gloves, and turn on the water. Push the pipe under the sidewalk and work it back and forth as the water pressure blasts a hole. Once the irrigation pipe has been inserted, stabilize its position by pushing as much soil as possible back under the slab.

Power trenchers are great for open areas, such as lawns, but you'll need a spade to trench in confined or irregularly shaped spaces.

A sharp-edged garden spade will make the trenching job easier.

Using water pressure to dig under a sidewalk is effective but can get messy.

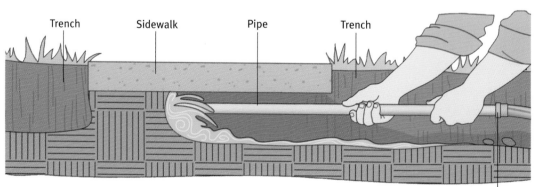

Trench   Sidewalk   Pipe   Trench

Hose-to-pipe adapter

Plumbing
considerations

Climate is the first factor to consider when deciding how deep to lay pipe. In temperate areas where freezing is not a problem, set pipes at any depth that is convenient, 6 to 8 inches being the norm.

In regions with freezing winters, burying all water lines below the frost line is ideal. However, the frost line extends down 40 inches or more in some parts of the continent, and digging that deep would be impractical. Fortunately, placing pipes below the frost line is not necessary if you install automatic or manual drain valves so that pipes can be completely drained before cold weather sets in. In that case, burying pipes in a trench about 12 inches deep is sufficient to protect the pipes from physical damage.

In lawn areas, place pipes deep enough under the turf to allow for full root growth and deep enough that such things as lawn aerators or the weight of landscape equipment will not damage them.

Lay irrigation lines on the surface of the ground in many areas of a landscape—usually where groundcover will hide them or where traffic is unlikely, such as on a steep slope. However, wherever there's foot traffic, bury pipes to keep them out of harm's way and to prevent tripping.

WHAT IS SLOPE?

A gradual downward slope—also called the pitch—of pipes, usually ⅛ inch per foot, prevents unwanted low spots that may hold water and contribute to many problems, including clogged emitters and accumulated debris inside the pipes. Slope is essential if your system has drain valves or you live in a cold region where you need to drain lines completely before winter.

Drain valves: a safeguard

Automatic drain valves protect your system from damage by automatically draining pipes when the pressure is off. If your system is properly sloped, there will be no standing water in the pipes that, in cold weather, could freeze and cause damage.

See pages 99 and 125 for options on installing automatic drain valves.

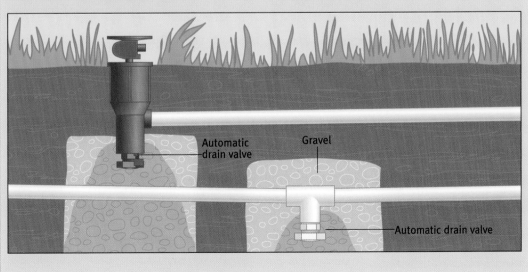

Automatic drain valve

Gravel

Automatic drain valve

Working with PVC and poly pipe

■ **PVC:** You cannot take solvent-welded joints apart. If you make a mistake, the only redress is to cut out the affected pipe and fitting and redo the installation, adding a coupling if necessary to extend the pipe to the length needed.

1 Cut the pipe to length using plastic-pipe cutters or a fine-blade saw. Use a deburring tool or file to remove burrs. Wipe the area to be "welded."

2 Apply the primer to the outside of the tubing and the inside of the fitting. Once the primer has evaporated, apply cement in the same way to each part. Quickly insert the pipe into the fitting, and give it a quarter turn to distribute the cement. Hold it in place for about 30 seconds, then wipe away any excess solvent from the joint.

3 Allow the cement to set for the length of time recommended on the can before turning on the water. If the pipe is to be buried, wait at least 12 hours.

■ **Poly:** Poly uses barbed fittings with hose clamps to create a secure connection. It is much easier to install than PVC.

Warming poly pipe in the sun for an hour or so will soften the pipe and make it easier to work with.

1 Cut poly pipe evenly to the proper length with a hacksaw or tubing shears (shown). Then slip a stainless-steel hose clamp over the pipe and insert the barbed fitting into the end of the hose.

2 Position the clamp over the ridged section of the barbed fitting and tighten it gently. (A heat gun can help soften the poly.) Many new poly fittings have hose clamps built into the fittings, so you may not need to purchase separate hose clamps.

Working with copper and steel pipe

■ **Copper:** Making reliable connections with copper tubing is not hard if you are careful. Soldered copper connections, also called sweat connections, require special equipment to do the job right: a multiuse wire brush, a roll of solder suitable for potable water systems, a container of flux, a flux brush, a propane torch, and a tubing cutter.

1 Cut the pipe using a tubing cutter, and dry fit your assembly. Pieces should fit together snugly but easily. Next, rough up the outside of the tubing with the multiuse wire brush (shown) or other wire brush. Use the brush to do the same to the inside of the fitting where it will be soldered.

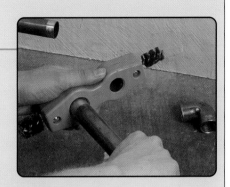

2 Using a small flux brush, apply flux to the outside of the pipe where you cleaned it and to the inside of the fitting. A thin, even layer on both areas is all you need. Then fit the pieces together.

3 Use a torch to begin heating the pipe and fitting on the side closest to you. Then move the torch to the back side of the fitting. When the flux begins to smoke and run out of the joint, apply the tip of a piece of solder to the joint. It should melt quickly and flow into the connection. Use a damp rag to wipe any excess solder into the joint. Let the joint cool completely before turning on the water.

■ **Steel:** When working with galvanized steel pipe, you will need a wire brush, pipe-thread tape or pipe compound, and two pipe wrenches. (If you are adding on to a steel system, buy adapters to make the transition to plastic or copper which is cheaper and easier to install.)

1 Use a small wire brush to remove any rust or dirt from the threads of the pipe. Add five or six clockwise wraps of pipe-thread tape. This seals the threads and eases the work of screwing on fittings.

2 Twist the fitting onto the pipe threads, and turn the fitting until it is hand-tight. Then use two wrenches to tighten further— one wrench to hold the pipe and the other to tighten the fitting a few more turns. Check that the fitting faces the right direction for the next pipe. Adjust as needed by tightening— not by loosening.

Laying out
your system

The more thoroughly and precisely you mark out your irrigation system, the less chance there will be for you or someone else to make a mistake.

To transfer your plan from paper to your yard, it's useful to have an assistant to help you mark the yard. You'll be using several supplies: string, wooden stakes, marking flags (available in a variety of colors from irrigation dealers), cans of marking paint, and a 50-foot tape measure.

If possible, color-code stakes, flags, and paint to match the colors used in your plan. That way, you will know at a glance which zone you are working on.

This is where you need patience. Don't be surprised if unexpected obstacles require you to alter your plan slightly.

Warning!

Before you start marking the locations of trenches, be sure your local utility companies have located and marked all buried utility lines. Remember: You may be held responsible for damage to unmarked lines and pipes.

Marking paint eliminates two problems common with marking strings: the tripping hazard and the problem of displaced strings.

Local utility companies will mark the location of buried pipes and cables in your yard. In many areas, it takes only one phone call to alert all companies concerned.

You need to dig trenches deep enough to allow the tallest sprinklers to drop to ground level when finished watering.

MARKING YOUR PLAN

Start by marking the main supply line, water meter, and valve manifold locations.

Next, mark the header lines and lateral lines.

Finally, mark the position of each sprinkler riser with a wooden stake. Check the sprinkler spacing using a string cut to the length of each sprinkler's radius. The string should just touch each sprinkler head adjacent to it.

Run string between the stakes to indicate the trenches for your pipes. Once the strings are in place, you will be better able to visualize the layout and maybe improve it. For instance, you might see a place where you could use a common trench to save digging work, or you might notice an overlooked obstacle.

Finally, stake out a trench leading from the zone valve manifolds to the irrigation timer box. You will need to bury wiring here.

Once you have laid out the project, use spray paint to mark the ground; then remove the string and stakes. Although this step is not absolutely necessary, it makes trenching much more accurate. You also won't have to worry about tripping over the strings.

111

Water hookups

To hook up your irrigation system to your home water supply, you will tie into the main supply line just past the water meter. The location of the water meter usually dictates where you place the tee for the irrigation system. You must cut into the line after the meter. If you don't have a water meter, tie into the supply line after the shutoff valve for the main service line.

Locate the cut as close as you can to the planned location of the backflow preventer.

Your home's water line, proceeding from the meter, is made of galvanized steel, copper, or PVC. Each type of pipe requires a slightly different method for adding a tee fitting. In most cases you'll use a transition fitting that lets you join schedule 40 PVC pipe—the pipe used in most irrigation systems—to your home's steel or copper line.

Check local codes before you begin. Some require metal piping and may insist that a licensed plumber handle this part of the job.

Before you break into the main supply line, turn off the water to your home. Shut off the valve on the house side of the water meter. Your shutoff may be in the outdoor "buffalo box" that holds your meter. In rare cases, you'll have to call your water department to turn off the water.

After you have shut off the water, open the taps in your house to let the water remaining in the pipes drain out. When you're ready to cut into the pipe, have a bucket handy.

STEEL, COPPER, OR PVC

The first thing to do after making the cut is cap your new line after the tee so you can turn on the water before proceeding with the system installation. Once that's done, you're ready to tie into the pipe. Here's how to prepare for tying into each type of pipe.

■ *Galvanized steel:* Because pipe threads go only in one direction, you cannot simply remove a pipe in the middle of a run. You must cut into it and, with the help of a fitting called a union, install your tee and rebuild the section of removed pipe. You may need to have a new piece of pipe threaded to suit your situation exactly. Often a stock piece of pipe (the shorter ones are known as nipples) will fit. If you plan to use copper in your watering system, make the transition from steel to copper with a fitting called a dielectric union to avoid corrosion.

■ *Copper:* Although a sweat joint is more permanent (see page 109), you can safely use a compression fitting with copper. Always cut copper with a tubing cutter because a hacksaw will

Tying into steel pipe

1 With water to the house shut off, cut the main service line just after the house-side stop valve. Use a hacksaw (shown) or a reciprocating saw with metal-cutting blade.

2 Using two pipe wrenches, unscrew both ends of the cut pipe. Wrap the threads of a 3- to 6-inch-long nipple with pipe-thread tape. Fasten the nipple and tee.

3 Add a short nipple to the tee. With the threads uppermost, slip on the nut for the union. Using pipe-thread tape, attach one half of the union. Set the second half of the union in place and measure to see what length of pipe will have to be added.

4 Install the length of pipe and attach the second half of the union to it. Slip the nut up and hand-tighten. Fully tighten the union with two wrenches.

dent the pipe out of round. You may have to sweat a cap onto a piece of pipe to seal off the tee temporarily.

■ *PVC:* Although PVC may have enough give in it to cement a tee in place, a compression tee is easier. Have a capped piece of pipe ready to seal off the tee temporarily.

SPIGOT CONNECTION

Making a permanent connection to an spigot can save digging and plumbing. However, this option works only in nonfreezing climates and only when the water flow is great enough to support your system design.

Shut off the faucet at the meter and remove the spigot. Install a threaded tee and reattach the faucet, using a threaded nipple of the appropriate length. Next, add a section of PVC to the remaining outlet on the tee. You will connect your main shutoff valve here.

Tying into copper

1 With the water off, cut the main service line, using a tubing cutter. Be sure to leave several inches of pipe on the meter side for making your connections.

2 Remove the nuts and ferrules from the tee, hold the tee against the pipe, and mark your second cut.

3 Complete the second cut. Slip the nuts into place, making sure their threaded ends face toward the fitting. Slip the ferrules onto the pipe, then tighten the nuts. No pipe-thread tape is needed.

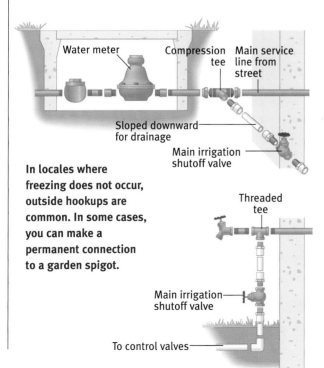

Water meter

Compression tee

Main service line from street

Sloped downward for drainage

Main irrigation shutoff valve

In locales where freezing does not occur, outside hookups are common. In some cases, you can make a permanent connection to a garden spigot.

Threaded tee

Main irrigation shutoff valve

To control valves

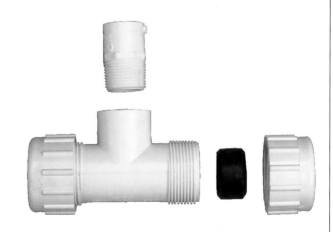

PVC is one of the easiest types of pipe to tie into. Purchase a PVC compression tee to suit the dimension of the main supply line. Take the nuts off the tee, hold the tee in place, and mark for your cuts. Use a plastic-pipe saw or other fine-tooth saw to cut into the line. Install the tee as shown.

113

Installing valves

The irrigation control valves are the obvious valves in your system. Less noticeable are the main shutoff, the master valve, and various drain valves.

When installing any valve, be careful that the water will flow in the correct direction. Arrows on the valve body indicate the direction of flow.

Before installing the valves for your irrigation system, check your water system calculations (pages 60 to 62). If your home's water capacity is greater than 80 GPM, you must first install a pressure reducer to lower the water pressure coming into the irrigation system. You should not add valves or drains to the main irrigation supply line until you have installed a pressure reducer, if needed.

The irrigation system's valves will include the main irrigation supply shutoff valve, a drain valve for emptying the main supply line for servicing or winterizing, and the irrigation zone control valves, which will deliver water to the individual zones as mapped on your irrigation plan. You may also be installing automatic drain valves to the water lines. (See page 125.)

MAIN SHUTOFF VALVE INSTALLATION

Once you have installed the compression tee, the next step is installing the main irrigation shutoff valve. This is true whether your meter is in the basement or the yard, or you are connecting to an spigot outside.

The main irrigation shutoff valve is usually a ball valve because these are easy and fast to open and close—requiring a simple quarter turn in either direction to go fully off or fully on. A ball valve also gives an immediate visual indication whether the valve is open or shut. When open, the valve handle is aligned with the supply line.

You can also use a gate valve for the main shutoff valve. On the plus side, a gate valve makes it easier to increase the flow gradually when filling the system in spring after winter shutdown. This reduces the possibility of a damaging pressure surge in the pipes. On the minus side, gate valves require several turns of the handle to open fully or close. Gate valves used in hard-water areas should be installed tilted to one side or the other to prevent particles from settling on the valve seat and causing leaks.

To install the shutoff valve, cement a piece of PVC pipe at least 3 inches long into the tee opening you will be using for your irrigation system. (If you have already done this to install a cap, just cut off the cap and proceed.)

Next cement your shutoff valve in place on the open end of the nipple. Pay attention to the water flow direction, which should be indicated on the valve body with an arrow.

Once the valve is in place, add another 3-inch or longer piece of PVC to the output side of the valve, and cement an in-line drain valve to that. Drain valves are sometimes called boiler drains and are usually gate valves. Gate valves are preferred because they let you control the flow of water more precisely as it exits the irrigation line.

Once both valves are in place, close them, turn the water back on, and check for leaks.

Main shutoff installation

1 With the water turned off at the meter, use a hacksaw to cut out a 3-inch section of the main service line just beyond the water meter. Be sure to leave at least 3 inches of pipe on the meter side of your cut.

2 Install a compression tee (see page 113) and tighten it down securely. Be sure the irrigation supply outlet of the tee is pointing in the right direction before tightening the compression nuts too far.

3 If needed, thread a slip adapter onto the tee, and glue a short PVC nipple to it. Then glue another adapter into place and thread on the main irrigation shutoff valve.

4 Finally, connect the valve outlet to the main irrigation supply line. Be sure the valve is closed, and turn on the water to check for leaks. If all is well, add several inches of gravel beneath the valve and enclose it in a valve box for protection. Backfill with dirt around the valve box.

Drilling through
foundations

Use a heavy-duty drill and masonry bit to drill through concrete or concrete block. Pull the bit out frequently and spray window cleaner on it to clean and cool the bit. Shoot some cleaner in the hole as well; the foaming action of the cleaner cleans out grit. A star drill and baby sledgehammer help if you hit a rock embedded in the concrete.

If your water meter is in the basement, you will need to run the main irrigation line out through the basement wall once you have installed the main irrigation shutoff valve and the drain valve.

■ **Going through the sill or rim joist—The easiest** way to run a water line outside is through the wooden sill plate or the rim joist of a house. The sill plate, often a 2×6, rests directly on top of the foundation. The rim joist, typically a 2×10 or 2×12, is a framing member that stands on edge on top of the sill plate. If access permits, you may be able to drill a hole here to feed the water line through and save yourself the trouble of drilling through the foundation.

Make the hole ¼ inch larger than the pipe diameter. Drill at a slight angle so that once the pipe is installed, it will slope slightly downward toward the main line drain valve. Seal any gaps with foam or insulation, followed by caulk.

■ **Going through the wall—If you need to feed the** line through the basement wall, first locate the spot on the outside of the house where you want the irrigation line to emerge. Dig a hole large enough so the pipe can slide through once the hole is drilled. If this spot is where the backflow prevention device or the first manifold will be located, you will need to dig deep enough to accommodate 8 to 12 inches of gravel as well.

Measure carefully so you can mark the location of the hole on the inside of the wall. Place it high enough to allow a slight slope (⅛ inch per foot) toward the drain valve so no water is left in the pipe once it drains. Mark the spot on the wall.

Using a masonry bit, ½ inch larger than your irrigation line, bore through the wall.

Now feed the pipe through the hole and make your connections to the drain valve. Once the PVC cement has set, fill any gaps around the pipe with epoxy, mortar, hydrocement, or expanding foam if the pipe is above grade.

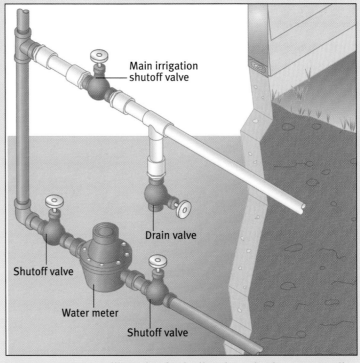

Main irrigation shutoff valve

Drain valve

Shutoff valve

Water meter

Shutoff valve

In some cases, you will need to feed a line through a basement wall.

Installing valves *continued*

INSTALLING THE BACKFLOW PREVENTER

Determine which type of backflow prevention device (BPD) will work best for your system—and whether a particular type is mandated by local codes. (See page 73.) You must install some BPDs to galvanized steel or copper plumbing. Codes may require that a licensed plumber install everything up to and including the BPD. If you plan to use a double-check valve (see page 73) or an air-gap system, be sure to check installation requirements before doing the work yourself.

If your system can't use antisiphon valves (which combine an atmospheric vacuum breaker with a zone control valve) and requires a separate BPD, you will need to install it between the main irrigation shutoff valve and the zone control valves. If a separate BPD is needed for each zone, you can install it after the zone control valves. (You would also do this to add atmospheric vacuum breakers to existing zones.)

When your BPD is installed below ground, as in the case of a double-check valve, place it in a valve box and use about 8 inches of gravel in a dry well for drainage underneath.

Install vacuum breakers and antisiphon valves above ground 6 to 12 inches higher than the highest sprinkler head. You should also place these inside a protective valve box.

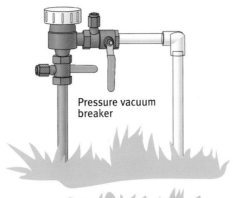

Pressure vacuum breaker

The backflow preventer you will use depends on your irrigation system water source and on local code requirements.

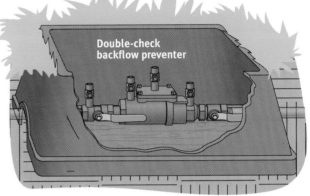

Double-check backflow preventer

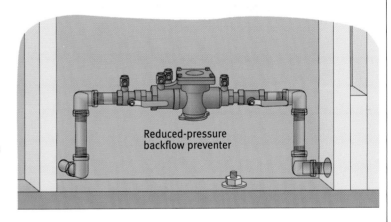

Reduced-pressure backflow preventer

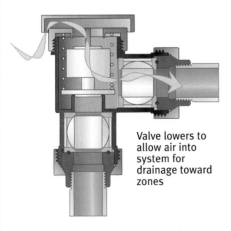

Valve lowers to allow air into system for drainage toward zones

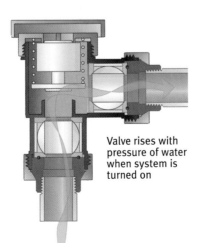

Valve rises with pressure of water when system is turned on

The atmospheric vacuum preventer is the most common type of BPD. It is often combined with an automatic zone valve to create an antisiphon valve.

117

Installing valves *continued*

Dig a dry well deep enough to accommodate the BPD, the 8 inches of gravel, and the valve box.

Add the gravel and tamp it down.

Run PVC pipe from the main shutoff or main supply drain valve, to the spot where you will be installing the BPD. Remember to pitch the pipe slightly toward the main drain valve to create positive drainage.

If you need to use plastic-to-metal adapters, install them onto the device *before* you connect the PVC pipe. Then, using PVC cement, make the connection to the inflow side of your BPD.

Adjust the gravel in the dry well to level and support the device.

To install an antisiphon valve, cement a 90-degree elbow to the supply line to turn it vertically. Add a piece of PVC pipe 6 to 12 inches long (or longer if needed) to reach the correct height, then cement the inlet side of the antisiphon valve to it. Do the same on the outlet side, ending with another elbow at the same level as the supply line. Be sure the elbow faces in the correct direction to connect with the zone plumbing line it feeds into. To assemble an antisiphon manifold, see page 121.

A pressure vacuum breaker is another type of BPD that might be mandated in your area. These can protect the entire system. You can choose between heavy-duty brass units (right) or more economical plastic types (below).

ZONE CONTROL VALVES AND MANIFOLDS

Zone control valves are the automatic valves that regulate water flow to the zones. They are either in-line valves or antisiphon valves. Because a separate control valve is required for each zone of your irrigation system, the valves are grouped together in manifolds to simplify installation. These reflect the area they are watering. Only one water connection is needed per manifold. With this approach, you can have one manifold grouping for the front yard, one for the backyard—as many as the layout of your lot requires.

When installing several in-line valves together, the manifold should sit atop an 8-inch layer of gravel. Space the valves at

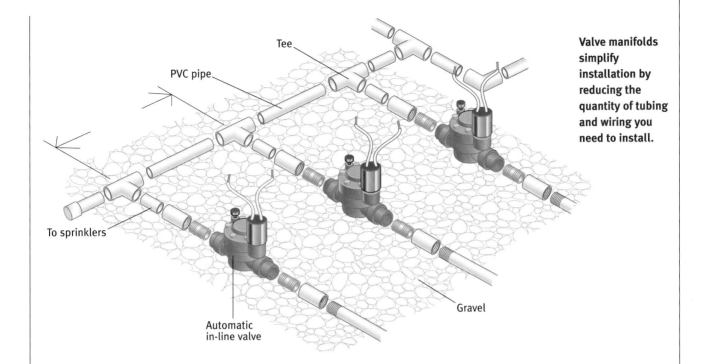

Tee

PVC pipe

To sprinklers

Automatic
in-line valve

Gravel

Valve manifolds
simplify
installation by
reducing the
quantity of tubing
and wiring you
need to install.

least 5 inches apart in the manifold for easy access, and locate them at least 5 inches from the side of the house. Observe these minimum spacing requirements with antisiphon and in-line valves alike.

ASSEMBLING VALVE MANIFOLDS

To assemble a manifold of control valves, you will need several tee fittings, end caps, and 5-inch sections of PVC pipe. (See page 108 for how to work with PVC.) If you are using antisiphon valves, you will also need two sections of pipe to use as risers for each valve.

Starting at the supply line, assemble a tee and then a 5-inch section of PVC pipe for each of the valves you are installing. Prime and cement the pieces together, being careful to align the tees properly with the zone outlets. Align the tees vertically for anti-siphon valves and horizontally for in-line valves.

Cement a cap on the last short piece of pipe. This allows the ease of adding a connection for another valve later if you want to add to your system.

In cold areas, use a manual drain valve instead of a cap to facilitate seasonal drainage.

Next, add short pieces of pipe—or, if using antisiphon valves, an elbow and a riser—to the outlet for each zone. This is where you will be attaching your valves.

Finally, cement the inlet side of the first tee to the supply line, rotating the manifold assembly into position on the gravel bed in order to spread the cement.

This neat assembly, complete and ready for wiring, ensures that you'll get the best from your components.

Building valve manifolds

1 Begin by assembling a tee and a PVC nipple for each valve in the manifold. The valves need to be at least 5 inches apart.

2 Glue the open end of the nipple to the inlet of the next tee. Repeat this until you have glued together enough tees for each valve. Add an extra nipple and cap at the end of the line to make future additions easier.

3 Once you have assembled the basic manifold, glue another short nipple and a zone control valve to the remaining outlet on each tee.

4 Once you have completed the manifold, attach it to the water supply line that will feed it. Be sure no dirt has fallen into any open pipe before you glue it in place.

5 Once you have made all the connections, turn on the water and check for leaks. Then manually flush each valve, using its bleed screw. Finally, add a valve box and backfill with dirt or gravel. (Note: Be sure you have enough irrigation wire in place to make your electrical connections to each valve later on.)

Installing valves *continued*

■ *Antisiphon and in-line valve installation:* If you are using antisiphon valves, assemble them into manifolds. The assembly is much like that for in-line valve manifolds (see opposite page) except that the outflow on the tees is vertical, rather than horizontal, in order to attach riser pipes. Cement PVC riser pipes into these outlets. The risers need to be long enough to position the valves above the highest sprinkler head in your irrigation system, typically 6 to 12 inches above the ground. Next, cement the inlet side of each valve to the vertical risers. Be sure the flow indicator on the valve body (see page 114) is pointing in the correct direction. If not, the valve will not protect your household water system from contamination. Give the valve a small twist on the riser to position it properly and to spread the cement in the joint.

Once you have all the valves in place, attach another riser pipe of the same length to the outflow for each valve.

Put an elbow at the bottom of each riser to turn the flow back to horizontal. Line it up in the right direction for connecting to your zone pipes. After you have connected the zone plumbing, complete the manifold.

■ *In-line valves:* Measure the width of the valve box you have purchased to be sure the manifold and valves will fit in the box once all is assembled. Assemble the manifold using the instructions on pages 119 and 120.

Once you have cemented all manifold and valve connections and the cement has set, turn off all the zone valves. Then turn on the water at the irrigation system shutoff valve to check for leaks. Open each zone valve's external bleed screw briefly to flush out any dirt before proceeding to the next step, connection of the zone plumbing.

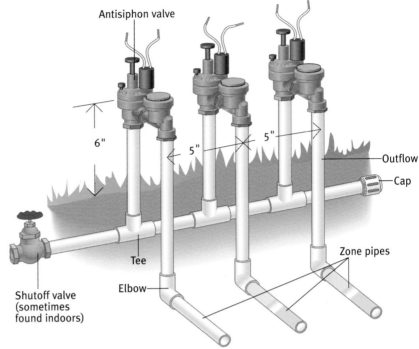

Antisiphon valves (shown) and in-line valves can be assembled into groupings called manifolds to control various zones in a yard.

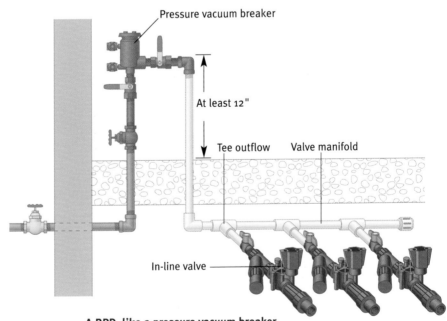

A BPD, like a pressure vacuum breaker, protects the system as a whole, allowing the use of simple in-line valves in the manifold rather than antisiphon valves.

121

Installing valves *continued*

VALVE BOXES

Plastic valve boxes, perhaps the lowest-tech components in an irrigation system, cover and protect expensive automatic valves. They are available in a range of sizes and shapes to cover everything from a single valve to a large manifold of valves. Some have locking covers to prevent tinkering and vandalism. Valve-box designs blend with their surroundings; some even resemble garden rocks.

Generally, you install the valve box last, after all connections have been made and confirmed to be leak-free. The box itself sits in the hole you dug for your manifold and has notches that fit over the water lines. Set the box into the hole and backfill with dirt to hold the box in position. Then add a few inches of gravel, slide in the lid, and lock it in place.

Valve boxes for aboveground antisiphon valves simply fit over the valves and rest on the gravel bed under the manifold.

Valve boxes provide protection from yard equipment as well as from vandalism.

A correctly installed valve box is level with the surrounding ground.

VALVE WIRING

Once you've installed the manifold, you will need to wire each valve in the manifold and run the bundle of wires to the location where you plan to install your timer.

For each manifold location, you will need a wiring bundle that consists of multiple colored wires, and one white wire known as the common wire. Use 18-gauge wire approved for underground use. A different-color wire notes each valve to make identification at the timer easier.

For each valve, attach one colored wire to one lead coming from the valve solenoid. To make the connection, you must use a special waterproof grease cap connector, so named because it is filled with silicone grease to seal the connection from moisture.

Connect the remaining leads from each valve to the white common wire using another waterproof connector. If the wires are not long enough to reach, add a length of white wire, splicing it onto the lead and the common wire. Be sure to use a waterproof grease cap for each connection.

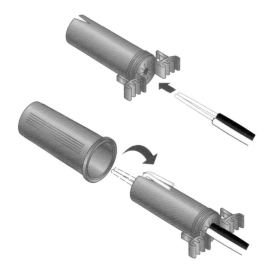

Waterproof connectors known as "grease caps" protect wire connections from water damage when a valve or plumbing failure occurs within the valve box.

Run the valve wire bundles along the bottom of the trenches under the irrigation pipes. Install the pipes on top of the wire bundles for added protection from shovels, hoe blades, or other yard tools. Once you have the pipes in place, secure the wires to them with electrical tape.

Be sure the wires will be buried at least 6 inches deep. If they need to run up the wall of a structure to reach your timer, secure them with plastic electrical staples. Leave them untrimmed until you are ready to make the final connections to the timer.

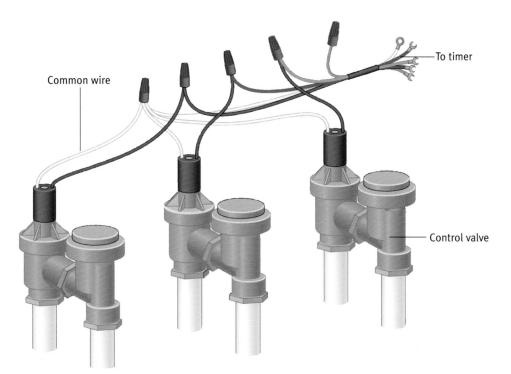

Common wire

To timer

Control valve

To wire the valves together correctly, connect each white valve wire to the white common wire. Connect each remaining valve lead to its own colored strand from the wire bundle. Use grease caps for all connections.

Laying
the pipes

p to this point it has been necessary to use PVC (or metal) pipe because it can handle pressure surges that sometimes come from the main water line. For the piping that comes after the zone control valves, you can continue with PVC or use flexible poly pipe. If you use poly pipe, you have the option of renting a pipe puller to install it rather than having to trench. To connect poly pipe to the PVC at the valves, you will need to use a PVC-to-poly adapter. The PVC side of the adapter is primed and cemented in the usual fashion; the poly side has a barbed fitting. Push the poly onto the barbs, then secure it with a pipe clamp.

Begin by installing a header line for each zone. Each header line will travel from the valve manifold as far as it needs to go to service all the lateral lines you will be installing for the sprinklers in each zone. Keep your runs as straight as possible, and give the lines a constant pitch of ⅛ inch per foot to facilitate drainage and protect against freeze damage. Next, use tees or elbows to attach the lateral lines to the headers. The lateral lines, which connect to the sprinklers, should also have as few turns as possible. A depth of 8 inches is usually sufficient for burying sprinkler lateral lines, but extra-high pop-up heads may require greater depth.

INSTALLING RISERS

A sprinkler riser is the pipe that rises up from the lateral line in a trench to the sprinkler. Adjustable risers are more expensive but you can adjust them quickly as needed. For example, a simple twist of the riser will extend its length when the soil builds up over time in a lawn or garden.

At each riser location, cut the lateral line and cement a tee in place. At the end of the line use an elbow rather than a tee. Most sprinklers use ½-inch or ¾-inch connections, so you may need a reducer tee depending on what size pipe you are using for the lateral line.

Add a riser to each tee. You can use precut threaded risers or install one end of the riser pipe into the tee or elbow. Then measure down to the proper depth below the ground surface. Cut the riser with a hacksaw or utility knife.

Use flexible swing-joint risers in heavy-traffic areas because they flex downward a bit when stepped on. (See page 129.)

Finally, use a torpedo level to check that each riser is vertical and at the appropriate height. The tops of stationary and pop-up lawn sprinkler heads need to be within 1 inch of the soil surface.

Mount shrub heads as high as the expected maximum height of the plantings they will water. Mount shrub heads on rigid PVC risers or on pieces of rebar that support a flexible poly riser. On slopes, always mount risers perpendicular to the slope.

When you are finished with each zone, flush it out with water to remove dirt and debris. Cap each riser until you are ready to install your sprinklers.

Laying pipe

1. Install the header line, then the lateral lines for each zone. Install tees and elbows wherever you will place a sprinkler riser.

2. Install the reducer elbow (last head on line).

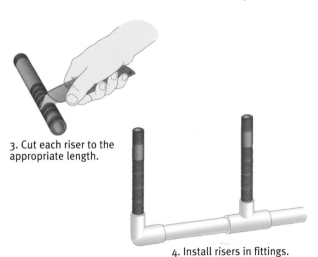

3. Cut each riser to the appropriate length.

4. Install risers in fittings.

INSTALLING AUTOMATIC DRAIN VALVES

If you live in an area with freezing temperatures, you need to protect your irrigation lines from the damage that can occur when water freezes and expands inside pipes. The best protection is keeping the pipes dry during cold months. Automatic drain valves installed on each zone are a convenient way to drain the system when it is not in use. An automatic drain valve is a small threaded device designed to remain shut when water under pressure is in the line. When the pressure is removed (as when the zone or system is turned off), the valve opens and lets any remaining water drain.

Although automatic drain valves are convenient, they do waste water, which may be a problem in areas where water is precious. See page 98 and 99 for other winterization options. Manual valves are usually used only on main lines that need to hold pressure at all times.

Automatic drain valves attach easily to any underground line by means of a tee fitting. Install them at a downward angle of about 45 degrees to allow for proper drainage. Add at least one automatic drain valve per lateral line, inserting it at the lowest point in the zone so that all the water in the pipes will drain between waterings. Beneath each drain valve location, dig a dry well at least 8 inches deep and fill it with gravel (see pages 99 and 107). This will give the drained water a place to go so the valve won't be resting in water. You can also add a short length of pipe as a protective header that can be slipped over the drain valve to prevent clogging.

An easy-to-install alternative to an automatic drain valve is the use of a self-draining sprinkler head rather than a drain valve. Many pop-up impact sprinklers models now come with two inlets—one on the side for the water connection and one on the bottom for an automatic drain valve. This allows each sprinkler body to drain after each use, eliminating any water from being trapped inside the sprinkler body. In warmer climates, you can just cap off and ignore the extra inlet. Beneath self-draining headers, remove 6 inches of soil and replace it with gravel.

Automatic drain valves prevent freeze damage, but they do waste water.

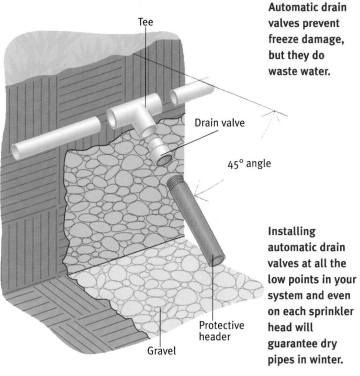

Tee

Drain valve

45° angle

Protective header

Gravel

Installing automatic drain valves at all the low points in your system and even on each sprinkler head will guarantee dry pipes in winter.

125

Installing
sprinklers

Once the risers and drains are in place, you're finally ready to install the heads and nozzles that will create your final spray patterns.

With some risers, you may need to add a threaded adapter to the riser to make the connection to the sprinkler head. If you are using a poly riser, you will need a conversion fitting that needs only a pipe clamp.

Thread the correct fitting into the sprinkler body. Adding a few wraps of pipe-thread tape over the threads before inserting the fitting makes it easier to tighten and seal the connection against leaks. Finish tightening the fitting with a wrench. If needed, angle the open end to connect with the riser properly.

Next, insert the upper end of the riser into the sprinkler fitting. Then cement, clamp, or tighten it to complete the connection.

Finally, hold the sprinkler in approximately the correct position and backfill around it just enough so it stays in place.

Pop-up sprinklers can water tall plants but recede neatly into place when done.

Pop-up sprinklers use water pressure and a retraction spring to raise and lower the nozzle when a zone turns on and off.

You can adjust most pop-up sprinklers to fine-tune the spray direction by twisting the riser one way or another.

Be sure to set your sprinklers vertically in the ground before refilling the trench.

FINAL POSITIONING

Once the sprinkler is freestanding, check its position relative to adjacent sprinklers and adjust as needed. Also, using a short torpedo level, check that it is vertical. Hold the level against the side of the sprinkler body and adjust as needed. It may be necessary to place a small block of wood under one end of the level to compensate for the overhang of the sprinkler body cap. Once the sprinkler is close to perpendicular, fill in with the rest of the dirt and tamp it down to secure the sprinkler in position.

Once all the sprinklers for a zone are in place, briefly turn on the water to that zone to flush out any dirt from the sprinklers. Check to be sure the sprinklers don't shift position as you flush them. If some do, you may need to reset and re-tamp the dirt.

Fill in the trenches for each zone as it is finished. Be sure you have laid all pipes and created any needed drainage pits. Shovel dirt into the trench, then smooth the residue with a leaf rake. Reset the sod.

Installation on slopes

There are two rules for installing sprinklers on slopes.
■ Position heads closer together on the uphill side of the pattern, because gravity will shorten the spray throw.
■ Always align sprinkler heads perpendicular to the slope to prevent erosion and uneven watering uphill.

Installing sprinklers *continued*

INSTALLING NOZZLES

Before installing nozzles into sprinkler heads, make sure you flush the risers of dirt. Many fixed-spray sprinklers come with flush plugs that make this process less messy. If flush plugs are lacking, turn on the water and flush out the sprinklers without the nozzles installed. Rotary sprinklers usually have factory-installed nozzles; for these, flush out the risers before you install the heads.

To maximize your system's efficiency, be sure to install the correct nozzle for the job. You may need to change nozzles after your system is up and running.

Once you have flushed the system, use your plan as a guide to thread on the correct nozzles one zone at a time. If a head comes with a flush plug, remove the plug and save it for future use.

Now it is time to check your installation. This usually involves getting a bit wet, so dress accordingly. Equip yourself with the tools needed for adjusting spray heads—typically, a screwdriver, key, or ratchet (often supplied by the manufacturer).

To check each zone, first be sure no water is running inside the house. Faucets, toilet tanks, and dishwashers should all be off. Then, turn on the water for the zone and check for leaks.

Make adjustments to spray patterns as needed, following the manufacturer's instructions. Start with the sprinkler closest to the control valve. You may need the special key or ratchet supplied by the manufacturer to adjust the pattern of rotary heads. To adjust an impact head, look for a friction collar at the base of the nozzle that you can reposition to change the spray pattern.

Low-gallonage heads

Unless otherwise specified by the manufacturer, it's safe to assume that sprinklers are of standard gallonage and designed for normal water pressure. Use low-gallonage heads for areas where water pressure is moderate to low (a static water pressure of less than 40 psi) or where water conservation is a priority. Because these heads apply water at a slower rate than other sprinklers, they are ideal for areas with soil that is mostly clay and may be subject to runoff.

SWING-JOINT CONNECTIONS

A swing joint is a flexible connection you can make between a lateral line and the sprinkler body inlet to add some give so the impact of foot traffic and lawn mowers will not damage the sprinkler or the connection (see illustration at right).

Make a standard riser connection by teeing in a one-piece vertical riser. The swing joint tees in a few extra pieces to absorb impact—a threaded nipple and street elbow. To install a swing-joint connection, attach to the tee in the lateral line a 12-inch nipple, either threaded or cemented depending on the fittings you use. Position this at about a 45-degree up angle to the lateral line.

At what is now the high end of the nipple, attach the threaded street elbow, then thread that into the riser.

The plastic nipple and the threaded street elbow flex when the sprinkler is hit. The sprinkler head then pops back to its original position. The final position of the sprinkler head is offset somewhat from where the tee is made on the lateral line, so adjust as needed to achieve proper coverage.

A well-constructed swing joint allows your sprinkler head to absorb gentle impact, such as hit by a mower.

FUNNY PIPE

Swing joints require several parts and can be a bit of a hassle to assemble. One alternative is highly flexible poly pipe, which has come to be known as Funny Pipe but is also sold under other names. It allows you to create a flexible joint that functions like a swing joint without all the extra fittings and threading, thus reducing the chance of leaks.

Another advantage of using flexible Funny Pipe is that it allows you to fine-tune your sprinkler installations. The flex of the pipe lets you move the sprinkler head several inches in any direction without the use of additional fittings. This is helpful for fine-tuning head-to-head coverage.

Funny Pipe (flexible tubing) connections are easier to make than swing-joint connections and easier to fine-tune for positioning.

129

Installing drip
and micro-irrigation

I nstalling drip and micro-irrigation is similar to installing the components used in a traditional sprinkler system. The major difference is that everything is smaller. In drawing up your overall plan, you should have already plotted the locations of the risers that will supply the water to your drip/microsystem. All that is left to do is define where you need the water and make the connections. This section reviews some of the layout options and offers some specific solutions for different planting areas.

Drip tubing is generally laid out in a series of relatively parallel lateral lines set 12 to 24 inches apart. At this distance, the moisture zones under each emitter will meet to create even water distribution. In general, the drip lines should be set closer (12 inches) in sandy soils and farther apart (18 to 24 inches) in loam or clay soils.

SELECTING TUBING

The material used for drip-irrigation tubing needs to be flexible and chemically stable so it doesn't leach damaging chemicals into the irrigation system water. Some manufacturers use reprocessed polyethylene (poly). Although stable for the short term, reprocessed poly may contain contaminants. Use virgin poly tubing for the best long-term results.

Vinyl tubing can also be risky. Although it is flexible, making it easy to work with, it may leach chlorine into the water passing through it. Even small amounts of chlorine can damage your plants' appearance and health. Instead of vinyl, use laminated poly tubing, which is made of several layers, each with different properties. Together the layers create a flexible, stable, and long-lasting tubing system. Pieces fit together easily and stay together a long time.

Drip and micro-irrigation can be used to water almost every area of your landscape— from flower beds to vegetable gardens to pots (above).

One way to hide the tubing is to pull it through the drain hole (right) and attach the emitter before filling a container.

SPIGOT INSTALLATION

Drip and micro-irrigation systems can be supplied from above ground by a spigot or hose-end connection, or inground through a riser connection.

If a spigot installation makes the most sense for your system, choose an outdoor spigot located as close as possible to your planned drip system. If you'd like to be able to use the spigot for purposes other than irrigation, you'll need to install a Y connection, which will add a second outlet for hose use.

If your spigot does not already have a vacuum breaker installed, you will need to attach one, to serve as the BPD device for your drip system.

Although most drip emitters and microsprays can operate at pressures up to 50 psi, that much pressure is more than is needed and puts undue stress on barbed fittings. As a precaution, install a pressure regulator, which will reduce the household water system to between 25 and 30 psi.

The next step is to install a mesh filter to trap small particles before they can get into the system and clog emitters. The filter is usually part of an elbow to which you will attach your tubing. Manufacturers select a mesh rating they feel delivers the best balance between particle filtration, flow rate, and ease of use. You can use a finer-mesh filter if desired, but it requires more frequent cleaning.

To span the distance from the water connection to the area to be irrigated, you can use a normal garden hose cut to the correct length or use a drip tubing adapter at the outlet of the filter with a ½-inch hose run to where you lay out your system.

Once the water is where it needs to be, the procedure for installing drip components is the same as for a permanent, inground drip connection.

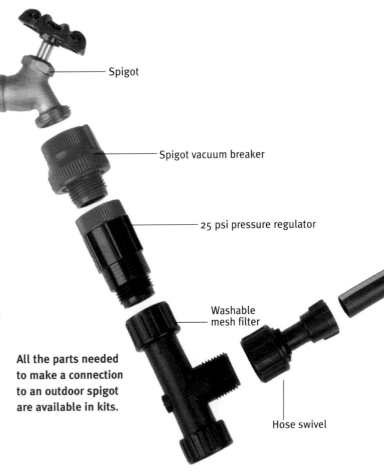

Spigot

Spigot vacuum breaker

25 psi pressure regulator

Washable mesh filter

Hose swivel

All the parts needed to make a connection to an outdoor spigot are available in kits.

DRIP EMITTER PLACEMENT

As easy as a drip system is to plan and set up, it is not one-size-fits-all. Use this chart to help you select your emitters.

Soil Type	Emitter Flow	Plant Spacing	Preferred Emitter Placement
Clay	½ GPH	Up to 24" 25" or more	Every 24" 1 per plant*
Loam	1 GPH	Up to 18" 19" or more	Every 18" 1 per plant*
Sand	2 GPH	Up to 12" 13" or more	Every 12" 1 per plant*

*For small- and medium-size plants. For shrubs, trees, and other large plants, see Number of Emitters per Plant Based on Canopy Diameter, page 138.

Installing drip and micro-irrigation *continued*

RISER OR INGROUND INSTALLATION

If you are planning to connect drip/microcomponents via an existing sprinkler riser, remember that the drip/micro will need to be on its own zone. That means you must cap any other sprinklers on the existing zone or convert them to drip as well.

Because of the large difference in flow rates between traditional sprinkler systems and drip systems, the two systems cannot exist on the same zone. You cannot create a workable watering schedule that efficiently runs drip/micro and conventional sprinkler systems in the same zone.

Connecting to a zone valve is a procedure similar to connecting to an outdoor spigot. You'll need to choose where to connect the several parts—the drip adapter, pressure regulator, and filter—and whether to connect inside the valve box, directly to the valve, or at the riser.

Installing all the components so they fit in the valve box can be a challenge. If you plan to use more than one riser as a water source, it makes sense to install a pressure reducer and filter to the valve feeding them, instead of adding a reducer and filter to every riser. You may need to install a larger valve box to accommodate the parts.

Drip manifolds are another option. You can mount these on any riser. They have the pressure regulator and filter built in, making them quick and easy to install.

Once you have attached the filter and regulator, you can use normal drip fittings provided by the maker to connect ½-inch drip tubing or fittings to the riser to begin your system. If you use a manifold, you will attach sections of ¼-inch tubing to the outlets on the drip manifold. These ¼-inch tubing runs should not be more that 10 feet long.

DRIP/MICROLAYOUTS

The layout for any drip/microsystem starts with the supply line. This is usually ½-inch poly tubing, also known as the header line. The header line is laid out in one of two ways, depending on what is most useful in your yard.

The *loop layout* has a header line that is teed into the water supply, then makes a loop around

Once you have converted a zone to a drip system, connecting to the risers in the zone is simple.

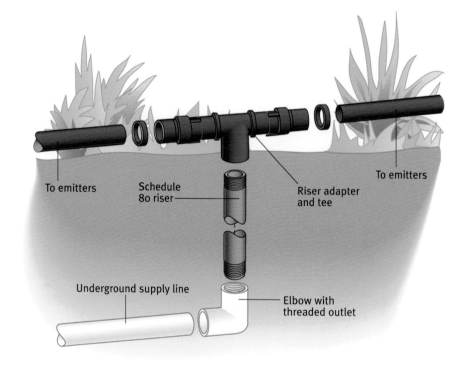

To emitters

Schedule 80 riser

Riser adapter and tee

To emitters

Underground supply line

Elbow with threaded outlet

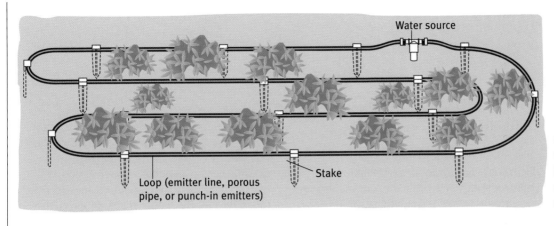

Water source

Stake

Loop (emitter line, porous pipe, or punch-in emitters)

A loop layout works well in flower beds and other irregularly shaped areas.

the areas to be watered, ending back at the tee. Because water enters both ends of the header line, even pressure is always maintained. This arrangement works well in flower beds and irregularly shaped areas.

The _parallel_, or _grid, layout_ has a header line or lines that run outward from the water source using a tee or an elbow. You can connect these to other lines called laterals at various intervals in parallel rows using additional fittings. Each lateral can terminate with its own end clamp, or you can close the rectangle by adding another piece of supply line to the ends to create a closed rectangle. This arrangement works well in large garden areas.

Connect emitters to laterals directly or with ¼-inch tubing that leads to individual plants. You can also use drip tubing for the lateral lines when you want to water the entire area evenly.

ISOLATED PLANTINGS

To water an out-of-the-way grouping of plants, add a lateral line of ½-inch poly. If the main PVC supply line must run across an exposed area such as a lawn, bury it 6 inches deep. At the planting area, add an elbow and a riser to feed the ½-inch poly. If you are able to snake it through planting beds aboveground to its destination, stake the line in place and cover it with mulch.

At the planting end, connect a manifold and place an emitter at every plant—or use one of the layout methods shown on this page. If you are watering only a small plant near the supply line, you can use ¼-inch poly as your lateral line.

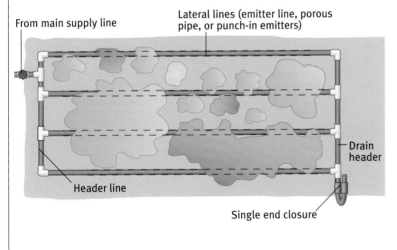

From main supply line

Lateral lines (emitter line, porous pipe, or punch-in emitters)

Drain header

Header line

Single end closure

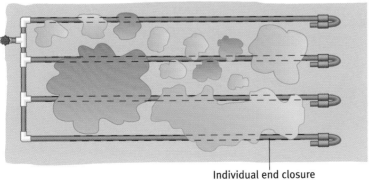

Individual end closure

Parallel, or grid, layouts such as these are well suited to watering evenly spaced rows of plants, such as vegetable gardens.

133

Installing drip and micro-irrigation *continued*

INSTALLING MICROSPRAYS AND EMITTERS

Begin your installation by assembling the sprinkler stakes that will hold your microsprays and emitters. There is sometimes a thin riser that must be screwed or pressed into the top. Push the stakes into position in the ground to mark the intended positions of the sprinklers.

If you have not already done so, lay out the ½-inch drip pipe using one of the layouts shown on page 133. Given the relatively high GPH (gallons per hour) needs of microsprays, you have to limit the length of your ¼-inch feeder tubes. Be sure the feeder tubes run no farther than 5 feet from the ½-inch drip pipe to full-circle microsprinkler heads and no more than 10 feet to half, quarter, or strip heads.

INSERTING AN EMITTER

To insert emitters into poly drip pipe, punch a hole with a hole punch. Some emitters have self-piercing barbs.

INSERTING TUBING INTO DRIP PIPE

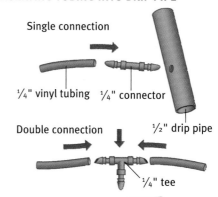

Single connection

¼" vinyl tubing   ¼" connector   ½" drip pipe

Double connection

¼" tee

TWO TYPES OF END CLOSURES

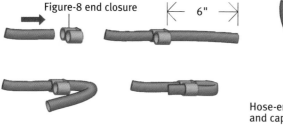

Figure-8 end closure |← 6" →|

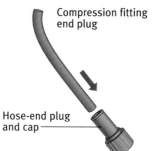

Compression fitting end plug

Hose-end plug and cap

TWO USES FOR ¼" TUBING

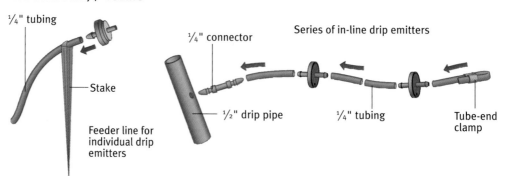

¼" tubing

Stake

Feeder line for individual drip emitters

¼" connector   Series of in-line drip emitters

½" drip pipe   ¼" tubing   Tube-end clamp

Cut the tubing to the length needed to reach from the stake to a convenient point on the ½-inch drip pipe. Leave a few extra inches to allow for repositioning later.

Punch a hole in the drip pipe with a hole punch, insert a connector in one end of the ¼-inch tubing, and plug the connector into the drip pipe. (See opposite page.) Attach the other end of the tubing to the barbed connection on the stake. If using emitters, lay the tubing on the ground in the correct position.

Turn on the water to flush the lines, then seal the end of the drip pipe with a closure fitting or an end plug. Insert the appropriate microsprinkler into the top of each riser, or push the emitter connector into the end of the tubing. Turn on the water again, and adjust the location and direction of the microsprinklers until you have the coverage you want. Finally, secure the stakes firmly into the ground.

VEGETABLE GARDENS

Micro-irrigation is designed to make it easy to find practical solutions to different watering needs. Because a vegetable garden needs frequent watering, it should be on a separate zone if possible. A separate zone is also a good idea because municipal regulations restricting watering usually allow you to water food plants whenever needed. For a garden divided into several beds, you might install a separate shutoff valve on the header line for each bed. That way, as your crops are cycled, you can open and close each section as their watering needs change. For example, when a bed of springtime radishes and lettuce has run its course and is lying fallow, you can water sprouting vegetables in the bed beside it.

Microsprays attached to risers gently apply water to plants that benefit from top-down watering.

Micro-irrigation emitters are an evolutionary step forward from drip irrigation. They are not quite as efficient but can be used in more applications.

Goofed? Try goof plugs

It is all too easy to punch a hole in the wrong section of pipe accidentally or, after testing the zones, to find that one section has too many emitters. You can easily correct this by removing the extra emitters and filling in the holes with hole plugs, often called goof plugs. Always have a few of these goof plugs on hand when working with a hole punch.

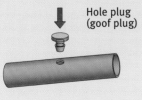

Hole plug (goof plug)

135

Installing drip
micro-irrigation *continued*

Because drip emitters get the right amount of water directly to the base of the plants, vegetables flourish with this watering system. And because a microsystem is flexible, you can alter it to suit the layout of your garden each year.

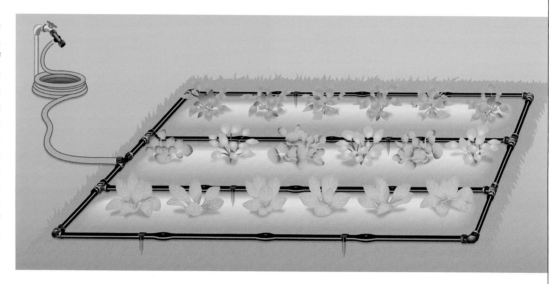

Vegetable gardens need frequent cultivation, which can damage irrigation lines. To allow for digging, hoeing, and rototilling, use PVC pipe, buried 18 inches deep, as the supply line. Bring it above ground with an elbow in a secure spot, and stake it heavily so it is solid. Then set up the header and lateral lines using a quick-connect hose-fitting system. This requires several adapters but is a system that can be pulled out quickly whenever the area requires cultivation. In cold climates, this also allows you to unclip the aboveground sections and bring them indoors for the winter.

Although a drip/microsystem is ideal for gardens, don't throw away your hand sprayer. Newly seeded sections still require gentle hand-watering until the seedlings are well-established.

Installing quick connects on vegetable garden headers makes it easy to activate and deactivate different areas of the garden as needed.

FLOWER BEDS

The arrangement of plants in a flower bed tends to be much more asymmetrical than in a vegetable garden. As a result, a free-form loop is the best layout for the water supply line. Once you've positioned it throughout the bed, you can attach ¼-inch feeding tubes for the emitters.

Start by laying out ½-inch hose in a loop that reflects the shape of the flower bed. Stake the tubing in place.

Use a hole punch to make holes in the drip pipe as close as possible to the spot you want to place a microspray and a riser stake. Spacing is dictated by the extent

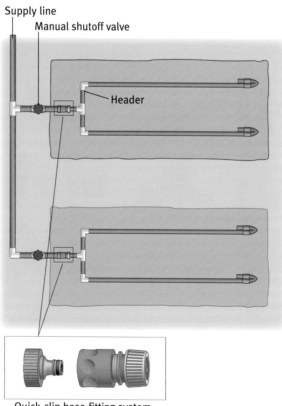

Supply line
Manual shutoff valve
Header

Quick-clip hose-fitting system

of the coverage from the chosen microspray.

Push the stake into the ground at the correct spot, then cut a length of ¼-inch tubing long enough to run between the hole in the drip pipe and the stake. Remember to cut the tubing several inches longer than needed to allow for repositioning.

Attach the ¼-inch tubing to the riser stake. Once all the stakes and tubes are in place, flush the system with water. Attach the microsprays to each stake, and turn on the water to fine-tune the patterns. Then secure the tubing to the ground and cover it with mulch.

Note: On smaller flower beds, it may be easier to place a manifold in the middle of the bed and run your ¼-inch tubing from it. Just be sure the manifold allows for enough emitters.

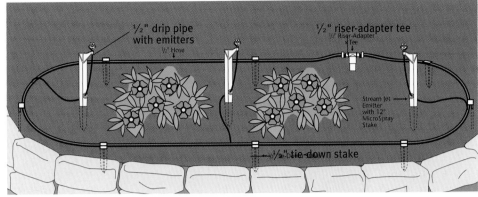

½" drip pipe with emitters
½" Hose
½" riser-adapter tee
½" Riser-Adapter Tee
Stream Jet Emitter with 12" MicroSpray Stake
⅛" tie-down stake

Flower beds are usually asymmetrically shaped. A loop layout (above) gives you flexibility for placing emitters where you need them. Water smaller beds with a central manifold from which supply lines radiate.

HANGING PLANTS

Installing a watering system for hanging baskets requires care to hide the tubing and position the emitter devices to make sure the plants receive adequate water.

If you will need more than one or two emitter devices, use a ½-inch drip pipe. Run the line up an unexposed side of the supporting structure of the porch or pergola, or along a door frame. Then run it across the top of the structure, again in a way that is least visible from below. Special clamps are available for holding the tubing to the structure.

Use a hole punch to add ¼-inch fittings to the tubing at the spots closest to and above your hanging plants.

Because they are exposed to wind and sun and are often hard to reach, hanging plants are good candidates for microsprays and emitters. Container gardens are easily overwatered. Micro-irrigation takes away the guesswork.

Installing drip micro-irrigation *continued*

NUMBER OF ½-GPH DRIP EMITTERS PER CONTAINER

This chart gives you a good starting point. Your own observations should dictate the final number.

Container Diameter	Number of Emitters
Up to 6"	1
7"–12"	2
13"–18"	3
19"–29"	4
Over 29"	1 every 6"

To each fitting add a length of ¼-inch tubing long enough to reach each pot. Use a stake or a clip to attach the tubing to the hanging pot. Once all the tubing is in place, briefly flush the lines. Attach the sprayers or emitters to each stake or clip. With the water running, position them to minimize overspray. This is important on hanging pots because there may be a seating area beneath them.

CONTAINER GARDENS

Because they are exposed to drying wind and sun, plants in container gardens need more water, delivered at more frequent intervals, than inground plants. In many cases, containers need a daily watering instead of the every two or three days needed by inground plants. For this reason, drip/microsystems used in container gardens should always be on their own control valves.

Depending on conditions and plant needs, micro-irrigation may need to be left on for up to an hour—enough time to moisten the soil in the container completely. When water begins to run out of the drainage holes, the container has been watered enough.

Generally speaking, one or two drip emitters per container is adequate, although long flower boxes may require more. Set the emitters at about 12-inch intervals. Low-flow (½ or 1 GPH), pressure-compensating emitters are preferred so that water is applied slowly to avoid overflow.

After installing micro-irrigation in containers but before adding end-closure fittings to the drip pipe, turn on the water and flush the tubing thoroughly.

Hide the drip pipe by running it under a deck or porch or along the edge of a patio. From the drip pipe, run ¼-inch tubing up the back of the container or even up through a drainage hole. Finally, clamp it into place with a small stake.

Because plants will need more water as they grow, all container systems require adjustment over time. Leaving the system on for a longer period of time works only if the needs of all the containers increase at the same rate. A better solution is to replace selected emitters with ones that provide a greater flow rate. Another option is to add extra emitters to increase the water amount fed to the containers.

TREES

Because trees use a great deal of water, many people assume that drip systems are not well-suited to watering them. But in reality, trees thrive on steady watering that saturates

NUMBER OF EMITTERS PER PLANT BASED ON CANOPY DIAMETER

Plant Canopy Diameter	Emitters per Plant
Up to 3'	2
4–5'	4
6–9'	6
10' and more	2 per 2½' of canopy diameter

IRRIGATING ISOLATED PLANTINGS

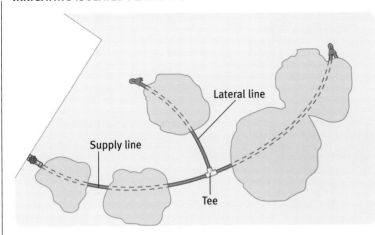

Lateral line

Supply line

Tee

THREE EMITTER SETUPS

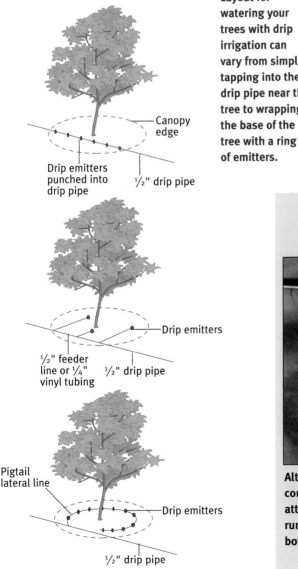

Canopy edge

Drip emitters punched into drip pipe

½" drip pipe

Layout for watering your trees with drip irrigation can vary from simply tapping into the drip pipe near the tree to wrapping the base of the tree with a ring of emitters.

Drip emitters

½" feeder line or ¼" vinyl tubing

½" drip pipe

Pigtail lateral line

Drip emitters

½" drip pipe

deeply—something a drip system is ideally suited to deliver. Because trees may require an almost constant flow of water, you may need to put your trees on a zone of their own.

To place the water where it is most needed, position the emitters at the base of the tree, halfway between the trunk and the edge of the canopy.

Use a loop layout plan to run a ½-inch drip pipe to all the trees and shrubs in a planting area. To apply the water to the trees, the simplest approach is to add a series of drip emitters to the drip pipe. However, this concentrates the water on one side of the tree.

A better method is to run three feeder lines from the supply, so you can position emitters at three points around the tree. If more water is called for, run ½-inch emitter hose around the tree trunk at a point halfway between the trunk and the edge of the leaf canopy, then plug the end back into the tee. This ensures even water pressure. Install multiple, evenly spaced emitters.

If it is not possible to run the ½-inch tubing close enough to the tree, you can attach a straight section of ¼-inch hose to the water line, run it to the tree, and then create a loop at the end of it. Secure everything in place with hold-down stakes, then cover with mulch.

A cooling mist

Although evaporative cooling misters use the same components as those used for hanging plants, avoid attaching them to the same zone. Your watering system runs on a schedule; misters are used on demand. Running both on the same system wastes water.

139

Timer installation

Before you begin installing the timer, be sure there is a suitable power connection within 6 feet. If you need to extend an electrical circuit and have a new receptacle installed, do this ahead of time. If you are installing it yourself, be sure to check the local codes before beginning.

To install most timers, you will need a pair of wire cutters and strippers, a straight-bladed screwdriver, a jeweler's screwdriver, a pencil, a tape measure, a torpedo level, and electrical tape. You may also need an electric drill/driver and bits. Specific installation instructions are included with each timer.

CHOOSING A LOCATION

You can mount your irrigation timer just about anywhere that is convenient for you. Many people mount their timers inside a garage to keep themselves and the timer out of the weather and inside the garage to have an available receptacle. If possible, choose a location that affords you a view of the yard. This will make it easier to check the operation of specific valves or zones. Fastening a timer directly to a wall stud is a much more secure base than simply using drywall anchors.

If it suits your plan better, you can mount the timer outside the house on an exterior wall. There are weatherproof enclosures available that will fit any timer on the market. They simply mount to the side of the house and are adapted to vinyl, wood, or other sidings.

Freestanding cabinets are also available that you can position anywhere that is convenient to your power supply.

An outdoor location also makes running wires to your timer easier. You won't have to drill holes through walls or nail wiring staples to secure the wiring. However, you will need to run the wires through conduit into the weather-resistant case, following local codes and using components specified for outdoor wiring. If you bury your power supply line, you will have to do so at depths required by your municipality.

Your irrigation timer is like the command center of the system. The terminal block on a sophisticated timer can appear rather complex, but every valve gets its own spot, as do all accessories.

WIRING

Making the wiring connections at the timer is a relatively easy process. Although you may need a jeweler's screwdriver for attaching the wires to the wiring blocks of most timers, some manufacturers have begun using tool-free snap-in connectors to make the task easier.

If you haven't already done so, lay the valve wires in the bottom of the trenches beneath the pipes. You can secure the bundle to the pipes with plastic tape.

Remember to install a few extra strands from each manifold now to make future expansion easier.

Next, connect the valve wires to the timer by taking the white common wire and attaching it to the COM terminal as marked on the timer. Then take each of the colored valve wires and connect it to one of the timer terminals in sequence. Finally, plug in the timer.

WARNING: Always use waterproof grease caps on all exterior connections that you make to your timer.

CONNECTING A PUMP START RELAY

If your system will use a pump start relay or a master valve, connect them to the proper terminals. The timer must be installed at least 12 feet from the pump and 5 feet from the pump relay to prevent any malfunctions.

CHECKING TIMER FUNCTION

Before you can begin filling in the trenches, check the operation of all your zone valves from the timer.

To do so, confirm that the system water is turned on. Check that there is power to the timer and the battery (if needed) is in place.

Use the timer to activate each valve manually according to the timer manufacturer's instructions. It is easy to get wires mixed up and attach them to the wrong terminals on the timer. When you turn on each valve, look at the yard to be sure the proper zone is running.

Wiring a timer

1 Mount timer and remove terminal cover. Pull wires to the timer; fasten to wall. If you use multi-color wires, you have a head start on getting the connections right.

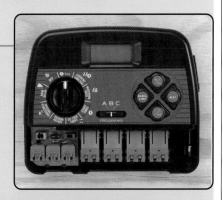

2 Strip each wire, removing ½ inch of insulation.

3 Connect the white wire to the COM terminal.

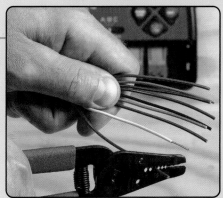

4 Connect each of the colored wires to a terminal on the terminal block. Plug in the timer power adapter.

Finishing up

O nce you have tested all the zones and have confidence that there are no leaks in any of your connections, finish refilling the trenches and resetting the sod. However, be sure you have allowed the entire system—and any last-minute repairs—at least 12 hours for the PVC cement used on the pipes to set completely.

A note on filling the trenches: Begin by covering the pipes with sand. This layer of sand will protect the pipes from the damage caused by compaction from above. Fill the trench with the soil you originally removed. Remember to fill the trenches high because the dirt will settle over time.

Next, carefully replace the sod that you cut out of the lawn. Be careful to match the direction of growth to the turf around it; otherwise, the patch may be visible. Gently hand tamp it into place as you go.

Once you have removed all the excess soil from the yard and replaced all the sod, you are ready to complete any final adjustments.

ADJUSTING THE SYSTEM

Turn on your sprinkler system and give it a careful inspection. The spray and water marks will make it easy to see whether the water is reaching the intended areas.

Needed adjustments in a micro-irrigation system aren't as easy to spot. You may have to get down on your knees to be sure that water is indeed dripping from each emitter. Buried emitter lines are more difficult to verify because the soil can be completely dry on the surface yet moist underneath. Puddles on the surface can indicate leaks, overly long watering periods, or excessive pressure.

Be sure to check all the wiring on any moisture sensors or other accessories you have hooked into your system. It's best to get in the habit of doing this. You should check the wiring at least once a year.

Making clean, square cuts when removing the sod makes it easier to replace. Finishing your installation is a big achievement. Now it is time to check the operation of all components and make any final adjustments before programming your system.

Completion checklist

Final steps:
- Check water connection for leaks.
- Make timer connections.
- Fill in trenches.
- Replace sod.
- Close up all valve boxes.
- Check operation of timer and zones.
- Perform "catch-can" test.
- Check drip emitters.
- Make final adjustments to the spray patterns and coverage of all sprinklers.
- Clean up tools and materials.

ADJUSTING COVERAGE AND PATTERN

Walk around the yard with the system running to see how everything is working. Run a catch-can test (see page 144) to assess how uniform your system's coverage is. As you inspect, look for the following:

■ Is there any overspray on areas that need to stay dry?

■ Is there even coverage?

■ Are all the sprinklers pointed in the correct direction?

■ Are the sprinklers high enough above the ground to clear the plants they need to water?

At this point you are somewhat limited in how far you can physically move the sprinkler heads. Even if you used flexible tubing for the risers, you will be able to move them only a few inches in any direction—unless of course you dig down and replace the incorrect riser with a longer one.

Although you are limited in how much you can change the physical layout, you can still adjust the radius, the pattern direction, and the pattern itself in order to fix any holes or misalignments in your coverage.

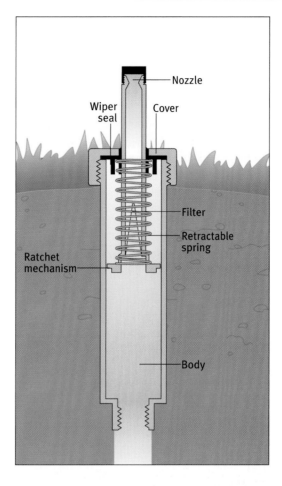

Sprinklers with ratcheting pop-up risers can be redirected by simply twisting the riser in the direction you want the spray pattern to move.

No system is perfect the first time it is run. You can always finely tune some system parts. Taking the time to adjust for small problems, such as this overspray onto a concrete curb, will save you water—and money—down the road.

Finishing up *continued*

Catch–can test

The catch-can test is a simple and effective way to check the performance of your sprinklers once they are all in place and working. Doing this test will let you know that your system is watering as planned and help you determine whether your irrigation schedule will have to be adjusted to create the most efficient watering cycles for your yard.

To do the test you will need a number of containers of the same size and shape. They should have a flat bottom and vertical sides. Using containers with sloping sides will throw off the measurements you get from the test. Soup cans or coffee cans work well for this; anything shorter allows too much water to splash out. Space the containers equidistant in a grid pattern throughout the zone you want to check.

(Don't worry if you don't have enough cans to cover the entire test area. You can perform the test in one area, then move the cans to another area and do the test again.)

Once the containers are in place, turn on the irrigation system and let it run for exactly 15 minutes. Then turn off the system and measure the depth of the water in each container. Add those amounts together and divide the total by the number of containers to get the average amount of water for each. Multiply that by 4 to calculate the precipitation rate of your irrigation system in inches per hour.

(You can use different run times, but you will have to multiply your measurements by something other than 4. For instance, if you let the system run for 10 minutes, you will multiply your average per can by 6 to get the rate in inches per hour.)

If you notice a large difference in the amount of water amount in the different cans, you know that you will need to adjust the sprinklers in that area to create matching coverage. Make the adjustments, then run the test again. You may have to test and adjust several times before the coverage is right.

Doing a catch-can test is an easy way to benchmark your irrigation system's performance and the only way to know how even your coverage really is.

After running the zone being tested for 15 minutes, measure the depth of the water in the container, using a ruler or tape measure.

ADJUSTING FAN SPRAYS

Of all the head types, fan sprays are the easiest to adjust. You simply change the nozzle on the sprinkler body. For those on pop-up sprinklers, you'll have to pull up the riser, hold it in place, then unscrew the old nozzle and replace it with a new one. For shrub heads where the riser is stationary, all you have to do is unscrew the nozzle. It may be necessary to change the filter when switching between different nozzles.

Nozzles generally come with the radius set in 2-foot increments. For adjustments of less than 2 feet, some nozzles have an adjustment screw that allows for fine-tuning of the coverage by allowing you to reduce the radius by up to 25 percent. You can do this by means of a small screw on top of the nozzle that you turn clockwise or counterclockwise, depending on which way you need the radius to adjust. You cannot increase the radius to exceed the specified radius—a nozzle with a 10-foot radius will always spray no more than 10 feet.

Adjustable-pattern fan spray nozzles are also becoming increasingly commonplace. They generally have an adjustment ring on top of the nozzle that you can twist to set the pattern anywhere from 0 to 360 degrees.

If you replace the nozzle, or if you installed the sprinkler with the pattern facing the wrong way, most pop-up fan sprays incorporate a riser that you can rotate within the sprinkler body to set the spray in the precise direction it needs to go. You can change the spray direction by small increments using these ratcheting risers, making it possible to set the pattern perfectly. Just pull the riser up out of the body with one hand, hold the sprinkler body in place with the other, and twist the riser into the correct position. Remember, not all fan sprays have this feature.

Turning the radius-reduction screw on the top of the nozzle lets you reduce the radius by up to 25 percent.

Pattern adjustment

When adjusting sprinkler patterns, be aware of the precipitation rate. This is the rate at which a sprinkler delivers water to the ground. On impact and rotary sprinklers this rate is not affected by an alteration in the pattern, but on some older fan spray designs it is. For example, cutting the pattern in half from a half circle to a quarter circle may not result in the same amount of flow going to that smaller pattern. Always use matched precipitation rate (MPR) sprinklers in your zones. This is the only way to be sure that every pattern in your zones is watering at the same rate as any other, if that is the intent.

145

Finishing up *continued*

ADJUSTING IMPACT ROTORS

You can set impact sprinkler for any arc from a full 360-degree circle down to about 20 degrees. Adjustment is simple. Just beneath the nozzle and the weighted swing arm that drives the head's rotation are two metal or plastic rings that wrap around the sprinkler body. (See below.) They have flanges on each end. Notice that a small wire lever sits between one flange from the top ring and one flange from the bottom. It is these flanges that determine the pattern and the direction of coverage.

If you move that wire lever up out of the way, or take both rings off of the sprinkler, the impact rotor will go in a complete circle. With the metal lever flipped down into position, all you need to do is move each ring in one direction or the other to set the direction and coverage. As the wire lever hits one or the other of the flanges, it reverses the sprinkler's direction, creating a repeating pattern.

A little experimentation is usually required to set the correct pattern and the correct direction. This is much easier to do with the sprinkler

You can add antibacksplash devices to riser-mounted impact sprinklers to correct some overspray situations.

The impact sprinkler is unique in that it can give you full 360-degree coverage and any increment up to 360 degrees with the same sprinkler head, making it very versatile.

Adjusting ring

Wire lever

running, so don't be afraid to get a little wet. Setting the radius on impact rotor sprinklers is not as easy. If your sprinkler has a removable nozzle, adding a nozzle with the radius you need may be the easiest approach. Unfortunately, not all impacts have interchangeable nozzles. In addition, changing the nozzle usually increases or decreases the water flow through the sprinkler, which affects the change in radius. Changing one nozzle may interfere with having even water coverage.

For making small adjustments to the radius, some impact sprinklers have an adjustable spray-reduction screw. To trim a little off the radius, turn the screw down into the water stream, slightly reducing the flow. Take care not to reduce the radius more than about 25 percent because it can cause the pattern to deform too much and interfere with your head-to-head coverage.

ADJUSTING GEAR-DRIVE ROTORS

The adjustment of gear-drive rotors is not nearly as standardized as with fan sprays and impact rotors. This may be because the gear-drive rotor is the newest type of sprinkler design and is still evolving as new design innovations are made. For specific information and instruction on final adjustments, you'll have to consult the manufacturer's materials supplied with your sprinkler.

Some types use changeable pattern disks in the top of the sprinkler. These disks allow for relatively small adjustments to the spray pattern. Some types have an adjustment ring on top you can turn to set the pattern. Various increments up to a full circle are possible.

You can handle small directional adjustments by rotating the entire sprinkler on its riser. You have to be careful when doing this because the potential for leaks increases when you twist the sprinkler body. Attempt only small changes.

Like the fan sprays, some gear drives have a radius reduction screw on the top of the sprinkler for trimming some distance off their throw to facilitate pattern matching. As with the other types, reductions of up to 25 percent are possible. Many other gear drives do not have this feature, and you can change the radius by changing the nozzles. Do this as a last resort. Unless your rotor has specially designed matched precipitation nozzles, swapping nozzles will affect the precipitation rate relative to the other sprinklers on the same zone.

Gear-drive rotors, perhaps because they are so new, have a more limited range of spray patterns.

Each gear-driven rotor has a slightly different method for adjustment. Refer to the manufacturer's instructions for specifics on your rotor.

Using your system

The purpose of irrigation is to get the right water amount to the right plants, at the right time. To do so, you have to analyze the yard's needs, prepare a watering schedule, then adjust the schedule as needed.

Now that your irrigation system is installed—the pipes are buried, the valves are working, and the sprinkler heads are all adjusted— it is time to set up the whole system so it does what you want it to do. This may be simple or complex, depending on the number of zones, the type of irrigation timer, and how precisely you feel you need to apply water.

You will need to decide how much water to apply to your plants and when to apply it for maximum effect. This chapter looks at the major factors to take into account when deciding both "how much" and "when." If you have a sophisticated timer, you can program it with virtually all of your watering information; if you have a simple mechanical timer, you'll just stick to the basics. No matter what timer you use, the process of setting it up is similar. The assumption here is that you are using a programmable timer for your system.

Basic annual maintenance procedures keep your system "well-oiled" and is the best way to save water, avoid inconvenience, and keep everything running and growing right for years to come.

Chapter 4

Scheduling your irrigation times correctly is the key to getting the efficiency and savings you should from your sprinklers.

Using your system

DIGEST

GREEN LIGHT FOR WATERING

Check these signals for planning your watering schedule:
Red (midday) Avoid watering in the heat of the day—too much water is lost to the sun's evaporation. (The opposite is true too. Avoid watering during or after a rainstorm.)
Yellow (4 p.m. to 8 p.m.) Watering in the evening is acceptable but may cause plant diseases because foliage tends to stay wet overnight.
Green (4 a.m. to 7 a.m.) Watering just before dawn is the best for your plants. There's far less evaporation.

To do

✓ Calculate water needs for the soil and the plants.

✓ Determine the best times for watering.

✓ Schedule the watering.

✓ Adjust the watering schedule as needed.

HYDRO-BABBLE
(WATERING TERMS WORTH KNOWING)

Start time: The time of day that your irrigation system starts to water. Most timers give you more than one start time every day.

Run time: The amount of time, in minutes, that each zone applies water.

Watering days: The actual calendar days on which the irrigation system runs.

CLEANING YOUR IRRIGATION SYSTEM

■ Turn off the system and remove the individual nozzles from one zone.
■ Run water through the zone for a few minutes until a clean, clear stream of water flows from each sprinkler head.
■ Turn off the water.
■ Take apart the nozzles (you can do this by hand or with a screwdriver, or using a special key depending on the type) and clean away any dirt or deposits.
■ Rinse out any filter screens or baskets.
■ Reassemble and replace all the parts.
■ Turn on water to the zone again to check that everything is leak-free and operating properly.
■ Repeat the procedure for the other zones.

BALANCING YOUR ET CHECKBOOK

A well-balanced evapotranspiration (ET)-based irrigation "checkbook" lets you accurately predict how much water your plants need every day. Like balancing your bank checkbook, it can be demanding. The rewards for doing it are usually worth the extra work. You need to know the following things:
■ the ET rate for where you live;
■ what types of plants you are watering;
■ something called the Kc (landscape coefficient) for each plant;
■ the landscape area (LA) of your property;
■ how much water your soil can hold; and
■ the precipitation rate of your sprinklers.

It all comes together using this formula:
(ET) × (Kc) × (LA) = How much water you need

THE RUNOFF TEST

This is an easy way to gauge the efficiency of your irrigation system.
■ Manually run the zone you want to test.
■ Watch the sprinklers, and keep track of how many minutes the system is running.
■ When you see any puddles or water runoff from that zone, turn off the system and note the amount of time it has taken to reach that point. This tells you the maximum number of minutes you can run that zone before the system starts wasting water.

MOISTURE SENSORS AND SOIL PROBES

A moisture sensor measures the water content at a certain depth below the surface and gives a reading that you can use to make accurate adjustments to the amount of water you are applying.

A soil probe can be as simple as a screwdriver or as sophisticated as a core extractor. No matter which type you use, the goal is to see how deeply the water is penetrating the soil.

Push a probe into the ground until you feel increasing resistance. This will tell you where the moist soil ends.

A core-extracting probe removes a deep cylinder of soil and lets you visually inspect the water content and other elements.

Rain sensors

Rain sensors tell when it is raining and turn off your irrigation system when it does. They are inexpensive, pay for themselves quickly, and protect plants from overwatering.

Scheduling

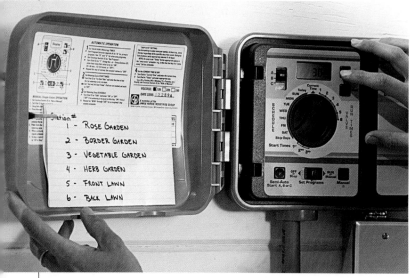

No matter how simple or sophisticated the timer, its purpose is to control when and for how long you apply water to your plants. Watering days, start times, and run times are common to every irrigation timer and schedule.

Irrigation scheduling is simple in concept. Regardless of how sophisticated or simple your system, scheduling is just a matter of when and for how long you run your irrigation system. In execution, however, this can get complex.

Here's the simplest schedule: Go outside, turn on the irrigation valve, and let the system run until you think it has run enough. Then turn off the valve, walk back inside and watch a football game, do some laundry, or contemplate your irrigation system. Of course, this will not work in the vast majority of watering situations.

One of the chief reasons for installing an automatic irrigation system is to water different plants with the exact amount of water each needs. Turning on a valve and operating the entire system at the same time won't accomplish that. Other than not watering your plants correctly, other reasons for setting a watering schedule on your timer are limited water pressure and flow, the need to use water in your house while the irrigation system is running, the local water-use restrictions, and different water requirements of various plant types in your yard.

INFILTRATION RATE FOR LEVEL GROUND AND SLOPES

When watering on hillsides or slopes, you should know the infiltration rate, which varies with the angle of the slope. This chart helps you figure out the infiltration rate to use when calculating the watering times for your sloping areas.

Average infiltration rate in inches per hour

Soil Texture Type	Percentage of Slope				
	0–4.9%	5–7.9%	8–11.9%	12–15.9%	Over 16%
Coarse sand	1.25	1.00	0.75	0.50	0.31
Medium sand	1.06	0.85	0.64	0.42	0.27
Fine sand	0.94	0.75	0.56	0.38	0.24
Loamy sand	0.88	0.70	0.53	0.35	0.22
Sandy loam	0.75	0.60	0.45	0.30	0.19
Fine sandy loam	0.63	0.50	0.38	0.25	0.16
Very fine sandy loam	0.59	0.47	0.35	0.24	0.15
Loam	0.54	0.43	0.33	0.22	0.14
Silt loam	0.50	0.40	0.30	0.20	0.13
Silt	0.44	0.35	0.26	0.18	0.11
Sandy clay	0.31	0.25	0.19	0.12	0.08
Clay loam	0.25	0.20	0.15	0.10	0.06
Silty clay	0.19	0.15	0.11	0.08	0.05
Clay	0.13	0.10	0.08	0.05	0.03

To arrive at a schedule, you need to know the following things about your yard, most of which you already know from doing your irrigation plan:

■ The soil type
■ The plant types you will be watering
■ The weekly water needs of each plant type
■ The precipitation rate of each of your zones
■ The watering restrictions, if any, that are in force in your area

Armed with this information and the information presented in the following pages, you will be able to develop and implement a basic watering schedule for your yard. First you will create a simple schedule and program your timer accordingly. Then you will track how well the program waters your yard. This will allow you to make adjustments over the course of a few weeks to achieve maximum efficiency. And you can do all this using almost no math!

(It is possible to develop a much more precise and specific watering schedule based on evapotranspiration rates and landscape coefficients, but that is more involved than many homeowners want or need.)

Scheduling concepts and terms

To understand irrigation discussions and advice from pros and salespeople, you need to understand some terms. Most are used in the upcoming chapter; some you may hear as you talk to irrigation specialists. Knowing what these words mean will help you get the most out of your system and schedule.

Watering days: The actual days on which the irrigation system runs. See page 33 for more information.

Start time: The time of day that your irrigation system starts to water. Most timers give you more than one start time.

Run time: The amount of time, in minutes, that each zone continues to apply water.

Root zone: The area below ground in which plant roots can take in moisture and nutrients from the soil. The root zone usually extends no deeper than 3 feet, even for large trees.

Watering deeply: Traditionally this has been a subjective term, meaning different things to different people. Think of "watering deeply" as watering to just beyond the depth of the root zone of the plant. This depth varies from species to species.

Infiltration rate: The rate at which soil can absorb water over a given amount of time. Some general figures are sandy soils, $3/4$ to $1\frac{1}{2}$ inches per hour; loam, $1/4$ to $3/4$ inch per hour; clay, $1/10$ to $1/4$ inch per hour. The rates vary with the exact composition of the soil.

62 gallons: The number of gallons it takes to cover 100 square feet of ground with 1 inch of water.

Square footage: The length of an area times its width.

Evapotranspiration (ET) rate: The rate that plant transpiration and evaporation remove water from the soil. This is a unique number for every plant species because they use water at a different rate.

Kc, or Landscape coefficient: This refers to the water needs of an individual plant or type of plant. To find the local ET value of specific plant species, multiply by another number, the landscape coefficient (Kc). These values are different for each plant type and are available from various sources; such as the Internet and your local county extension service.

(ET) x (Kc) x (LA) = Site water budget: This formula estimates the exact water usage of an area of one plant type. ET is the evapotranspiration rate, and Kc is the landscape coefficient for the plant in question, and LA is the measured area of the field or garden or flower bed.

PWR (plant water requirements): The amount of water a plant needs is measured in inches of water.

PAW (plant available water) = AW (available water) x RZ (root zone): The plant available water refers to the amount of water that is present in the soil—the moisture that is actually available for use by the plants.

PWR=ET x Kc: The plant water needs (PWR) for any plant is the current ET rate multiplied by the Kc, or landscape coefficient, for that plant.

Scheduling *continued*

If you see puddles in any of your zones after watering, reduce the number of minutes you are irrigating that zone. For more precise tests for runoff, see page 162.

HOW MUCH TO WATER

The goal of any irrigation system is to replace the water lost from the soil to evaporation and transpiration, and to supply additional water for plant growth. For noncommercial applications, determining how much water to give the plants is not overly complicated but requires some figuring and testing.

In the past, watering to the point of saturation and not watering again until the soil was dry became a common practice. With drip systems, gardeners would run the system for hours, then allow the plant to dry out almost to the point of wilting before watering it again. This practice is no longer recommended. It results in irregular growth, and much of the water doesn't even get to the plant but goes to rehydrate the parched soil around it.

Watering needs change over time. So be ready to make adjustments to avoid either over- or underwatering. Overwatering is wasteful and can lead to disease or rot; underwatering stunts growth and can kill sensitive plants. Fortunately, there is ample room between these two extremes. Most plants will not only survive, but also grow and thrive even if the ground varies between very moist and almost dry.

The goal is to keep the soil around the root zone of the plant moist at all times. Follow these guidelines for the various plant types on your property:

- For turfgrass, the root zone depth is 4 to 6 inches.
- For small flowering plants, the depth of the root zone may be only 2 or 3 inches.
- Many groundcovers have a root-zone depth of about 4 to 8 inches.
- For mature trees, the root-zone depth is several feet.

Take time to fine-tune your system to give your plants the water they need without wasting water that drains lower than the root zone.

Adjust watering to match your soil

- **Clay** holds the most water but is slow to absorb and release it. Apply water no faster than it can soak in, or water in cycles. Run the system until water runs off. Program the system to turn off long enough for water to soak in, then cycle on and off until you apply the full amount.
- **Sandy soil** is porous, and water readily flows in and out of it.

To wet very sandy soil 6 to 8 inches deep, water in $\frac{1}{2}$-inch increments.
- **Loam**, the ideal soil, is porous yet retains moisture. Water normally.

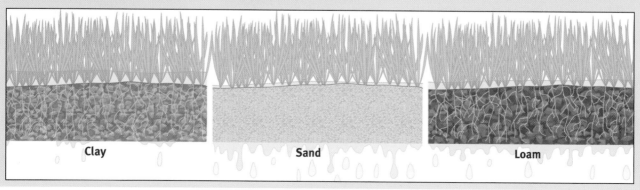

Clay   Sand   Loam

Early morning is the best time for watering because there is little wind and water pressure is at its peak.

WHEN TO WATER

One of the reasons you divided your irrigation system into zones was to meet the needs of individual plant types. To give all the plants the water they need when they need it, each zone in your system must run independently of the other zones. These various irrigation schedules can be hard to keep track of and are the best reason for choosing a programmable timer that runs them for you.

For most plants, the ideal time of day for sprinkler irrigation is just before dawn. There is usually little wind to divert spray, and water pressure is at its maximum in the morning. Because there is no direct sun to cause water to evaporate, more water enters the soil and the plants' cells than during the heat of the day.

The second-best choice is in the evening. This is often the time people with manual systems choose to run them—nobody wants to get up at 3 a.m. to turn on the sprinklers one zone at a time. Evening irrigation, however, has two disadvantages: Water pressure is usually slightly lower than before dawn, and diseases are more likely to infect susceptible plants when leaves stay wet all night. With early-morning watering, the leaves soon dry under the heat of the sun.

The least efficient time of day to water is midday. On a hot, dry day, much of the water applied evaporates before it enters the soil, especially if there is wind. An exception is drip and micro-irrigation. With emitters underground or under a layer of mulch, there is little water lost from evaporation. As a result, you can run your micro-irrigation system at any time.

Avoid watering when it is raining. Combining natural precipitation with irrigation greatly increases the chances of overwatering your plants. Attaching a rain sensor to your automatic timer will take care of this problem by turning off the system during rain.

SPRINKLER EFFICIENCIES BY CLIMATE

This chart illustrates how sprinkler efficiency lessens the hotter and drier the climate. The same thing happens in your yard as the sun and the temperature rise throughout the day.

Climate	Average Efficiencies
Low desert	60%
High desert	65%
Hot, dry	70%
Moderate	75%
Cool	80%

Source: Ministry of Agriculture, British Columbia

Scheduling *continued*

Also, avoid watering during high winds. This creates excess evaporation as well as water spray blown onto areas such as walkways, driveways—even the neighbors yard. Finally, set your system based on the absorption and holding qualities of your soil so you are confident you are watering only when the root zone of the plant is almost dry. (See the Soil Basic Intake Rate chart on the opposite page.)

CALCULATING WEEKLY NEEDS

Most people simply turn on the sprinklers when the plants look as though they need water and off when the soil appears wet enough. Often this gets the job done. However, this approach is always slightly irregular. As a result, plant growth will be uneven. It is much better to have a schedule that provides your plants with fairly even soil moisture at all times.

One approach is to use a few simple figures to approximate watering needs, then use the estimates to develop a weekly watering schedule that you can program into a timer. For example, most lawn areas need about an inch of water a week to maintain healthy growth. However, the other plant types in your yard will have different needs. Consult your county extension service, local nursery, or local garden center to find out how much water these various plantings need. In hot, dry weather you might have to double that, or in cool weather cut that time in half. Do a catch-can test (see page 144) to determine the exact precipitation rate of your system or start with these estimates. Typically, most fan spray sprinklers deliver an inch of water in about 60 minutes; rotary head sprinklers need about 180 minutes to deliver an inch of water.

If you can't find generalized weekly watering rates for your plants, you can dabble in the high-tech world of evapotranspiration rates, or ET. To calculate the weekly watering needs of your plants, call the county extension service and ask for the ET rate for your area. (ET numbers are constantly changing with the weather. They are measured daily or weekly, so ask for an average. Additional sources of ET information include the local weather service, local irrigation dealers, or plant nurseries.) Then get the landscape coefficient (Kc) for each plant type you are watering. Multiplying these two numbers together, gives the approximate weekly water needs for your plants. This is enough to get you started. These numbers are also available from various sites on the Internet. Simply type in "landscape coefficient" to find a number of listings from universities and others for thousands of plants.

Once you know how much water your plants need per week and how fast your sprinklers can apply it, plan watering days, start times, and run times to arrive at a final irrigation schedule that gets the correct amount of water to the plants.

Aside from the days you cannot water because of watering restrictions, select your watering days to consistently create even watering for each plant type.

WATERING GUIDELINES FOR MICRO-IRRIGATION SYSTEMS

You can use these general guidelines as a starting point for your drip and micro-irrigation schedule. Always check these settings after a week or so, using a moisture probe.

Weather	Duration in Minutes	Number of Times per Week
Cool	10	Every other day
Warm	15	Every day
Hot	20	Every day

Do this for each zone you are watering. Once you have built a schedule based on your estimates, adjust it up or down to account for the other microclimate elements unique to each zone, such as shade, sun, and wind exposure.

Micro-irrigation is simpler. Water is applied so slowly, with little danger of runoff. Most people find they can irrigate efficiently using drip or micro-irrigation without doing any complicated calculations. Use the guidelines in the chart above to select an appropriate initial run time for drip and micro-irrigation zones. You may need to increase the run time for trees and large shrubs, and decrease it for arid-climate plants.

ASSIGNING WATERING DAYS

Once you have figured out how much water each zone needs every week, you have to decide how best to get it into the ground. A watering schedule will give the watering days, start times, and run times. The start time and the run time are closely related. Together they tell the timer when and how long to water on the you have chosen.

The watering days are the days of the week that your irrigation system actually waters, using the start times and zone run times you have selected. Choose your watering days to meet your landscape's weekly water needs and to apply that water as evenly as possible. For instance, avoid bunching the days in one part of the week. Instead, space them out for even coverage. The moisture level in the ground should remain as even as possible. It should not be wet for three days, then dry for four. A multiple-program timer lets you create, store,

and run more than one set of these variables, allowing for different zone combinations and schedules.

For example, suppose you need to put 1 inch of water on your yard every week. If you have well-drained soil, you could do it all on one day. However that would probably cause the soil in the root zone to dry out before the next watering day. Watering two or three days a week is preferable. Sandy soil dries out even more quickly, so you may need to water on four days. With heavy clay soil, the ground might stay moist all week using just one or two watering days.

If your area has water-use restrictions imposed, those must take priority over all other criteria for choosing the watering days. Watering restrictions in your area may eliminate half the days and half the available hours of those days. If you need three watering days per week and watering restrictions forbid watering on three days of the week, your options are pretty straightforward. You'll have to choose watering days from the four available days that will give you the most even watering schedule.

ASSIGNING START TIMES

Once you know how many days you will be watering per week, you can decide how many start times to use on each watering day.

For example, assume that the plants in a zone in your yard need 1 inch of precipitation per week. Also assume that the precipitation rate of the system is 1 inch per hour. Because of local

SOIL BASIC INTAKE RATE

Soil water intake, or infiltration, tells you how fast, in inches of water per hour, the soil can absorb the water you apply. Knowing this helps you determine how long you can run your sprinklers before you start wasting water.

Soil Textural Class	Basic Intake Rate (inches per hour)
Clay	0.10
Silty clay	0.15
Clay loam	0.20
Loam	0.35
Sandy loam	0.40
Loamy sand	0.50
Sand	0.60

Source: Irrigation Association

Scheduling *continued*

watering restrictions, you know you can water only three days out of the week. Because you need a total of 60 minutes each week to apply enough water to your zone, watering on three days means you need to water for 20 minutes on each of these days.

However, you'll also have to factor in the soil type, the plants' root-zone depth, and the other variables discussed on pages 152 to 157. If the zone has clay soil, it can't absorb more than about ¼ inch in 15 minutes. So you'll need at least two different start times per watering day to get a cumulative total of 20 minutes per day. (And you'll want to leave at least 60 minutes between the waterings to allow for absorption.)

If the plants in your zone have a shallow root zone, watering for more than just a few minutes at a time will flush water past the roots. The remedy is to reduce the amount of water applied at one time. You can accomplish this by adding an additional start time and running the sprinklers for fewer minutes each time they turn on. This means three start times per watering day.

One, maybe even two, of these start times can be in the early morning although you need to avoid start times that coincide with household activities. For example, you may

Watering in the heat of the day wastes a great deal of water. The best time to run an irrigation system is right before or at dawn.

GENERALIZED SOIL PROPERTIES

This chart summarizes the water-holding capacity (available water, or AW) of various soil types. It is recorded as inches of water for every inch of soil, so the higher the number, the more water the soil can hold.

Soil Class	AW
Sand	0.08
Sandy loam	0.15
Loam	0.21
Clay loam	0.17
Clay	0.12

not want the system running when you leave for work or when the kids play in the yard. You may have to schedule a watering or two in midmorning.

DETERMINING RUN TIMES

The run times you select are adjusted according to the number of start times you use. Run times are set for each zone, whereas start times and watering days are for the whole system. The net result will be the total number of minutes of watering per day required by your plants. Run times also need to take into account any microclimate features present in your yard, such as slope, shade, and soil infiltration rates.

If you have three watering days and two start times per day, that means six irrigations on that zone per week. In order for the water applications (known as cycles in irrigation parlance) to be even, you need to know the run times—how many minutes each irrigation on that zone should last. Divide 60 minutes by six irrigations and you get about 10 minutes per irrigation—the run time you need to use for that zone.

The equation works out like this: Multiply the number of watering days (3) by the number of daily start times

(2). Divide the result (6) into the weekly watering need (60 minutes) to get a run time of 10 minutes for each watering cycle.

Double check the figures to make sure you end up with the correct amount of weekly water—1 inch per week is a common requirement. If the number of irrigations is changed, the run times will need to change to compensate.

Finally, remember that start times and watering days affect every zone in the system. Run times address the individual water needs of each zone. Therefore, each zone must run by itself. If two zones run at the same time, the precipitation rate for those zones will change drastically, completely messing up your watering calculations. This is because residential water systems do not have enough capacity to handle the water flow needs of two zones at once, not to mention the precipitous drop in water pressure that would occur inside your house.

Run times are set for each zone independently, allowing you to tailor the amount of water you apply to every zone. In this yard, turf in a rain shadow (see page 29) is being watered while the zones covering a flower bed and a more exposed area of turf are shut off.

SAMPLE WATERING SCHEDULE

This is an example of one type of simple irrigation schedule. See page 160 for how to draw up a slightly different but easier-to-read version of a watering schedule.

	Sunday	Monday	Tuesday	Wednesday	Thursday	Friday	Saturday
First Cycle							
Zone 1		5:00–5:27			5:00–5:27		
Zone 2		5:28–5:45			5:28–5:45		
Zone 3		5:46–6:25			5:46–6:25		
Second Cycle*							
Zone 1		6:27–6:54			6:27–6:54		
Zone 2		6:55–7:12			6:55–7:12		
Zone 3		7:25–8:04			7:25–8:04		
Third Cycle*							
Zone 1		8:05–8:32			8:05–8:32		
Zone 2		8:33–8:50			8:33–8:50		
Zone 3		8:51–9:30			8:51–9:30		

*Note that the second and third cycles don't start until at least one hour after the previous cycle is completed. An automatic system will not repeat irrigation on the same zone until one hour has elapsed to allow time for the water to soak into the soil. For example, the first cycle of Zone 1 ends at 5:27 a.m., and the second cycle doesn't begin until 6:27 a.m.

Scheduling *continued*

If you water manually or with an automatic timer, having a watering schedule to refer to is essential.

A schedule option

This example shows the essentials of a workable schedule. It indicates the start and run times, shows that only one zone is running at a time, and makes it clear that all zones are receiving even water.

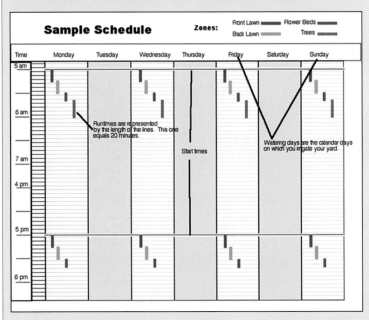

DRAWING UP YOUR SCHEDULE

Once you have determined the watering days, start times, and run times necessary to get the proper amount of water on the ground in each zone, you can draw up a schedule. Whether you are going to program a timer or use the schedule to run the irrigation system manually, you will need to write it down.

The schedule will actually be a fairly simple chart. All you need are sheets of graph paper, perhaps a ruler, and colored pencils to represent each zone. The graph paper will make laying everything out much easier.

■ Divide the paper into eight equal columns.

■ Label the first column "Time."

■ Mark the "Time" column with the hours of the day. It is usually enough to break the hours into no more than 10-minute sections. Marking smaller intervals than that can be tricky.

■ Label the remaining columns with the days of the week.

■ Indicate local watering-restrictions times on your schedule.

■ Mark the start times you have chosen to use on each day by drawing a line across your chart at the correct times for each day. For clarity and readability, use a different colored pencil for each of the zones in the system.

■ One by one, mark out the run times for each zone. Draw a line with a colored pencil that corresponds to the run time for that zone.

Post this schedule at the control valves if you will be operating the system manually, or use it to program your automatic irrigation timer. Leave a copy of it near the timer for easy reference later on.

THE ET CHECKBOOK

The ET checkbook is a more involved but more precise method for deriving a watering schedule. It is similar to maintaining a checking account at the bank.

Transactions are recorded regularly, perhaps even daily, tracking water instead of currency. The correct value for the account is established using precise soil property information and plant data that allow you to derive the correct water content for the soil for any type of plant. "Deposits" to the account include any precipitation; "withdrawals" are the sum of any water loss from the soil—the evapotranspiration (ET) rate and how much water the plant actually uses.

The goal is to keep the actual water content as close to the calculated optimal balance as possible by balancing the deposits and withdrawals of water.

To create an irrigation checkbook, you will need the following information:

■ Local ET rate
■ Plant types
■ Landscape coefficient (Kc) for your plants
■ Soil type
■ Root-zone depth for each zone
■ Soil water-holding capacity in inches of water per inch of soil
■ Available water in inches of water per inch of soil
■ Allowable depletion in inches of water per inch of soil
■ Precipitation rate of each zone

Using local ET information and the Kc for the plants in a yard, you can arrive at an accurate prediction of the water you will need on a day-to-day basis for each zone.

The local ET rate, available from local weather stations, is multiplied by the Kc for the plant you want to water and by the square footage of the area the plant occupies, represented by LA (land area). Because you need a Kc value for every plant type, as well as the square footage planted in that plant type, it is not as easy to use this method in a small yard with highly varied plants. You can, however, find Kc averages for plant groups, which are a bit less accurate but for the homeowner much easier. The basic formula goes like this:

ET multiplied by Kc multiplied by LA equals water for that zone.

Once the water needs have been calculated in this way, you can monitor water use. Then make irrigation changes until the predicted and actual water use coincide. Because ET values change daily, the arrived-at water use requires ongoing monitoring to stay as efficient as possible.

This is more work than most home gardeners want or need. Although using ET information is complex at the moment, the advent of software-based controllers that can do all the required calculations automatically means the precision of this type of scheduling will soon be saving water in neighborhoods all over the continent.

Irrigation checkbook

The irrigation checkbook resembles a regular checkbook. The deposits and withdrawals are made in water rather than money.

The irrigation checkbook can be precise and predictive, but it requires technical knowledge and user management to keep it working properly.

Day	Rainfall (deposit) +	Irrigation (deposit) +	Water Use (withdrawal) −	Amt. to apply (balance)
	1.05			1.05
1			0.20	0.85
2			0.20	0.65
3			0.20	0.45
4		0.45		0.90
			0.20	0.70
5	0.15			0.85
			0.20	0.65
6	0.38			1.03
			0.20	0.83
7		0.45		1.28

Scheduling *continued*

A moisture sensor is an inexpensive investment that will prove valuable when you fine-tune your irrigation schedule.

EVALUATING AND ADJUSTING

No matter how you create your schedule, you will need to evaluate it and make changes over the course of a few days to get the watering just right. There are several simple ways to evaluate your schedule. One of the most basic is the runoff test. (See below right.) If your system produces puddles or runoff, you need to reduce the run times for those zones and perhaps even add a new start time.

Another indication of an incorrect schedule is wilting. Although slight wilting is normal with certain vegetables, if you notice that plants in any of the zones are wilting before the next watering session, correct the schedule. You will most likely need to add a watering day to your schedule to spread out the irrigation more evenly or to move one watering day later in the week to close the weekly watering gap that is wilting the plant.

Don't overlook natural precipitation. If it is raining more than you anticipated, you may be able to shorten the run times of your system. Conversely, if it has been hot and windy, you may have to add to the run times of all your zones. A timer with a seasonal adjustment or a "water budget" feature can make this simpler.

There is no way to evaluate the efficiency of your schedule without some first-hand observation on your part. If there is a problem, make modest adjustments. Drastic changes may just create other problems. Take several weeks to fine-tune your watering gradually. The goal is to have no runoff or standing water, with the soil in each zone staying slightly moist until the sprinklers come back on.

MOISTURE SENSORS AND PROBES

The most precise way to evaluate your schedule is to use a moisture sensor or probe to measure the water content below the surface. Either device will give you a reading that you can use to make timing adjustments to the schedule.

To use a soil probe, simply push it into the ground until you feel increasing resistance. That resistance tells you where moist soil ends and dry soil begins. Measure the distance the probe has gone into the ground, and compare this to

Runoff tests

Runoff tests are an easy way to gauge the efficiency of your system. Start each test with the soil dry, not after a rainstorm or soon after you have irrigated.

Method One

Manually run the zone you want to test. Watch the zone, and keep track of how many minutes the system has run. When you see any puddles or water runoff from that zone, note how long it took to reach that point. This tells you the maximum number of minutes you can run your zone before you start wasting water.

Method Two

Activate your irrigation program for the zone you want to test. After the zone program has turned off, inspect for puddles and runoff in that zone. Any puddles and runoff indicate that the run times on the zone need to be reduced, or you will be wasting water. It may also mean adding an additional cycle to get the proper amount of water on the plants without oversaturation.

the root-zone depth you desire. If you need water to sink deeper, you will need to adjust your schedule.

A core-extracting probe is more reliable. Drive it into the ground and pull it out to obtain a core of dirt that you can examine to see how much more or less water is needed to get to the proper depth.

RAIN SENSORS

The most useful option you can add to a new or existing irrigation system is a rain sensor. This inexpensive add-on could well pay for itself in one season, no matter what part of the country you live in.

Rain sensors shut off your irrigation system in the event of natural precipitation. This saves water by avoiding unnecessary artificial precipitation and protects your plants from overwatering.

There are many different models available, from a number of manufacturers. They are all compatible with any timer that has a rain sensor port on its terminal block. A rain sensor connects in the same way that a normal automatic irrigation valve does.

Until recently, all rain sensors had to be hardwired to the timer. This limited where they could be mounted because installation entailed running a new wire from the sensor to the timer. In the last few years, wireless technology has changed all that. Now, for about the same price you would have paid for a hardwired rain sensor several years ago, you can buy a wireless unit. This saves you the trouble of running wire from the sensor to the time it gives you more flexibility in positioning it well away from overhanging eaves or trees so it can quickly turn off the system when significant rainfall begins.

Older sensors overrode your system at the first drop of rain, which could keep the irrigation system from watering even if the rainfall was inconsequential. Newer rain sensors are easily adjustable. You can set them to shut off the system only after a predetermined amount of natural precipitation has fallen. This allows you to make better use of the rain as part of your irrigation schedule. Timers with rain sensor ports also allow you to set the amount of time that the system will be deactivated, once the sensor has turned it off.

Rain sensors are so effective at saving water that they are now mandated equipment in many parts of North America.

A rain sensor is an inexpensive but valuable addition to any automatic system. It detects rainfall and signals the timer to suspend its operation when it senses a preset amount of precipitation has fallen.

Watering suggestions

Lawns are usually the most needy water users in the yard. Without consistent moisture, many will go dormant and lose that lush green look everyone wants.

Figuring how often and how much to water all your different flower beds, garden plots, lawn areas, and groundcover plantings isn't always easy. However, most problems can be solved with a bit of patience and careful observation.

WHAT PLANTS NEED

Landscape coefficients (Kc) have been calculated using the individual evapotranspiration (ET) rates of each plant. The local ET rate is multiplied by the Kc for each plant to determine how much water it needs. Because water needs change with conditions, landscape coefficients are usually given in three values—high, average, and low—that represent the range of water used by a certain plant.

Plant type	High	Average	Low
Trees	0.9	0.5	0.2
Shrubs	0.7	0.5	0.2
Groundcover	0.9	0.5	0.2
Mixture of trees, shrubs, and groundcover	0.9	0.5	0.2
Turfgrass	0.8	0.75	0.6

Source: Irrigation Association

Follow the instructions in the first part of this chapter to water to root depth, then reapply moisture just before the root zone dries out. A moisture sensor or probe (see page 162) is your most useful tool for checking this.

To further evaluate and fine-tune your system's efficiency and coverage, keep in mind the specific needs of various types of plants. This section will help you do just that.

No matter how many sophisticated tools you have at your disposal, a basic understanding of your yard and the plants in it and the most useful tools of all. It is well worth your time to consult gardening books that describe plants and their needs in detail. Remember, the more you know about your plants, the easier it will be to use your watering system to full advantage.

Here are some simple tips and guidelines for various plant types in your yard.

LAWNS

You know your grass needs water if you walk across the lawn and your footprints remain visible for more than a few seconds. Another sign of thirst is a dull appearance, caused by the grass blades folding up and exposing their base.

Watering daily versus weekly

Applying ¹⁄₁₀ inch of water daily supplies nearly 1 inch of water a week, but the lawn will not be as healthy as

it could be if you had applied the water in one 1-inch or two ½-inch waterings. The more water you apply at one time,

the deeper and healthier the root system grows and the more resilient the grass becomes.

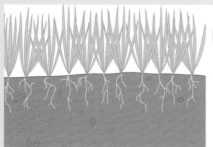 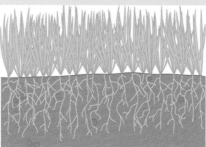 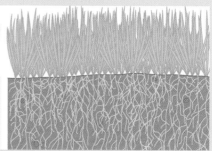

During warm weather, most lawns demand abundant water—between 1 and 2 inches per week—for healthy growth. If you live in a dry-summer climate, you must supply the necessary water. If you're in a summer-rainfall area, you will have to irrigate only when rain doesn't come abundantly enough or at the right time.

If your area has a good supply of natural precipitation, you can use bluegrass, ryegrass, or St. Augustine grass. These grasses are unsuitable in drier, hotter climates. It is usually a good idea to plant grasses that are native to your area and adapted to local conditions.

FLOWER BEDS

In a mixed planting bed, pay attention to the different needs of all the plants. A flower bed may contain annuals, perennials, bulbs, or a combination of all three. Check a flower bed's root zone at various locations with a moisture sensor when adjusting the irrigation system.

Annuals grow, bloom, and die—all in one year. Most annuals require constant moisture if they are to bloom vigorously. That means a consistent supply of water is needed until flowering is finished.

Perennials can live for years. They need regular moisture from the onset of growth until they finish blooming. Once they go dormant, some perennials tolerate routine watering while others prefer—or even require almost no watering.

Deciduous bulbs typically enter dormancy a month or so after flowering. Because some dormant bulbs can take moist conditions and

others can't, it is important to know a bulb's needs before planting it near annuals and perennials that will be watered. Evergreen bulbs have no true dormant period; and can be watered as needed throughout the year.

Some flowers, such as azaleas and petunias, are prone to disease when kept constantly moist. A sprinkler system that wets the flowers should be run early in the day, allowing the flowers to dry quickly.

Grouping plants with similar needs makes your irrigation scheduling easier and more accurate. The result will be better-looking plants and less work for you.

Watering suggestions
continued

Water has a powerful effect on the growth of most garden vegetables and berries—and affects their taste and size.

VEGETABLE GARDENS

The delectable flavor and crispness of homegrown vegetables depends greatly on watering them according to their stage of growth. Underwatered vegetables can be stunted, bitter, and tough. Overwatered vegetables may rot before they make it to your table.

You can water more efficiently if you group your vegetables according to their water needs. The bigger and faster growing they are, the more water they'll use. Shallow-rooted plants such as beets, carrots, lettuce, spinach, and radishes grow at about the same rate and use similar amounts of water. Corn, melons, and squash all grow rapidly and need more water.

Larger plants need more water at a greater depth. Small, shallow-rooted young plants need watering as often as two or three times a day in some conditions to stay moist.

You can estimate the water needs of your vegetables by multiplying the local ET rate (available from your local county extension service), by its crop, or landscape, coefficient. (See pages 160 and 161 for more on ET.) Crop coefficients for several vegetable families are shown in the chart on this page. Notice how their watering needs change for different periods of growth.

CROP COEFFICIENTS (KC) FOR VEGETABLES

Crop Type	Kc (early season)	Kc (mid season)	Kc (late season)
Solanum Family (potatoes, eggplants, tomatoes)	0.6	1.15	0.80
Cucurbitaceae Family (melons, squash, cucumbers)	0.5	1.00	0.80
Small vegetables	0.7	1.05	0.95
Roots and tubers	0.5	1.10	0.95
Legumes	0.4	1.15	0.55

TREES AND SHRUBS

Water must reach the root zone of large plants. It's sometimes thought that you have to soak the soil for hours to do this, but the absorption roots of even very large trees are no deeper than 2 to 3 feet.

Mature trees benefit most from water applied at or just beyond the drip line of the canopy rather than close to the trunk. The drip line is the outside perimeter of the canopy formed by the leaves. However, when first establishing a

large plant, be sure to get water directly to the root zone, which will be close to the trunk. If the water is applied farther out, the roots may die before they have a chance to spread out and reach the moisture.

The best watering techniques are those that keep the root crown (the roots closest to the surface) and the trunk dry. Effective methods include filling a soil basin with water, inserting a deep-root irrigator, or using a drip system.

A soil basin is an effective way to prevent runoff when watering a plant growing in open soil, with no lawn or groundcover planted around it. To make a soil basin, mound two concentric rings of soil and flood the area between them.

Deep-root irrigators attach to a garden hose and are pushed down into the roots of the tree. Each irrigator injects water into the root zone, shooting it out horizontally in several directions below ground. This is an easy way to get supplemental water to a lawn tree. Avoid pushing the irrigators deeper than 18 inches, and position them about a third of the way in from the drip line. Place one every few feet around the tree.

Watering trees is not as water- or time-intensive as with other plants. But trees still need adequate moisture to grow at their best.

GROUNDCOVER

Groundcovers are dense, low-growing plants that blanket the ground and bind the soil together. Many perennials, shrubs, and vines qualify as groundcovers. Used as alternatives to high-maintenance turf, they are less demanding of water because their root zones are deeper than those of turfgrasses. Also, variations in watering are not as noticeable in groundcovers. Some groundcovers have horizontal branches, giving the impression of a uniform planting when closely spaced. This thick foliage reduces evaporative losses, which making them more water efficient than grass.

Fan sprays and micro-irrigation are ideal choices for watering groundcovers.

ROOT DEPTH AND EFFECTIVE WATERING

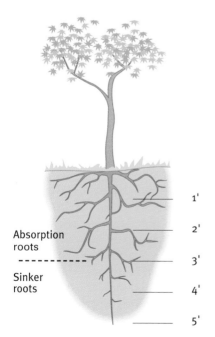

Absorption roots

Sinker roots

1'
2'
3'
4'
5'

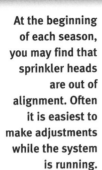

At the beginning of each season, you may find that sprinkler heads are out of alignment. Often it is easiest to make adjustments while the system is running.

Maintenance

A properly designed and installed irrigation system requires only minimal maintenance. However, periodic upkeep is vital. And as time passes, you may find that you want to adapt or update your system.

SEASONAL ADJUSTMENTS

At the beginning of each growing season, turn on your system and check that each spray head is delivering the desired coverage. The heads may have been knocked out of alignment by foot traffic, a wayward lawn mower, or a snow shovel. This can cause them to spray sidewalks or other unintended surfaces while leaving part of the garden unwatered.

You might find there is too much or not enough overlap between heads. To adjust this, move the nozzle to redirect its spray, turn the spray-reduction adjustment screw on the top of the nozzle (see pages 147 and 169). In the case of a ratcheting riser, turn the riser. Most impact rotary heads have rings at the base of the spray head that adjust the pattern and a diffuser screw to adjust the distance of throw. With microsprinklers, simply twist the head to change its direction.

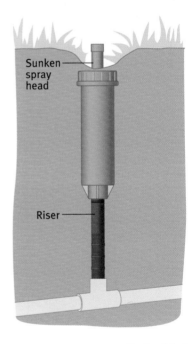

Reposition spray heads so they are flush with the surrounding ground. Also, keep grass and other foliage trimmed away from the sprinkler nozzle.

Sometimes spray heads produce a mist or fogging action rather than the larger drops necessary for watering. This indicates that the water flow is too strong. Adjust it at the zone control valve. If the system is manual, turn the zone shutoff clockwise until you see large drops. Some automatic valves have a special knob for this adjustment called a flow control that adjusts the flow to minimize misting and fogging.

ADAPTING TO CHANGING NEEDS

Your yard and its watering needs will probably change over time. Usually this will require no more than readjusting the watering schedule or the flow rate of sprinklers. But if you've added new beds or radically altered the use of any part of the yard, significant changes may be needed.

Modifications to aboveground micro-irrigation systems are easy to carry out, especially if you left room for expansion on each drip zone. Simply add a line and punch in new emitters, as described in the drip installation section (see pages 130–139). You can also replace emitters and microsprinklers with units of higher or lower GPH ratings. Be sure to recalculate the zone's capacity before adding any component to avoid overloading it.

To remove lines or emitters, install new barbed fittings and hole plugs as needed. Underground micro-irrigation installations will require digging, but the connections are the same.

Adding on to sprinkler systems is not complicated as long as you have left space on each manifold and zone for future expansion. Before adding an extra sprinkler head or lateral line to a zone, check that enough water pressure is available. When adding whatever trenches are necessary for the new pipes and sprinklers, dig carefully so you don't break the pipe or other fixtures already in place. For future reference, be sure to draw any new components and pipes onto your plan.

PVC connections cannot be taken apart and reused, so be sure you have all the fittings you need before you start rearranging PVC plumbing. Polyethylene fittings, however, can usually be reused.

Sprinklers and risers can be reused as well. Changing nozzles may be the only adjustment needed; a full-circle nozzle can be replaced with a part circle or even a strip nozzle in a matter of seconds. When converting lawns to shrubs or flower beds, the system change can be as simple as putting the sprinklers on taller risers. However, be certain that any sprinklers that will be added or changed are compatible with others in that zone.

If you didn't leave room for expansion on your valve manifold, you may need to rebuild the whole manifold and install a larger valve box. If so, refer to the installation section on pages 114 to 123.

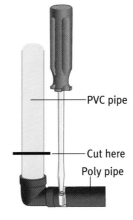

Adapting to changing needs can be as simple as adjusting spray (left) patterns, or as involved as adding an entire new zone to an existing system. If you left space for adding on to your manifold, the connections are relatively simple (below).

CHANGING CONNECTIONS

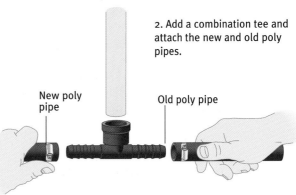

PVC pipe

Cut here

Poly pipe

1. Cut PVC pipe above the fitting. Unscrew the clamp and remove the poly pipe.

2. Add a combination tee and attach the new and old poly pipes.

New poly pipe

Old poly pipe

169

Maintenance *continued*

CLEANING AND FLUSHING

You need to clean all irrigation systems occasionally to remove dirt, debris, or plant materials that have built up over the months. And there are a few basic steps that you can take at any time of the year to be sure the water can always get through your system unfettered.

from the head; overhanging grass can interfere with the spray pattern. Also, prune vegetation growing around pop-up and shrub spray heads in garden, groundcover, and shrub areas.

Clean the mesh filter each month. You can clean most filters simply by turning on the flush outlet (dump valve). If your system has no dump valve, take out the filter and rinse it thoroughly. At least once a year take apart, clean, and inspect even filters that have a dump valve. If the filter screen shows any sign of damage, replace it.

Micro-irrigation systems are more sensitive to blockage caused by dirt and debris because they don't have enough flow to push out a blockage. Clean them more frequently. Once a month during the irrigation season, remove the end closure from each line and flush the line thoroughly until the water runs clear, then put the end closure back in place.

Irrigation lines can be flushed simply by removing the sprinkler nozzle (shown). Some sprinklers have a flush plug, which saves water and preserves water pressure.

To prevent buildup in the pipes, risers, and nozzles, use the following method to flush each zone in the system at least once per year.
■ Turn off water to one zone, and remove all of that zone's individual nozzles and/or sprinkler heads.
■ Run water through the zone for a few minutes until a clean, clear stream of water flows from each sprinkler head.
■ Turn off the water.
■ Take apart the nozzles (depending on the type, you can do this by hand or with a screwdriver or special key). Clean them to remove any dirt or deposits.
■ Rinse out the filter screen or basket.
■ Reassemble and replace all the parts.
■ Turn on the zone again to check that everything is leak-free and operating properly.

Be sure to keep the grass around the stationary and pop-up lawn heads trimmed back

When cleaning your sprinklers, it is important to rinse the filter baskets in running water. Clogged passages in the filter can cause sprinkler performance to drop substantially.

WINTERIZING

To cope with sustained freezing temperatures, you must completely drain and dry your system to prevent damage to the components. One approach is to drain the system using drain valves. You should have one drain valve per zone. In poorly drained soils you may need to dig a dry well below each drain valve to ensure that no water collects and freezes there.

To winterize a system using manual drains, begin by shutting off the irrigation water supply. Open all the manual drain valves downward from the zone valves to allow the lines to drain. Leave the valves open for a few days to be sure all the water has escaped, then close them again. Finally, open the manual drains ahead of your zone valves to allow the main irrigation supply line to drain. (Even if this line terminates in your basement, you should drain it.)

With automatic drains, all you need to do is close the main water-supply valve. The lines down from the automatic zone valves will drain by themselves. To check that the drains are working, remove a sprinkler from its riser and check that there is no water in the pipe.

Be sure to drain the main irrigation supply line as well. To check that the supply has drained, remove the valve bonnet (cover) and look inside. The valve should be dry.

SPRING START-UP

Neglecting to properly start up your irrigation system in spring can cause damage to the system. Fortunately, a few simple steps before you start watering again will protect your system and keep it reliable year after year.

The greatest threat to your irrigation system is water hammer. It is produced by a pressure spike caused by water rushing into an empty pipe, giving the air in the pipes no time to escape. When this happens, the pressure inside the pipe can reach 15 times normal operating pressure. This is enough to burst fittings and even blow sprinklers out of the ground.

Before refilling your system, use a shovel to confirm that the soil is frost-free to a full 12 inches below the surface. Filling your system while the ground is still frozen can cause unseen and hard-to-fix freeze damage to your pipes.

If your irrigation system isn't equipped with automatic drains, remove the nozzle or sprinkler head located at the highest point of each zone. Start filling the system very slowly, beginning with the main line of the irrigation system

Using a compressor

If you own a compressor that handles 25 cubic feet per minute (cfm) or more, with a pressure regulator adjustable to 50 psi or less, you can winterize your irrigation system using compressed air. To avoid damage to the system, do not exceed 50 psi (3.52 kg/cm$_2$) of air pressure.

1. Shut off the main water supply.

2. Connect the air compressor hose to an appropriate air fitting located down from the irrigation supply valve. Install a tee fitting just after in the main line. Put a threaded nipple and cap on the extra leg, and use it as the connection to the air hose. If your backflow preventer is installed on the main line, be sure you make the connection just below it.

3. Activate each automatic valve manually from the controller. Blow out each zone valve until all the water is expelled.

4. Disconnect the air hose and open any drains that are installed between the main shutoff and the valve manifolds.

(located between the water source and the zone valves). Slowly open the shutoff valve that controls the water supply to the entire system—just a quarter turn is enough. Take your time; remember that the water has to travel the entire length of the main line.

Next, slowly fill each zone by manually opening the zone valve using the bleed on the valve. When the water pouring out of the open riser (where you removed the nozzle) runs free of air bubbles, close off the zone valve.

It may take as long as 30 minutes to fill a zone carefully. Once the zone is filled, replace the sprinkler head you removed. Repeat the process for each zone. Once you have filled the entire irrigation system, run each zone for two minutes. This lets you test your automatic timer, flush out any remaining air, and check that all the heads are spraying properly.

Be sure you have a collection of spare irrigation parts on hand before turning the water back on. Include some extra PVC and/or poly pipe, primer, and cement as well. Finally, if you have an automatic controller, replace the batteries and make sure your timer programs are still accurate.

Troubleshooting and repair

Fortunately, little is likely to go wrong with a properly installed irrigation system. Malfunctions are the exception rather than the rule. Even if things do go awry, it is usually a simple matter to correct the problem. Most malfunctions are apparent and involve no more than twisting a pop-up sprinkler riser to correct a wayward spray pattern. But when something more involved occurs, such as leaks or nonfunctional zones, it is good to know where to start looking for the problem. The pages that follow discuss some of the most common problems you might encounter and steps you can take to correct them.

Troubleshooting and repair

DIGEST

TROUBLESHOOTING CHECKLIST

Got a problem? Always proceed "outward" on your system when trying to determine why something doesn't work. Start at the timer first, then follow the water flow. For instance, if you find you have inoperative zones and sprinklers:

- Check the timer for power.

- Check the timer programming.

- Check the zone control valves.

- Check for sprinkler damage.

- Check for plumbing leaks.

Repair Tools

- ✓ Hacksaw
- ✓ Tubing cutters
- ✓ Sprinkler riser puller
- ✓ Screwdrivers
- ✓ Electrical multitester
- ✓ Continuity tester
- ✓ PVC cement
- ✓ Poly fittings
- ✓ Plumbing tape
- ✓ Garden shovel or spade
- ✓ Extra wiring, fuses, and grease-cap fittings
- ✓ Plastic pipe shears

BEING PREPARED

Let's face it: A watering system will get a lot of abuse, so it's inevitable that pieces will break. Stock up on spare parts (often components go on clearance at the end of the watering season) to have them handy when a repair is needed.

And the most common problems are?

Timer not connected to the power supply.
Plant matter clogging the sprinklers.
Damage from lawn equipment.
Incorrect timer programming.
Water supply not turned on.

AN OUNCE OF PREVENTION

■ Inspect drip systems monthly for leaks and clogged emitters.

■ Clean mesh filters in drip/microsystems and sprinkler filter baskets often to prevent clogs.

■ Use the bleed valves on your zone control valves to evacuate dirt that builds up inside the valve body. Do this at least yearly.

■ If your timer requires backup batteries, replace them annually.

■ Before putting your system to bed for the winter, be certain that all water is out of the system. This will save repairs later.

REMOVING A POP-UP SPRINKLER HEAD

■ Dig out all dirt from around the head so you have access to the head and the riser or the connection beneath it.

■ Reach under the sprinkler head with one hand and hold onto the riser or tee connection at the base of the sprinkler.

■ With your other hand, loosen and unscrew the sprinkler from the riser.

■ Thread the new or repaired head onto the riser, and hand-tighten it plus a quarter to half a turn. Be sure to hold the pipe beneath it to stabilize it. No pipe dope (a type of sealant) or tape is needed with plastic fittings.

LEAKS

Leaks are the most insidious problem because they usually are not detected until it is too late.

You can use repair (dresser) couplings for most leaks. They need no cement and can fix a small leak in just a few minutes.

Large leaks may require extensive digging, cutting, and gluing to fix.

175

Servicing components

Most potential problems with an irrigation system do not require immediate attention. They can be noted and corrected during routine maintenance. Regular flushing and cleaning, especially of filters and sprinkler heads, will eliminate most problems before any serious damage to plants occurs. But there are a few instances where more vigorous intervention may be needed.

DIAGNOSING AN IRRIGATION TIMER

Automatic irrigation systems depend on the efficient operation of the timer to fulfill their mission. They are subject to a number of problems, most of which are from faulty wiring. When the circuit breaker controlling an automatic irrigation system trips or when valves fail to open or close even though they have been thoroughly cleaned and inspected, the cause is generally a poor wire connection or a shorted wire.

When inspecting and making wiring repairs, be sure the circuit breaker controlling power to the irrigation system is off. Then check all wire connections, including those at the automatic timer, zone valves, and master control valve. Repair any that look faulty. Water in contact with a bare wire is a common cause of malfunction. Make sure the connections are properly sealed and waterproofed with a grease-cap fitting. If the connections seem intact, you may have to dig up part of the malfunctioning zone to trace the location of a break in the wire.

Using a continuity tester or a multitester (sometimes called a multimeter) may be the best way to track down breaks in the wiring circuit. It could also save you from exploratory digging. These tools are easy to use, but be sure you follow manufacturer's instructions at all times.

SERVICING IRRIGATION VALVES

If none of the zones operates, check the master control valve. You may simply have forgotten to turn it on after last servicing or draining the system for the winter. If only one of the zones is not operating properly, the problem is likely with the valve to that zone. Because of advances in materials, modern valves are less likely to stick than older ones. They are also easier to adjust. You can usually correct problems caused by high or low flow conditions by adjusting the flow control on the valve. Each valve model has a different type of flow control, but you can adjust most by hand or with a wrench.

When a zone doesn't shut off automatically or won't operate, the problem may lie with the zone control valve. Try using the external bleed screw while the water is running to dislodge any dirt that may be stuck in the valve diaphragm. If that fails, turn off the water and take the valve apart according to the manufacturer's instructions. Clean out any debris or buildup, and check for damage to the diaphragm. If a valve diaphragm fails, it is easily replaced. The exact procedure varies with manufacturer, but the general steps are as follows.

Continuity testers and multitesters can be helpful when tracking down bad wiring connections in your irrigation system.

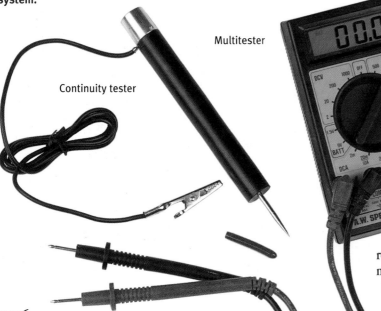

Multitester

Continuity tester

■ Turn off the water supply to the irrigation system and unscrew or unthread the valve bonnet from the valve body.

■ Remove the valve bonnet assembly and the spring. Gently pry the diaphragm from its seat in the valve body. Flush out the seat and valve body with clean water and inspect for damage. If the valve is damaged, replace it. Otherwise proceed.

■ Press the new diaphragm into place in the valve body, then replace the spring and the valve bonnet.

■ Tighten the screws or hold-down ring, turn on the water, and check for leaks.

Cracked or damaged valve bonnets or bodies can sometimes be repaired but are best replaced by new ones.

If a manual control valve leaks or becomes hard to turn, before replacing the entire valve stem, check the packing nut. The packing nut sits at the top of the valve bonnet where the stem enters the valve—a classic location for a leak. Often, this nut is tight to prevent the valve from operating inadvertently. First, be sure you have loosened the packing nut. If that isn't the problem, check the threads on the valve stem for damage. If the threads on the stem or the valve body are damaged, you will need to replace that piece.

Have the zone running if you need to change the flow control setting. This allows you to check the results visually as you go.

Valve designs can vary. This valve is fairly typical, but when repairing a valve, check the Internet. Most manufacturers have online manuals.

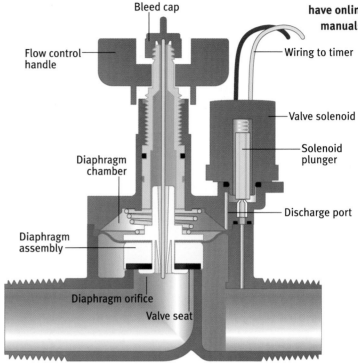

Bleed cap / Flow control handle / Wiring to timer / Valve solenoid / Solenoid plunger / Diaphragm chamber / Discharge port / Diaphragm assembly / Diaphragm orifice / Valve seat

Servicing irrigation valves

After turning off the power, remove the hold-down ring by removing the screws or unthreading it.

Remove the valve bonnet and spring. Then carefully pry out the diaphragm and flush the valve body with water.

Gently push the new diaphragm into its seat. Then reassemble the valve and test for leaks.

Servicing components *continued*

SERVICING SPRINKLERS

Regular inspection of your sprinklers will prevent most spray head problems. Make sure you clean and replace damaged or worn-out nozzles and filters. Don't be surprised to find that filters have not been installed on your sprinklers, as they should be. Missing filter baskets are responsible for many a clogged sprinkler nozzle.

Pop-up spray heads present special problems. If they refuse to pop up or retract, the problem is usually the wiper seal. This is a rubber or plastic gasket designed to keep dirt and debris out of the pop-up mechanism. When this gasket wears out, small particles of dirt can jam the pop-up riser in place.

The other major mechanical reason a pop-up sprinkler won't pop is a damaged riser retraction spring. If the riser has no spring tension at all, the entire sprinkler should be replaced.

Do not open the sprinkler body. Due to safety concerns over the danger of the riser retraction spring being ejected from the sprinkler body, you can no longer replace the wiper seal yourself. If it goes bad, you will need to replace the entire sprinkler body. This is one more reason why it pays to keep this area of the sprinkler clean—free of any dirt or debris.

Any repair that requires opening the sprinkler body or repairing connections to it, will require you to take the sprinkler out of the ground.

Removing a pop-up sprinkler head

1 Dig out all dirt from around the head so you have access to the head and the riser or the connection beneath.

2 Reach under the sprinkler head with one hand and hold onto the riser or tee connection at the base of the sprinkler.

3 With your other hand, loosen and unscrew the sprinkler from the riser.

4 Thread the new or repaired head onto the riser, and hand-tighten it plus a quarter to half turn. Be sure to hold the pipe beneath it to stabilize it. No pipe dope or tape is needed with plastic fittings.

SERVICING EMITTERS

Emitters and microsprays are fairly worry-free. Because they have no moving parts and low flow rates, all there is to think about are clogging and physical damage to the components.

If you suspect a leak in an aboveground drip/microzone, check along the lines for obvious wet spots where they should not be. Remove any mulch covering the tubing, turn on the water, and check for any bubbling or spraying from the pipe itself or around the emitters.

If the pipe is leaking, cut out the cracked or punctured section with plastic pipe cutters and attach a repair coupler in its place.

If an emitter is leaking, first make sure it is well seated into the tubing. If it will not snap firmly into place, you can punch a new hole for it and snap the emitter into the new hole. Fill the old hole with a goof plug. (See page 135.)

In areas with hard water (high in mineral content), an emitter may get clogged with mineral deposits from the water. You may see a whitish deposit where the water should be dripping from the emitter. Although certain types of emitters such as flag emitters, as well as some older-style drip emitters, can be opened and cleaned out. Newer emitters are permanently sealed. Sometimes soaking the

Flag drip emitter

Some emitters, such as this flag type, can be opened to facilitate cleaning. However, most are permanently sealed, limiting what you can do to clean them if they clog.

clogged emitter in a mixture of ⅛ cup white vinegar per ½ gallon of clean water will dissolve the deposits and restore the correct flow and function. Generally, it is easiest to replace badly clogged units with new ones.

Check the system monthly. Regularly clean out the mesh filter screen at the water connection, and replace it if it is ripped or shows signs of wear. Also, inspect your system by walking around to check the emitters for proper operation and to be sure they are not being overrun by plant matter. Replace any damaged emitters.

The best thing you can do for your drip irrigation components is to rinse and inspect the mesh filter every year. Replace it at the first sign of wear. This will help avoid clogs in the first place.

Servicing components *continued*

Leaks in irrigation plumbing often show up as puddles of standing water in your lawn. If you notice any such wet spots, investigate immediately. If a large break occurs, major damage can result.

TRACING PLUMBING LEAKS

Repairing PVC is no harder than installing it in the first place. Most repairs take only a few minutes to complete.

Plumbing leaks usually go unnoticed until there is a major failure or water-pressure loss. Even when the problem becomes more serious, the only sign of impending failure is water saturation of the ground above the leak.

When you suspect a leak in underground irrigation pipes, remove the sprinklers from

REPAIRING PVC PIPE WITH A REPAIR COUPLING

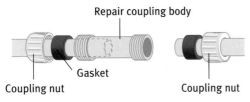

Repair coupling body

Gasket

Coupling nut

Coupling nut

REPAIRING PVC PIPE BY REPLACING THE DAMAGED SECTION

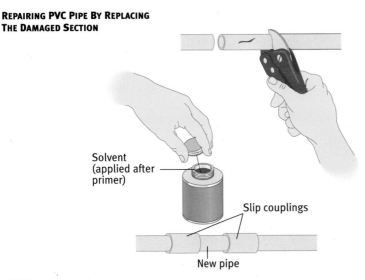

Solvent (applied after primer)

Slip couplings

New pipe

their risers in the suspect zone and cap them. Then turn on the zone. Inspect any aboveground connections and fittings for leaks. If none are found, wait until water starts appearing on the surface of the ground. The leak should be underneath it. (If you can't find the source of the leak, call in a professional. Special equipment can trace the problem.)

Once you have tracked down the location of the leak, you will need to dig down to the damaged pipe. Be careful of any timer wires running under or alongside the pipes—you don't want to cut them and create another repair job.

REPAIRING MINOR LEAKS

Minor leaks at the joints of poly pipe usually require no more than tightening the hose clamps at the site of the leak. You can easily fix small leaks in the pipe itself by cutting out the break and replacing it with a new piece of tubing and some couplings. Likewise, you can remedy leaks in PVC pipes with a repair coupling, also sometimes called a dresser coupling. It is a compression-type fitting, so you do not need cement. To install a repair coupling, turn off the water and use plastic-pipe shears or a hacksaw to cut through the pipe at the leak. Slip on the dresser coupling components, center the coupling body over the cut, and tighten the coupling nuts and gaskets until firmly in place.

REPAIRING MAJOR LEAKS

Large breaks in poly, PVC, or any other pipe preclude the use of repair couplings. Remove the damaged piece and install a new section of pipe in its place, using couplings at both ends of the new piece. Making the actual connections is no different than cementing the pipe together during installation. Always turn off the water before making repairs, and flush the system thoroughly before reburying the pipe.

You can reuse poly pipe fittings near damaged sections if they are still in good condition. Avoid reusing or repairing fittings on damaged PVC pipe. Cut off any suspect parts and replace them.

Troubleshooting: water supply

House water is contaminated with bacteria.	No backflow prevention on the system.	Install the mandated backflow prevention.
There is water runoff after a zone finishes watering.	System is overwatering.	Reduce the run times for the affected zones.
	System is watering a slope.	Irrigate slopes for shorter periods but more often, or reduce the sprinkler precipitation rate for that zone.
Water is puddling in the yard.	Leak in the system.	Locate the leak and repair it, or replace broken part.
	Punctured drip irrigation line.	Use a plug to repair the leak.
	System is irrigating too long.	Reduce the minutes of run time for your zones.
There is no water in one part of one zone.	Poly supply line may be kinked.	Inspect the lines and straighten any kinks.
	Rock or other debris is deforming the supply pipe.	Inspect the line, remove any rocks, and bed the pipe in sand.
	Buildup of debris and sediment has blocked the line.	Flush out the zone lines thoroughly.
Freeze damage occurs during winter.	System was not properly winterized.	Add drain valves at the lowest point in each zone.
		Use compressed air to blow out system before winter.

Troubleshooting: valves

A zone valve will not turn on.	Incorrect watering days, start times, or run times.	Check the timer program.
	Water supply is off to the zone valve.	Turn on the water supply.
	Faulty valve solenoid.	Replace the solenoid.
	Closed control at valve.	Open it counterclockwise.
A zone valve will not turn off.	Zone valve wires are not connected.	Connect the wires.
	Timer programming is incorrect.	Check the timer program.
	Debris in valve, solenoid, or metering orifice.	Disassemble the valve and clean with fresh water.
Water is leaking from a valve.	Valve diaphragm is faulty.	Replace the valve diaphragm.
	Valve body is cracked or broken or the valve bonnet is broken.	Replace the valve.
Leak from lowest sprinkler in zone.	Damaged valve diaphragm.	Replace the diaphragm.
A manual valve is stuck or hard to operate.	Dirt in the valve.	Clean and lubricate the valve stem.
	Damaged threads on stem.	Replace the valve stem.
Misting of the spray occurs.	Flow is too high.	Adjust the flow control on the irrigation valve.
The spray pattern is too small.	Flow control is set too low.	Adjust the flow control to increase the water flow.

timers

The watering cycle repeats.	Too many start times.	Disable redundant starts.
	Season adjust is set at more than 100 percent.	Set the season adjust to 100 percent or less.
The fuses blow too often.	Valve solenoid is faulty.	Replace the solenoid.
	Wires to valves damaged.	Repair the wiring.
	Timer is faulty.	Replace the timer.
The timer's display is blank.	No power to the timer.	Check the outlet for power.
	Transformer is faulty.	Replace the transformer.
	Blown fuse in the timer circuit.	Repair damaged wiring or replace the bad solenoid.
	Timer is faulty.	Replace the timer.
The irrigation system does not water the yard.	Timer is off, or it has a blown fuse.	Replace the fuse and turn on the timer.
	No power at outlet.	Reset the circuit breaker.
	No 24-volt power from transformer to timer.	Replace the bad wiring or the transformer.
	Wire to valves damaged.	Repair any damaged wiring.
	Faulty transformer, timer, or rain sensor.	Replace any faulty components as needed.
	Incorrect watering days, start times or run times.	Check timer program settings.
Zone not working.	Damaged zone connection.	Repair the wiring.

Troubleshooting: sprinklers

Problem	Cause	Solution
The sprinklers on a zone don't pop up correctly.	Not enough water pressure to run the zone.	Split the zone in two.
	Main system shutoff valve is not fully open.	Open the system shutoff valve counterclockwise.
	Flow control on the zone valve is partially closed.	Open the flow control counterclockwise.
Sprinkler pops up, but no water sprays.	Radius adjustment screw may be turned fully off.	Turn the screw counterclockwise.
	Nozzle clogged by debris.	Remove and clean nozzle.
	Internal nozzle filter may be plugged by debris.	Flush out nozzle screen.
	Broken sprinkler.	Replace the sprinkler.
A rotor sprinkler won't rotate.	Too little water pressure.	Increase water pressure.
	Sprinkler is broken.	Replace the sprinkler.
There is a gap in the spray pattern.	Debris stuck in sprinkler nozzle and/or head.	Clean out the sprinkler head and nozzle.
	Sprinkler is faulty.	Replace the sprinkler.
Sprinkler rotates in one direction, then stops.	Not enough pressure to rotate sprinkler.	Increase water pressure.
	Faulty sprinkler head.	Replace the sprinkler.
Water floods from a sprinkler.	Sprinkler nozzle missing.	Replace the missing nozzle.
	Cracked or missing sprinkler head.	Replace the sprinkler.

A sprinkler will not retract after watering.	→	Debris is stuck between the sprinkler riser and the riser seal.	→	Remove any debris from the seal.
		Damaged riser or riser seal.	→	Replace the seal or replace the sprinkler.
		Damaged retraction spring.	→	Replace the sprinkler.

micro-irrigation

There is no water coming from an emitter.	→	Emitter is clogged.	→	Clean or replace the emitter.
One part of the drip zone is dry.	→	Not enough emitters in that area.	→	Add emitters or replace with higher-flow emitters.
		Kinks in the poly tubing.	→	Inspect the lines and straighten if needed.
Part of the zone is too moist.	→	Too many emitters in that area.	→	Reduce the number of emitters in that area, or replace them with lower-flow emitters.
Emitters come loose	→	Too much pressure in the system.	→	Add a pressure regulator to the line.
Container plants are too dry.	→	Not enough irrigation.	→	Add more emitters.
		Not enough irrigation.	→	Put containers on a separate zone; increase irrigation time.
Container plants are too wet.	→	Too much irrigation.	→	Remove emitters.
			→	Put containers on a separate zone; decrease irrigation time.

Index

Note: Page references in **bold italic** type refer to photographs, illustrations, and information in captions.

62 gallons, defined, 153

A

Adapters
insert, *85*
male, *85*
plastic-to-metal, 118
Aeration, 27, *27*
Air circulation, on slopes, 30–31
Air gap systems, 74, 117
Annual plants, watering guidelines, 165
Anti-backsplash devices, *146*
Anti-siphon valves, *83*
about, 71, *73*, 103
installing, *71*, 121, *121*, 122
See also Backflow prevention devices
Aral Sea, water management practices, 17–18
Atmospheric vacuum breakers (AVBs), 73, *117*
Available water (AW), 153, 158, 161

B

Backflow prevention devices
about, 72–73
air gaps, 74, 117
atmospheric vacuum breakers, 73, *117*
design symbols, *88*
double-check valves, 73–74, *73*, 117, *117, 118*
installing, 117–118, *117*
pressure vacuum breakers, 73, *73*, 117, *117, 118*
for pumps, 53
reduced-pressure, 74, *117, 118*
troubleshooting problems, 181
See also Anti-siphon valves
Barbed connections, 72
Bubblers, for drip and micro-irrigation systems, 82
Bubbler sprinkler heads
about, 49, 74, 77, *77, 93*
advantages, 44
coverage, 93
design symbols, 88
flood, 77

Bulbs, watering guidelines, 165
Bushings, reducer, *85*

C

Carbohydrates, photosynthetic role, 10, *10*, 11
Carbon dioxide, photosynthetic role, 10, *10*
Catch basins, 27
Catch-can tests, 143, 144, *144,* 156
Clamps, stainless steel, *85*
Clay
clay loam, 36
composition and structure, 34–35, *34*
infiltration rates, 152
water-holding capacity, 12, 158
watering guidelines, 78, 154
Climate
ET weather stations, 32, *33,* 156
as grass selection criterion, 165
humidity, 30
plant adaptations to, 6
sprinkler efficiencies and, 155–156
temperature, 28–29
weather patterns, 6, 9
in weekly water needs calculations, 156–157
See also Cold damage; Microclimates; Precipitation; Wind
Cold damage
insufficient water and, 6
pipe depth and, 107
troubleshooting problems, 181
See also Winterizing irrigation systems
Compressors, to winterize irrigation systems, 99, *99,* 171, 181
Condensation, role in water cycle, 7–8, *7*
Container gardens
hanging pots, 137–138, *137, 139*
irrigation system installation, *130,* 138
irrigation system planning, 63
irrigation system repair, 185
Controllers. *See* Timers
Couplings
insert, *85*
to repair leaks, 175, 180, *180*
threaded, *85*
Crop coefficient. *See* Landscape coefficient (Kc)

D

Diseases of plants, 6, 165
Drainage
on slopes, 31
soil type and, 12
subsoil and, 38
testing, 38, *38*

Drainage pits, 102
Drain caps, *85*
Draining irrigation systems
in cold weather, 98–99, 107, 175, 181
compressors for, *99*
procedures, 171
Drain valves
about, *85*, 171, 181
automatic, 99, 107, *107*
installing, 103, 125, *125*
manual, 98–99, *99,* 107, 171
Drip lines, of trees, *11*
Drip systems
about, 21, 48, 50, 79, *81*, 130
adjusting systems, 142
bubblers, 82
buying components, 50, *79,* 80, *80*
for container gardens, 138
emitter tubing, 80–81, 130
filters, servicing, 170, *170,* 175, 179, *179*
for flower beds, 136–137, *137*
for hanging pots, 137–138, *137*
hookups and conversions, 83, *83*
installing, 50
layouts, 132–133, *133*
manifolds, 81, 89, *89*
microtubing, 80
misters, 82, *139*
mulch to cover, 41, 50
pipe fittings, *85*
plumbing terms, defined, 84
preventing problems, 175
risers, installing, 132, *132*
spigots, installing, 131, *131*
for trees, 138–139, *139*
for vegetable gardens, 135–136, *136*
for water conservation, *14,* 16, 27
weekly water needs, calculating, 157
See also Emitters, for drip and micro-irrigation systems; Micro-irrigation systems
Drought and drought stress
causes, 18
impact on plant growth, 6, 10, 13–14
management strategies, 18–19, 27
symptoms of stress, 19
water restrictions, local, 26, 52, 157–158
Drought-tolerant plants
adaptations, 9, *9*
hydrozones for, 24–25, *24*
selecting, 27
xeriscaping, *19,* 22–23, 22, *23*

Scotts Sprinklers and Watering Systems
Editor: Michael McKinley
Contributing Editor: Veronica Lorson Fowler
Contributing Technical Editor: Ashton Ritchie
Photo Researcher: Harijs Priekulis
Copy Chief: Terri Fredrickson
Publishing Operations Manager: Karen Schirm
Edit and Design Production Coordinator: Mary Lee Gavin
Editorial and Design Assistants: Kathleen Stevens,
    Kairee Windsor
Marketing Product Managers: Aparna Pande,
    Isaac Petersen, Gina Rickert, Stephen Rogers,
    Brent Wiersma, Tyler Woods
Book Production Managers: Pam Kvitne,
    Marjorie J. Schenkelberg, Rick von Holdt, Mark Weaver
Contributing Copy Editor: Barbara Feller-Roth
Contributing Proofreaders: Lorraine Ferrell, Nancy
    Wallace Humes, Stephanie Petersen
Contributing Map Illustrator: Jana Fothergill
Indexer: Ellen Davenport

**Additional Editorial Contributions from
    Greenleaf Publishing**
Project Editor: David Toht
Writer: Perry Vayo
Graphic Design: Jean DeVaty, Rebecca Anderson
Editorial/Design Assistant: Sarah Tibbott
Associate Editors: Steve Cory, Diane Slavik
Copy Editor: Barbara Webb
Illustrators: Tony Davis, Rebecca Anderson, Mike Grundy
Photo stylist: Eila Heinz

Meredith® Books
Executive Director, Editorial: Gregory H. Kayko
Executive Director, Design: Matt Strelecki
Executive Editor/Group Manager: Benjamin W. Allen
Senior Associate Design Director: Tom Wegner
Publisher and Editor in Chief: James D. Blume

Editorial Director: Linda Raglan Cunningham
Executive Director, Marketing: Jeffrey B. Myers
Executive Director, New Business Development:
    Todd M. Davis
Executive Director, Sales: Ken Zagor
Director, Operations: George A. Susral
Director, Production: Douglas M. Johnston
Business Director: Jim Leonard

Vice President and General Manager: Douglas J. Guendel

Meredith Publishing Group
President: Jack Griffin
Senior Vice President: Bob Mate

Meredith Corporation
Chairman and Chief Executive Officer: William T. Kerr
President and Chief Operating Officer: Stephen M. Lacy

In Memoriam: E.T. Meredith III (1933–2003)

Note to the Readers: Due to differing conditions, tools, and individual skills, Meredith Corporation assumes no responsibility for any damages, injuries suffered, or losses incurred as a result of following the information published in this book. Before beginning any project, review the instructions carefully, and if any doubts or questions remain, consult local experts or authorities. Because local codes and regulations vary greatly, you always should check with authorities to ensure that your project complies with all applicable local codes and regulations. Always read and observe all of the safety precautions provided by manufacturers of any tools, equipment, or supplies, and follow all accepted safety procedures.

Thanks to: Janet Anderson, Staci Bailey, Thomas E. Blackett, Gina Hale, The Toro Company, Brenda Witherspoon

Photographers
(Photographers credited may retain copyright ©
to the listed photographs.)
L = Left, R = Right, C = Center, B = Bottom, T = Top, i = Inset

© Craig Aurness/CORBIS: 13T; © Yann Arthus-Bertrand/CORBIS: 14B; Campbell Scientific, Inc.: 33B; Bruce Coleman: 34B; CORBIS: 8B, 24T; Grace Davies: 12B; Getty Images, Inc.: 4–5; Judy White/GardenPhotos.com: 16B, 19B, 31B, 53T; Linda & Alan Detrick: 10BR, 17B; © John & Dallas Heaton/CORBIS: 15T; © Patrick Johns/CORBIS: 98T; Dency Kane: 34T; Charles Mann Photographer (Designer/Owner Dan Johnson): 22B; Orbit ® Irrigation Products, Inc.: 2T, 27CR, 28B, 51T, 70TL, 71BL, 78CL, 84B, 93CR, 118T, 125T, 127CR, 128CL, 135T, 147BL, 179T; Jerry Pavia: 9BL, 9BR; Jerry Howard/Positive Images: 29B; Lee Lockwood/Positive Images: 36B; Peter Symcox/Positive Images: 24B; © Photowood Inc./CORBIS: 7T; Rain Bird Corporation: 33T, 49B; © Richard Hamilton Smith/CORBIS: 19T; Richard Hamilton Smith: 165BR; Dan Stultz/Greenleaf Publishing, Inc.: 3CR, 3BR, 25T, 27T, 27B, 32B, 37 all, 39BR, 40B, 41T, 42–43, 45BL, 45BR, 46TR, 47B, 50B, 52B, 53B, 64T, 87T, 91T, 99T, 103TL, 103TR, 103C, 104T, 104B, 105 all, 106CL, 108 all, 108B, 109 all, 109B all, 109 all, 111T, 112 all, 113 all, 114B, 131T, 135B, 143B, 144T, 144B, 150–151, 150C, 156B, 158B, 159T, 160T, 161B, 162T, 168T, 170CL, 170B, 172–173, 174–175, 174B, 176B, 177 all, 178 all, 179B, 180T; The Toro Company: 3T, 20T, 21B, 46B, 50T, 60T, 65T, 65B, 66T, 66B, 67T, 67B, 67B, 68B, 69C, 70TR, 71TL, 71BR, 72B, 73T, 73C, 75T, 77T, 77C, 77B, 78T, 79T, 81T, 82C, 83T, 89T, 92T, 102B, 111B, 114T, 115 all, 118B, 119B, 120 all, 122B, 126 all, 129B, 141 all, 145T, 147BR, 148/149, 155T, 163B; Watts Regulator Company: 73B; Judy White: 16B, 19B, 31B, 53T.

All of us at Meredith® Books are dedicated to providing you with the information and ideas you need to enhance your home and garden. We welcome your comments and suggestions about this book. Write to us at:
    Meredith Corporation
    Meredith Gardening Books
    1716 Locust St.
    Des Moines, IA 50309–3023

If you would like to purchase any of our gardening, home improvement, cooking, crafts, or home decorating and design books, check wherever quality books are sold. Or visit us at: meredithbooks.com

If you would like more information on other Scotts products, call 800-543-TURF or visit us at: www.Scotts.com

191